Derleth
Hawk...and Dove

Derleth
Hawk...and Dove

by
Dorothy M. Grobe Litersky

THE NATIONAL WRITERS PRESS

Published in the United States of America by
The National Writers Press
1450 S. Havana St.
Auorora, CO 80012

International Standard Book Number 0-88100-093-0
Library of Congress Catalog Card No. 97-66715

About the Cover

Every May, Derleth took to the prairie to harvest his favorite mushrooms.

The hunt became an almost ritualistic event, a time he additionally used to welcome and enjoy the arrival of Spring's flora and fauna.

The wicker basket under his arm served two functions. It carried the mushrooms he gathered, and its wicker construction allowed mushroom spores to filter down through the bottom of the basket to reseed the area as he picked.

The cover photograph was taken by Jeri Schwartz.

Dedication

This biography of August Derleth is dedicated to all people who seek the truth about the human condition...and who, like Augie's friend, Elky, continually question "Why?"

Acknowledgments

I wish to thank all those loyal friends and generous strangers who helped make my dream of one day publishing this biography come true. I especially wish to mention two friends: the late T.V. Olsen, author; and the late Dorothy House Guilday, friend, writer, and educator, who encouraged me all through the last 25 years.

Norbert Blei gave critiques of Derleth: Hawk; and Dove, with valuable suggestions and insights that helped in the revision of the original manuscript. I am also indebted to teachers of the Rhinelander School of Arts in Wisconsin who taught me the craft and tools invaluable to a writer; Barbara Vroman, author, publisher, agent, consultant, and friend who never lost faith in the book; Jeri Schwartz and Cedric Vig, who shared their outstanding photography talents; Meric Davis, typist; Ruby View Word Processing (Teresa); and especially my beloved daughter, Barbara Ann Sadler, for suffering through cleaning up my manuscript and getting it on disk, with Matthew Sadler, my grandson, and his friend, Christopher Schulte, contributing their computer expertise. And of course, the publishers of Derleth: Hawk; and Dove, the National Writers Press, its operating staff and the production coordinator, Harald Prommel.

The staff of the State of Wisconsin Historical Society Museum Archives in Madison were gracious, and extremely helpful in guiding my research there.

A word of caution to the readers: A good portion of this biography has August Derleth as a source of credits. Any expressed views and descriptions are from his perspective. Others involved in his various relationships and activities might not agree with his accounts of them.

As Derleth's biographer, I have, to the best of my ability, tried to present as accurate a profile as possible. He wanted a portrayal of the whole man, free of the closet of lies he had been forced to hide in throughout his lifetime.

Without the devoted services of my personal caregiver, Donnie Bucklew, the final revisions of this biography would not have been possible. I have been blessed with priceless services and incredible miracles. One doctor saved my life twice. One eye surgeon rescued my eyes from almost total blindness and cured a 40 year case of color blindness. Two physicians helped me coax my body back to life after I had begged them to help me die. Mere words cannot express my gratitude.

Dorothy M. G. Litersky

Prologue

"I have made no steps in the direction of marriage. I would have to have a woman who could both care for the children understandably and sensibly and also understand that it would be a primary task for her to further my work by every means possible....American women have an exaggerated, highly romantic view of life; they are in the main spoiled...."[1]

August Derleth sat at the circular desk in his studio trying to keep his mind on the proofs spread out before him. tedious job...tic-toc Unbelievable he'd suffered through this over 150 times. But it had to be done, and he was the only one to do it. There, another one. Idiot editor must have been an English teacher, correcting the grammar in quotations, tic-toc, tic-toc.

The clock's eternal ticking pushed into his brain *the publishers want them by the end of the week. tic-toc, tic-toc, louder and louder, as though trying to tell him something. Of course! It must almost be time for Caitlin.* Derleth glanced at the clock. *A quarter after two. Already fifteen precious minutes wasted. Only three hours before the children return from school. Where the devil was she?*

Derleth dropped his pen, pushed himself to his feet, paced about the huge room. His blood pressure was rising. *No need to get upset. It could be anything. Tic-toc, tic-toc.*

He shook his head, impatiently. *What could have delayed her? Or was this just another ploy in her emasculation maneuver?*[2]

His mind began to race. Doubts about Caitlin raised their ugly heads. Fear and panic were not far behind. *It couldn't be her husband delaying her – he knew all about their affair – poor chump – a nice lad, really – and so good looking – not yet 30 and already well up the ladder to financial success – a rotten lover, though – so naive – so clumsy – so ignorant about a women's needs – neglected her, too – no consideration – tic-toc, tic-toc – she had to come – today was the day he had to tell her he couldn't*

1

marry her as they'd planned – couldn't go to Vegas with her for the divorce after his week as Writer-in-Residence next month – or honeymoon in England.

Derleth was better known in England than in the States. His Sherlock Holmes pastiches, his Peck mysteries, the "Joan" stories of his affair with Maris and his earlier macabre and science fiction had already made fans in four different genre. His anthologies, the Lovecraft letters, and hard cover fiction, his poetry collections, and even the Sac Prairie and Wisconsin sagas were attracting notice in the more prestigious literary groups. His reputation as author and publisher was rapidly solidifying in Europe, Mexico, and Japan. Much as he hated leaving his home in Sac Prairie he had always yearned to visit England.

Tic-toc, tic-toc. No sense getting panicky. A number of little things could have delayed her

Derleth paused in his pacing to watch a redwing settle on the branch of the lilac tree outside the window. The bird held a long, fat worm in his beak – food for his mate who sat on her unhatched clutch of eggs, nested in the crotch of the tree.

How many years had the faithful monogamous pair nested there? One brood after another to add splashes of bright crimson to the beauty of the prairie. Why couldn't he and Caitlin....

August turned abruptly and reached for the phone. There was no answer.

Tic-toc, tic-toc – precious moments slipping by – an accident? – his blood raced faster with every tic-toc – she had to be all right – how could he get along without her? – without her quick mind – her lust for life? her beauty? "The most beautiful woman in the state," they were calling her. His heart quickened at the thought of Caitlin's beauty. *How could he live without her? – her long, shapely limbs entwined in his – her soft, eager lips – all the perfection of her melting into him – consuming him – tic-toc, tic-toc.*

He picked up the phone again. Still no answer – *an accident surely – nothing less could keep her from him.*

He reached into his pocket for his blood pressure pills, popped two into his mouth, gulping them down, then resumed pacing. *an accident?*

2

He turned and reached for the phone again. It rang as his hand touched the receiver. "Derleth, here," he barked in irritation. *some stupid idiot wanting to know if the swallows always returned to Capistrano on the same date – a nuisance – these pseudo-naturalists – calling from all over the country lately*

"Aug?"

It was Caitlin finally. her voice was muffled yet he could sense her impatience – no, more than that – her anger

"Caitlin, thank God! I've been frantic. Are you OK? – not sick or – I've envisioned an accident...."

"It was an accident all right."

"Oh, my poor darling. Where are you – the hospital?"

"No, I'm fine – just mad as hell."

He could scarcely hear her.

"If you're in trouble with a traffic officer or judge, don't worry, I can fix it."

Caitlin giggled. "Not that kind of accident, Mr. Fix-it. My mother and cousin 'accidentally' happened to be in the neighborhood and dropped in to warn me not to have anything to do with you. You're a dangerous man. The whole town's talking about us. On and on for almost two hours. I couldn't get rid of them. Now it's too late, darling. Nothing will keep me away from you tomorrow. I need your arms around me, your loving...'til then. Tomorrow."

Tic-toc, tic-toc. the beat was slower, fainter – the clock would all but stand still until tomorrow. Oddly enough, he was relieved. like a stay of execution – no. only a day's delay. he couldn't go on living the way he'd had to do all his life – living a lie, walking a tight line knowing one little slip – one misstep would bring his world crashing about him

Derleth settled in his desk chair, picked up his pen. His eyes strayed from the proofs to a corner of the window. A spider web shot darts of multi-colored sunbeams into the studio. A common black spider was busily spinning a cocoon of web around a still wriggling fly. The spider stopped spinning momentarily, to shoot a discharge of tranquilizer into his victim's abdomen.

trapped – in a soft cocoon of the strongest fiber once known to man – trapped – the poor fly doesn't have a chance – the

3

gossamer web would keep it trapped until its captor was ready to devour it alive

Derleth deserted his desk. He was tired, suddenly so very tired. He reached to startle the spider away from the fly, then plucked the cocoon out of the web and crushed it between his fingers. *an act of mercy – better than being consumed slowly, painfully*

Derleth moved to the bed, sat down, removed his shoes, neatly placing them side by side on the floor. He relaxed against the mountains of pillows. *why couldn't he be like the red wings, blissfully loving the same mate year after year – instead of falling into one relationship after another from the early age of 15 – from Margery to Caitlin – tomorrow – how could he explain why he couldn't marry her? – she'd be fully of why's – why indeed?*

He tried to use her extravagance as an excuse. *but no. Caitlin was used to pretty clothes beautiful houses jewelry – he'd enjoyed giving her what he could – wished he could do more – it wasn't her extravagance.* He could afford Caitlin's wants now.[3] His rising profits the last three years had him out of the red, financially, and even accumulating a sizable bank account – not to mention the stock of books filling his two warehouses. Awards, prizes, acclamations were pouring in from everywhere. *everything looked rosy ahead – or it should – tomorrow – his old excuse of not wanting to break up a family – to break one of his own firm principles – was not valid either. the marriage was breaking up before she came to him – no more lies – it was time to face the real truth*

this compulsion to control. where did it come from? his royal ancestors? when did it start or was it there from the beginning? in his genes?

Derleth's eyes were getting heavier. His brace and truss were cutting into his torso, the skin underneath was itchy with heat and sweat. He wiggled out of his shorts, jerked the heavy rubberized support off.

ugly, smelly torture chamber – his bloated body, criss-crossed with livid scars – held together inside with wires – disgusting. why would a twenty-eight year old raving beauty want to marry a sixty-two year old wreck like him?

4

August had voiced his protests to Caitlin, after the surgery. Her answer, "Shush." "It still works, your body, better than ever." *she was right – the extensive surgery, the long months in the hospital had definitely not harmed that portion of his bodily functions – on the contrary, he was hornier than ever[4] – Caitlin matched his passion, as though she, too, heard the tic-toc relentlessly ticking the seconds of eternity away*

He stretched out on the bed with a sigh of relief as his burning body absorbed the cool comfort of the sheet.

was it his compulsive control – the need to exercise his power – prove his superiority – feed his ego that made this marriage impossible?

His eyelids grew heavier. *so tired – so many problems – how he longed for a simpler time – for a time when he was a child and all of life was thrilling – beckoning – when he had always been so curiously sure of himself*

He closed his eyes in utter weariness. Far off in the distance he could see a small figure marching up a familiar tree-lined street in his beloved Sauk City....

SOURCE NOTES
PROLOGUE

[1] A. D. to Ian Law, 1927.

[2] A. D. Journal, 3 Aug., pp2ff; 9 Nov., pp47ff; 2 Dec., 1969 pp54ff (August admits to his best friend, Hugo Schwenker, that he is helpless in Caitlin's hands when she takes "...superior..." control in their coupling and Derleth's "unmasculine, ardent desire...for such possession was obvious to him); 13 Dec., 1970. page 59 August, reviewing passages in his journal, realizes Caitlin is becoming more important to him than his work, an admission that "...sent a tremor of alarm through him..."

[3] Note 2, page 27; 2, 7, 19, 21 Sept. pp24ff; 5, 18, 20, 25 Oct., 13 Nov. p. 48, Augie lost his head buying 36 pieces of jewelry and at least 12 dresses for Caitlin. Her closets at home were already filled with lovely flowing gowns; (Biographer viewed 10 or more very feminine gowns at the Rhinelander School of Arts.)

[4] Note 2, 12 Nov. 1970.

Chapter One

"The conviction of continuity is strong..."[1]

Five year old August Derleth marched resolutely past the flourishing garden fragrant with camomile, sweet William, thyme, sage, roses, geraniums, mint, cosmos, clematis and grape hyacinths; past the stone smokehouse; past the temptation of Grandma Derleth's ground cherry sauce and homemade rye bread; across the street separating his grandparent's home from a limestone, L-shaped building in front of which hung a bright red wagon with black letters.[2]

DERLETH & SONS

August knew what the sign over the blacksmith shop said because August could read.[3]

"We used to laugh at him," August's mother, Rosella, ninety-one years young, an attractive woman still, recalled 61 years later, as she relaxed in a wheelchair, enjoying the seclusion of a grassy nook outside the Maplewood Nursing Home in Sac Prairie. Silver-white wisps of what had once been heavy chestnut brown hair peeked out from a deep pink, lacy straw bonnet. Her skin was smooth with a surprising look of youth. Her mind was sharp, her memory clear, her voice firm.[4]

August loved the peculiar blend of odors in the shop: the pungent smell of scorched horse hooves mixed with the sweet aroma of freshly shaved wood chips from the wagons Grandpa Derleth, his Uncle Charlie, and August's dad, William, fashioned there. The dark mystery of the gabled storage room and its air of forbidden and secret places had a special lure for the lad.

Once again, Grandfather Derleth indulged his namesake's desire to explore the gable room. When they'd finished, he paused before descending the broad stairway to the smithy below, and bent over. August eagerly accepted the familiar gesture to climb aboard. Too eagerly. As he jumped up on his grandfather's back, his momentum vaulted him over the old man's head hurtling his body down the stairwell to land, with vicious force, on the machinery below. The sharp end of a row of iron bars cut deep into his skull.

A priest was called into administer Extreme Unction as the child hovered between life and death. He was unconscious for two nights and two days.[5]

August could laugh about it years later. When an interviewer asked what August attributed his genius to, he gave the flippant answer, "Being dumped on my head at the age of five, perhaps."[6]

It wasn't the first time the Derleth family had faced a possibility of untimely death. Three years earlier, Rosella had a close brush with the Grim Reaper as she struggled to give birth to his sister, Hildred. In later years, August maintained that his mother's strong will power pulled her through.

August, himself, showed early evidence of having an even stronger will. His Grandmother Volk regarded his tendency to do as he pleased, a result of naughtiness and stubbornness. She claimed his temper was evident even when he was a baby at his mother's breast, shaking his head in impatience and anger when the milk came too slowly.

From early years, a sense of independence led August. Without Rosella's permission, often without her knowledge, he made trips to visit his Grandmother Volk or went downtown to beg candy from his Aunt Virginia, working at the grocery store. One day when he was still only five, he went fishing in Dickerson's Slough with a neighbor boy, Karl Ganzlin. He did not come home until after nine in the evening. Grandma Volk and Mrs. Ganzlin, fearing the boys may have drowned, set out to search for them. They found the boys near the creamery, directly north of the railroad bridge. When reprimanded, August became quite indignant at the suggestion that he and Karl couldn't take care of themselves, even close to the river.[7]

After the fall in the blacksmith shop, August was forbidden to enter the shop again. Rosella undoubtedly overcompensated trying to prevent any future injuries to her son. August never developed an interest in basketball, football or rough physical sports even though he had the physique of a wrestler. He roller-skated but never owned a bicycle. He preferred to walk, even as a child. He thought himself too clumsy to ride a bike or learn the tools of his father's trade. His tall, strong, handsome father, William, often lost patience with August's ineptness.[8]

August's family background was predominantly Teutonic. Great-grandfather Michael Derleth moved from Bavaria in 1839 to America, from Philadelphia to Sac Prairie in 1852. Grandfather Volk's grandfather was a count who fled from France to Bavaria when the "terror" (revolution) came. On February 24, 1909, William Julius Derleth and Rosella Louise Volk Derleth gave birth to a son of French, Bavarian, Prussian and Pennsylvanian ancestry.[9]

Michael Derleth had been a skilled locksmith, silversmith, and goldsmith in Zinl, Bavaria. The lock and key on the old catholic church building of St. Jude's Parish in Sauk City was made by Michael shortly before his death. His skills had been passed down to August's grandfather, uncle, and father.[10] After his father's death, it was to his skillful hands August addressed this poem:

A LITTLE ELEGY FOR MY FATHER

"...How he loved the feel of wood in his hands.
He built to last. Strange in this house he wrought.
With such capable hands, to think of him as past...."[11]

August's lack of skill may have been due to a lack of interest in the wood-working craft. As an adult he became a graceful fencer and dancer; his fingers were nimble enough to dash off neatly typed letters at a hundred words a minute.

Derleth's enthusiasms took a different tack than his progenitors. He loved to collect things, tin cans to begin with. They had colorful wrappers and were shiny. The Derleth family was too poor to afford many toys; the tin cans were a substitute. Too, there was a challenge and a feeling of accomplishment in collecting. Years after his own tin can collection had long rusted out of existence, August could still get a thrill from the sight of tin cans piled in a box.[12]

He graduated from tin cans to stamps, and shared his new

hobby with Hugh, a "...thin, hawk-faced youth with silky hair, wryly, humorous eyes...." Hugo was the son of a local harness maker, Bill Schwenker, and his "bird-like" wife. The boys would watch for incoming mail and hurry to the post office to rummage through the wastebasket as postal customers ripped open and discarded envelopes, so they could retrieve the precious stamps.[13]

He started collecting comics at an early age: Windsor McCay's light and masterfully drawn fantasies in "Little Nemo in Slumberland"; Johnny Gruelle's whimsically charming "Mr. Tweedle Dee"; Outcult's "Buster Brown"; Dirk's "Katzenjammer Kids"; Dwiggen's "School Days"; Fisher's "Mutt and Jeff"; and Herriman's "Krazy Kat". His later literary, critical, and anthropological interests were already in evidence in these early selections.[14]

August seized every opportunity to page through old newspapers, even at the town dump. His Aunt Bertha sent him comics from Minneapolis. He hounded other relatives and neighbors to save papers for him.[15]

"I was salting away my sense of humor," August said years later when asked why he collected the comics.[16]

When August was five, his family moved to a snug, cozy, white building located three blocks north and one block west of his former home. Built by his Great-grandfather Damm, it was shaded by a huge, century-old soft maple, young red cedars, and blackberry trees. The spacious front yard had a lawn swing, and a clump of bridal wreath graced the northwest corner. A woodshed, hen house, and a "two-holer" lay east and northwest of the house. A rose trellis climbed one wall and grape arbors surrounded the gardens in the back yard. Fido's dog house nestled under a sturdy black ash south of the house. A trap door in the kitchen floor led to a cellar with stores of canned and preserved food. A wooden walk ran north across the garden to the home of Grandmother Volk.[17]

Elizabeth Volk, born in Scranton, Pennsylvania, in 1856, in the heart of the hexerie country, believed in dreams, owned a dream book, was superstitious, and had a fear of a "...curious book of cabalistic lore, which she believed unlocked the secrets of heaven and earth, and was owned by every witch...."

Elizabeth Volk had a good reason to believe in dreams. Back in July, 1889, she'd had a dream of her husband, Adam, standing with a smoking pistol over the body of another man. In July, 1890, a mouthy Irishman from Chicago came into Adam Volk's saloon and taunted him all day, trying to pick a fight. Adam, enraged finally, went home to get his Winchester. Elizabeth tried to stop him. He hurled her away with such force she later lost the child she was carrying. The young heckler, Danny Ahern, gun in hand, awaited Adam in front of the saloon.

"Shoot!" Volk commanded.

Ahern shot. Volk's shot came "...as soon after as distinguishable..." according to a witness. The Irishman's bullet missed Adam, but the tavern keeper's shot was fatal. Since a law had only recently been passed in Wisconsin making duels illegal, Volk was charged with murder. The jury consisted of natives of English and Irish descent without one German among them. Unable to produce proof of self defense, Volk was found guilty of second degree murder and sentenced to 14 years in the Wisconsin State Prison at Waupun. On July 6, 1891, just three months later, he died of Bright's disease.[18]

Grandmother Volk took in laundry in order to support her six children for the many years before she married Adam's brother, Phillip. Her own stepfather, Grand-grandfather Westle, was a teacher and instilled a respect for education in Grandmother Volk which she passed on to Rosella. August's mother was determined that both her children should have a good education. Grandma Volk hoarded pennies so that August might buy magazines and books; she encouraged him to write, had a strong faith in his future, and predicted he would be great someday. She also had an influence on his early reading tastes. These leaned toward macabre tales and the adventures of Sherlock Holmes, who was her favorite fictional detective.[19]

Other strong influences helped shape young Derleth's life. One of these was Sauk City itself. The town had regular spacious streets similar to those of the important and unusual Sac Indian Village that had occupied the site in 1766. Sauk City is today the oldest incorporated village in Wisconsin, its original charter having been granted on March 30, 1854. When August was born, it had a population of about 2,000.[20] Howard P.

Lovecraft, noted author of the macabre genre and later correspondent of Derleth's, described it as "...rather an unusual place: a prairie town peopled about 1830 by a group of Germans of the haute-bourgeoisie and lesser nobility, and sharply differentiated both from such Yankee towns as good old Appleton, (Wisconsin), and from the peasant German areas. Small and self-contained, it has cherished ancient manners and heritage and memories and has developed a sometimes enjoyable and sometimes exasperating clannishness..."[21] Here, with the Wisconsin River to swim and fish in, the marshes and hills to tramp through, and the wide, wonderful world of nature spread around and above, with relatives and grand parents nearby, with friends like Hugo Schwenker and Karl Ganzlin, August spent an ideal childhood. Here he had security, love, friendship, and wholesome adventure at his doorstep. His roots flourished and reached deep into the soil of Sac Prairie, so that all his life he was reluctant to leave it, and never felt at ease when he did.[22]

The Ganzlins and Derleths were close neighbors. Karl and August grew up together, haunting the alley that ran from the lumberyard to the creamery. They spent hours playing about the neighborhood barns, fishing down at the dam, spying on the town characters like Minnie Meyer, as she netted chunks of butter out of buttermilk churns. They even put on plays, using the summer kitchen at the rear of the Derleth home for a dressing room, the wooden platform and part of the wooden walk beneath the grape arbors as a stage. They charged pins or pennies for admission. Karl was a bright lad, more adventurous than August; he enjoyed macho activities such as hunting, as he grew older.

Another neighborhood playmate, Mark Schorer, was the son of a prominent Sauk City family. Mark was closer to Karl than to August when they were very young. It wasn't until their mid-teens that Sauk City's two leading authors became friends.[23]

It was Hugo Schwenker who became Derleth's closest and life-long friend. Hugo, or "Hugh", as August called him, was much quieter, shyer, more introspective than Karl or Mark. He was excellent at mathematics, not one of Derleth's better subjects. In addition to sharing August's passion for philately, he collected postcards. He had a small office behind his father's harness shop, where he and August spent many hours. Though Hugo helped his father with harness-making, he was usually available for a hike or a fishing jaunt.

The two boys combed the countryside, laying up a store of Tom Sawyer and Huck Finn type memories that would one day form the basis for a series of juvenile adventure stories by August.[24]

After young Derleth entered St. Aloysius School, his relationship with Karl and Mark, both Protestants, deteriorated. There was running feud between the students of the Catholic and the public schools and a widening gap in the social and financial status of August's and the other two's families. Also, Mark and Karl were a grade ahead of August. Though Hugo was Protestant, too, he and August shared a philosophy that transcended conditioned beliefs and knit them together for life. Both were strong individualists, disinclined to follow the crowd; each was intent on living life in his own way.[25]

Miss Annie Maegerlein, another neighbor who lived across the street from the Derleths, helped influence young August's future reading tastes by supplying him with clippings she saved from the daily *MILWAUKEE JOURNAL*. These included "The Bedtime Story" by Thorton W. Burgess, illustrated by Harrison Cady. It related the adventures of Mother West Wind's neighbors in "Green Meadow" and "Old Briar Patch", "Peter Rabbit", "Johnny Cluck", "Uncle Billy Possum", "Hoot Owl", and "Grandfather Frog". Such clippings ultimately led August to Thoreau by way of Ernest Thompson Seton and John Burroughs.[26]

Derleth's reading was encouraged and shaped, too, by Sauk City's first librarian, Josephine Merk, who guided the reading of all children in the area. Recognizing the superiority of August's budding mind, she accorded him special attention, and there developed a warm friendship that lasted until Josephine Merk's death. The librarian and the future author spent many interesting and fruitful hours of discussion on an intellectual plane that few Sauk City natives could achieve. The only time August was upset with Miss Merk's guidance was when she once refused to let him take out a currently popular novel titled *THREE WEEKS*.

Never one to be thwarted, August persuaded an older student to withdraw the book for him. After reading it, he was angry with the librarian for not having explained beforehand that it was "bilge", thus saving him time and trouble.[27]

August's Catholic schooling ingrained an early training in disciplined work habits. It expanded his interest in nature, which had first been stimulated by Miss Maegerlein's clippings and by his many hours tramping through the countryside.

Sister Anaclete patiently tried to impart to August some of her own talent and appreciation for art and music. Because she had an "angel face and disposition", August heard her out with less impatience than was his usual want. One day in the fourth grade, when Sister Anaclete read Longfellow's "The Children's Hours", and explained the Bishop of Bingen's motives to the class, August's face in the back of the room held such look of horror that, as she told him several years later, she could never again bring herself to relate horror stories to children. Little did Sister Anaclete realize that at the time she was merely nurturing a passion that was destined to help shape the whole future of the macabre genre in world literature.[28]

It was Sister Isabelle, August's teacher in grade seven and eight – a stern disciplinarian, tall and sturdy, almost masculine figure with deep brown eyes and a fine sense of humor and fairness, who added to Derleth's store of nature lore. Sister Isabelle took her classes out to the fields and woods. August recalled that she "...knew the trillium, the small wood violet, the May apples, the scarlet tanager, the rose-breasted grosbeak, the pee-wee, oak, black elder, and hard maple...."[29]

It was Sister Isabelle who, after reading August's first detective story about violent death and deception, urged him to write more short stories.

He could write as well as other authors featured in current issues of *SECRET SERVICE MAGAZINE*, August decided. He would allow himself the time it would take him to write forty stories, to make his first sale. If he'd gained no acceptance in that period, he would cast about for something other than writing for his life's work.[30]

[1] August Derleth, <u>Walden West,</u> (N.Y., 1961), p. 54.

[2] Ibid., pp. 18-ff.

[3] A. D. to Phillip Colehaur, May 12, 1952.

[4] Interview of Rosella Derleth, Maplewood Nursing Home, Prairie du Sac, Wisconsin, July, 1976.

[5] Note 1, p. 16.

[6] Katherine Klipstein, "August Derleth, Brusk, Cynical, Rules Sauk City with Powerful Pen", <u>Madison Tower Times,</u> April 8, 1939.

[7] A. D. Journal, 12 December, 1937, Box 68, p. 235.

[8] A. D. to Inez Weaver, February 16, 1965.

[9] Note 8, op. cit.

[10] Note 8, op. cit.

[11] August Derleth, <u>COLLECTED POEMS – 1937-67,</u> (N.Y., 1969), p. 246.

[12] Note 8, op. cit.

[13] Note 1 & 2, op. cit.

[14] Bill Blackbeard, "Wham! Biff! Sauk! August Derleth and the Comics", IS#4 postmortem memorial issue (fanzine).

[15] Ibid.

[16] Note 14, op. cit.

[17] Note 1,

[18] August Derleth, "Hell hath no fury" <u>Wisconsin Murders,</u> (Sauk City, Wis., 1968), pp. 120ff; A. D. Journal, 2 December 1954, January 22 and 28, 1960; Bright's disease – kidney disorder caused by cold and dampness, scarlet fever, pregnancy, or violent intemperance. Scholl, <u>Library of Health,</u> pp. 395-ff.

[19] Note 13.

[20] Plaque, Sauk City bridge (now named August Derleth Bridge), erected by the Dane County Conservation Committee in 1969. Biographer's visual research, July, 1979.

[21] H. P. Lovecraft to (we were unable to locate the letter to determine the recipient, but the style and language are unmistakably H. P. Lovecraft's).

[22] Biographer's opinion.

[23] Carl Ganzlin tape, Derleth room, Sauk City library, Sauk City, Wisconsin.

[24] Note 1, pp. 21-25-ff; pp. 59-ff.

[25] Note 23, op. cit.

[26] Note 1,

[27] August Derleth, lecture to librarians, miscellaneous papers, SWHS museum archives, Madison, Wis.

[28] Sister Anaclete to August, reprint in August Derleth Society newsletter, Vol. 2, No. 2, July 31, 1969.

[29] Ibid.

[30] August Derleth, Writing Fiction, (Boston, Mass., 1946); fiction classes of August Derleth, Rhinelander School of Arts.

Chapter Two

"I lost most of my illusions before I was 20."[1]

In high school, August's attractive, blonde English teacher, Miss Frieda Schroeder, lured him into extensive reading in order to gain her favor. *EMERSON'S ESSAYS* and *WALDEN POND* were among the books he first devoured. At fourteen, he was reading Galsworthy as well as Doyl, Hardy as well as *WEIRD TALES,* Chesterton as well as Poe. In time, Alexander Dumas and Sabatini left their influences.[2]

Meanwhile, he persisted in his story writing. He sent out one macabre tale after another, only to have them rejected. In two years, 39 of his productions met the same fate.

One of the last of them, entitled "The Locked Box", was rejected by Farnsworth Wright, the patient, long-suffering editor of *WEIRD TALES* with the comment that it was "...not very even...." August rewrote and resubmitted it. Wright returned it with the notation that it was "...almost ready for *WEIRD TALES*...." With a little more work, Wright suggested, it MIGHT make the grade. Such was Derleth's naivete of manuscript submission at the time, Wright advised that henceforth, would August please number his pages to avoid confusion.[3]

"Might" was not good enough for August Derleth. The fortieth story had to succeed. August thought that one of his stories, "Bat's Belfry", was better than the others. It had been the eighteenth of his tales to be rejected. As usual, Wright had made pertinent remarks and suggestions for improvement. The English innkeeper in the story had used a cockney accent and cockney dialect was limited to a certain area in London; not prevalent in the "down country". This was August's first lesson in paying close attention to detail, a lesson he scrupulously followed thereafter and passed on to students in his future writing classes. He revised the story according to Wright's suggestions, and resubmitted it. Wright suggested a few other changes, and August rewrote once more.

On the 15th of October, 1925, Wright's letter of acceptance

arrived, stating that August would get $18.00 on publication. It was one of the most exciting moments of his life: his first sale. The initial hurdle in a long line of hurdles was behind him. Acceptance did not mean money in the bank the next day. August had to wait seven months to see "Bat's Belfry" in print and to cash the check he received for it.[4]

Wright's acceptance was the first of 139 stories by Derleth to be published in *WEIRD TALES*.[5] Farnsworth Wright patiently nurtured the budding writer's talent. Again and again he returned August's manuscripts, coached, encouraged and corrected him, and primed his idea pump to such an extent that the stories published under August Derleth's byline were almost collaborations.

Some of the stories, no matter how many times Derleth reworked them, never did make it with Wright. "The Chicago Horror" was one. After eight or ten rejections, he sent it to "Ghost Stories", where it was also rejected by editor Daniel Wheeler.[6]

Although August was busily writing, reading, collecting things, attending school, and becoming involved in class politics, he also found time to fall in love. He did so with the same intensity he had exhibited as a little boy leaping over his grandfather's back. Sitting behind Margery in class, August had teased her by pulling her long golden braids, never quite aware that he was doing so to attract her attention. It wasn't until those golden braids were worn up around her head like a crown that he became consciously aware of how pretty she was, and how closely she resembled Laura La Plante, his favorite movie star. He took to combing his hair upwards too, in a six inch coif, which made him appear much taller.

August and Margery would meet after school and walk the village streets hand-in-hand. Puppy love like theirs was a perfectly natural and innocent experience between two young teenagers of that era, but not in the eyes of beholders such as a bigoted, frustrated, lonely aunt of August's, a town busy-body, who found titillation in imagining what went on between two young people of the opposite sex and two sets of parents who belonged to two groups of arch enemies – the Catholic and Lutheran congregations of Sac Prairie. The shy meetings of the young couple, at first so innocent and natural, soon turned into elaborately arranged, secret and forbidden rendezvous as the Catholics and Lutherans, including their own families, joined forces to keep them apart.

Derleth was furious at the townsfolk's interference. He felt they didn't try to understand the beauty and magic of that first love, and the depths to which he would go to keep the crystal of that love untouched, unblemished; he was furious, too, that anyone would think he, himself, would do anything to destroy the sweet innocence of Margery.

What followed proved to be Sauk City's baptism in locking horns with someone who, all through his lifetime, would battle to counteract the ignorance, the bigotry, the malicious gossip, and the stubborn viciousness of small mentalities. Even at sixteen, August Derleth was intelligent enough, and ruthless enough, to turn his antagonists' own weapons against them. His crag-like jaw, still scarcely noticeable under a lingering layer of baby fat, was nonetheless manifest in a metaphorical way as he pursued his own ends.

He enlisted fellow students to spy upon people who had been spying on him. He dug up ancient and current gossip for the purpose of blackmailing those who were gossiping about him. He bullied the school principal and threatened to disrupt the entire junior class, compeers he'd had under his thumb for years.

All of it was to no avail. Not the town, but Margery herself, defeated August. Her strength was not equal to the struggle. She gave in to her family's pressure and began to date a Protestant boy. Loss of his first love, like his fall down the smithy stairs, left him almost mortally wounded. Margery's betrayal would one day form the basis of his first novel, *EVENING IN SPRING*. The book, August often told others, was almost completely autobiographical.[3]

Apparently, August turned his back on the fair sex at this time. Margery, he felt, had betrayed his love.

His relations with his sister Hildred had never been particularly close, to judge from his journal. It seems almost as though Hildred didn't really exist for him in their earliest years, except as a touchpoint of irritation from time to time; the kind of relationship often found in siblings where one has been unfavorably compared to the other. Hildred, in contrast to August, was a less difficult, less stubborn, and less exasperating child. The contrast may have been emphasized constantly by Rosella to Derleth, resulting in a deep resentment of his sister.[8] Like August, Hildred was interested in literature in high school. She joined the Literary Society and served on the *SAUKWIS* yearbook staff. Unlike August, she also participated in athletics, played on the girls' basketball team, and was a member of the Sauk City High School Athletic Association.[9] Her sports activities, along with singing in the high school girls' glee club, may have stimulated a feeling of jealousy on August's part.[10] He developed a taste for both jazz and classical music over the years, but was involved in the more passive role of listener. He did play the piano on occasion, but claimed he could not sing in tune.[11]

Although, during his junior year, August could almost pick and choose his companions at will, being president of his class and pretty much in control of both the junior and senior students, he was lonely. His feeling of isolation from his peers stemmed from several sources. The effects of his experience with Margery made him shy away from girls. One of his close companions, Karl Ganzlin, like most of the male students, was interested in seeking female companionship. In Wisconsin, beer flowed like water before prohibition. There was no law restricting students from imbibing at taverns or dance halls. The largely German population of the area served beer with meals, as did the Derleth family. It was up to parents to teach their offspring the evils of overindulgence in intoxicating beverages. No doubt Rosella educated her son thoroughly on the subject. William Derleth, in his later years, was inclined on occasion to overindulge in martinis. Derleth mentioned in his journal that he sent his father a bottle of whiskey for his birthday.[12] August had his extensive reading, his writing, his duties as class president, his schoolwork, and his growing correspondence to keep him busy. He had little time or interest in beer bashes.

Hugo Schwenker was busy helping his father in the harness shop after school, and had less time for fishing jaunts and walks through the marshes and prairie.[13]

Young Derleth, at this time, also became more and more aware of a new development in his life, the puberty changes taking place within his body. In the process of exploring and coping with the awakening of his sexuality, he did what many teenagers of his era did. He masturbated. During one of these episodes of "jerking off", he found someone to not only fill the void left by Margery, but to share this wonderful new awareness.

He had hurried to the school lavatory to relieve a sudden embarrassing burgeoning in his groin, and did not at first notice the room was already occupied. When he finally became conscious of another presence and looked around, there stood Mark Schorer, busily engaged in the same process.[14]

Both August and Mark had undoubtedly been exposed to the horrible consequences of indulging in such sinful behavior. Now, suddenly, they shared a guilty secret. With August, however, there probably was very little guilt. He lived, all his life, believing that if you had an itch, you should scratch it.

Gradually, through the days that followed, the boys' secret became a strong bond between them. When August needed to relieve his "itch", Mark would also ask the teacher's permission to leave the room. Their relationship flourished, and expanded, as they moved from exploring their own erogenous zones, to investigating each other's. By the time summer vacation rolled around, they were completely involved not only sexually, but emotionally as well. They were in love![15]

During this period, August first made contact with an important pen pal, Howard P. Lovecraft, a middle-aged recluse in Providence, Rhode Island, whose weird and outre fiction Derleth had long admired. WEIRD TALES was one of the few outlets for the genre of macabre fiction, and Lovecraft's material was published therein. Although it was not the policy of WEIRD TALES to give out the addresses of their contributing authors, Farnsworth Wright made an exception when Derleth requested Lovecraft's address.[16]

August's first letter to Lovecraft contained a single question about Arthur Machen's fantasy novel, HILL OF DREAMS, a favorite work of both authors. That epistle set off correspondence that began in 1926 and ended with Lovecraft's death in 1937.

Still young and impressionable, August absorbed every-thing "Grandpa" Lovecraft, in his spidery script and fascinating eighteenth century style, had to say, not only about writing, but about almost every other subject that came up. They dis-cussed various books August was reading and the classic and macabre oriented material that Lovecraft thought he should be exploring.

They shared their ideas about religion, which Lovecraft con-sidered a totally mythical matter, with no basis in fact; and astronomy, a subject in which Lovecraft was a lay expert and in which he succeeded in arousing August's interest, one that lasted a lifetime and crept into many of his future writings. August's ability to assimilate the contents of four to eight books a day caused Lovecraft to exclaim "...Bless my soul..."

Lovecraft suggested that August add dime novels to his collections of stamps, comics, detective fiction, weird and macabre fiction, regional American literature, and records. They argued about the supernatural, Lovecraft writing at great length to support his belief that there was no supreme deity and that man had no consciousness that would persevere after his demise.

They discussed the works of many writers, among them, Oscar Wilde, whose homosexual lifestyle and works were well known. August, with his newly acquired personal experience, still maintained that Wilde's lifestyle was decadent; that he acted like an alley cat, and love was not at all part of Wilde's debauchery.

Howard criticized August's writings. He encouraged August to write poetry as an exercise to improve his prose. Though August had dabbled a bit in poetry during his romance with Margery, he'd made no real attempt at serious poetic composi-tion until Lovecraft urged him to do so.[17]

Derleth was one of many aspiring young writers who kept up a constant stream, of correspondence with Lovecraft. Many of them later became famous in the field of fantasy and friends of one another. Among them were: Frank Belnap Long, Clark Ashton Smith, Alfred Galpin, Robert E. Howard, Donald Wandrei, Robert Bloch, Maurice W. Moe, J. Vernon Shea, Robert

Barlow, and others whom Lovecraft referred to as his "grandsons". Through Howard they began to correspond with each other, exchanging story critiques, books, and pertinent information; occasionally collaborating, and sometimes getting together for visits. Lovecraft was particularly impressed with August Derleth from the beginning. To Clark Ashton Smith he wrote, "I have just discovered a boy of seventeen who promises to develop into something of a fantaisiste...August William Derleth, whose name you may have seen as author of some rather immature stories in WEIRD TALES...turns out to be a veritable prodigy..." Over and over again, Lovecraft, expressed awe, delight, admiration, and incredibility concerning August Derleth in his letters.

To J. Vernon Shea he wrote, "When I say Derleth will soon lead all the rest of the gang, I speak seriously and advisedly....He has a profundity, seriousness, simplicity, and human insight that none of the rest of us can ever begin to duplicate. In comparison to his promise-laden sketches, my own tales are the superficial tinsel of a played-out never-ran...."[18]

Though called juvenile and prosaic fillers, hastily written, most of Derleth's early fantasy offerings sold. This encouraged him to continue writing, perfect his craft, keep his mind alert to new ideas, techniques, everything essential to turn out readable fiction. Farnsworth Wright was the kind of editor whom authors idolize. He was infinitely patient, constantly encouraging, throughly knowledgeable about the macabre genre. The Derleth-Wright association was mutually beneficial. WEIRD TALES gained a steady, reliable contributor who gradually built up a fan following in the United States and other countries as well.

Some of Derleth's stories bore the pseudonyms of Steve Grendon, Tally Mason, Eldon Heath, Simon West, Michael West, Kenyon Holmes, Will Garth, and Romily Devon: a necessary ploy to disguise the enormous amount of work contributed to WEIRD TALES alone. Will Garth was a name shared by other authors.[19]

Basil Copper, an English journalist, editor, collector, and avid fan of the macabre, was an overseas admirer of August's work. Copper wrote that he "...became enamored of an excellent writer of stories whose delicate-hued narratives had something in them of Algernon Blackwood and Lord Dunsany...a man named Stephen Grendon...." Copper thought that Derleth's ghost story, "Mister George", was one of the finest of its kind in the English language. Copper didn't know when he wrote that letter, the tremendous influence Derleth's work would have on his own writing career years later. When Derleth was unable to handle any more of the pastiche of Sherlock Holmes, Copper continued the genre with his own imitations of Derleth's Solar Pons. August graciously gave Copper his wholehearted permission to do so.[20]

As the boys' love affair flourished, they spent more time together, getting to know more about each other. They discovered they had two mutual interests. Mark, like August, was planning to attend the University of Wisconsin after finishing high school. Mark was a senior, August a junior, when their relationship began. Mark, like August, was determined to write serious literature someday. Derleth, with the self confidence, born of his successful sales so far, promised to tutor Mark. They would begin by collaborating on mysteries.

Although Wright was still buying regularly, the pay was small. He needed a job during the summer vacation to help accumulate his tuition. The boys would only be able to work on their collaborations in the late afternoons and early evenings. But where? The Derleth home was too crowded. The Schorer's house was much larger, but would not provide the quiet and privacy they needed to create and most important to indulge in their forbidden lifestyle. What to do? They put their heads together and came up with a perfect solution. They would rent a studio. August knew of an ideal place right near his favorite swimming hole. The upper story of a small building on Water Street, north of the harness shop, was for rent. It was close to a small undeveloped park alongside the Wisconsin River where Derleth had played since he was five. Somehow both young men managed to sell their parents on the idea; August with little trouble since he was by this time in complete control of his own life, in spite of Rosella's valiant and consistent efforts to talk him into some semblance of conformity. Mark's parents, richer and less strict than Derleth's, were also inclined to be more indulgent. Once settled, August was in seventh heaven. Mark was genuinely interested in learning everything he could about the writing craft, and August had much to offer, thanks to Farnsworth Wright's patient tutoring.

While August and Mark collaborated, August dreaming up the plots, and Mark making a rough first draft, then August writing and rewriting the final version, they were also having fun. They played cards with their landlady, ate her stale, though still tasty, cookies, swam nude in the holes along the river, and grew closer everyday.

The summer ended all too soon, and Mark had to leave for college, while August went back to high school. He did not give up the studio, however. Mark had joined a fraternity and would stay at its quarters there during the week, but would go back to the studio during the weekends. Derleth invited two of his friends, Karl Ganzlin and Pete Blankenheim, to stay at the studio during the week, for a portion of the rent. Mark still paid his share also, thus relieving Derleth of any financial responsibility.[21]

[1] A. D. to Ian Law, Aug. 4, 1958.

[2] August Derleth, Walden West, (N.Y., 1961) p. 56.

[3] Farnsworth Wright to A. D., Sept. 24, 1929; August Derleth, Writing Fiction, (Boston, Mass., 1946, pp. 163ff.

[4] Ibid., Oct. 15, 1925 (F. W. to A. D.); Biographer's notes taken while attending or auditing A. D. classes, 1963 to 1969.

[5] Rauth, "A listing of pulp stories", State of Wisconsin Historical Society Museum (SWHS) archives, Madison, Wis.

[6] Daniel Wheeler to A. D., March 31, 1931.

[7] August Derleth, Evening in Spring, (Sauk City, 1945) summary.

[8] Biographer's conclusion.

[9] Sauk City High School yearbook, 1928.

[10] Note 8, op. cit.

[11] Note 2,

[12] Ibid.,

[13] Carl Ganzlin tape. August Derleth Room, Sauk City Library.

[14] A. D. letter to

[15] Note 8, op. cit.

[16] A. D. to Farnsworth Wright, Sept. 24, 1929.

[17] Biographer viewed tape of all the Lovecraft letters to A. D. through courtesy of SWHS (State of Wisconsin Museum archives, Madison, Wis., and the Florida Atlantic University Library at Boca Raton, Florida.)

[18] August Derleth, Volumes I, II, III, IV, V, Lovecraft's Collected Letters, (Sauk City, Wisconsin).

[19] Note 3, (Writing Fiction); Note 4, (Biographer's notes); Note 2, p. 24.

[20] Basil Copper "A Giant Remembered", August Derleth Society newsletter, Vol 1, #2, pp. 1-ff.

[21] A. D. Journal.

Chapter Three

*"...I take my friends for what they are, faults and all, but
I'll be damned if I'll be put upon..."*[1]

Although William Derleth contributed a good portion of his
wages to help his son through college, and *WEIRD TALES*
purchased over 25 of August's macabre stories in those four
years, Derleth was hard pressed for money.[2] Of the $8.15 per
week from his father, $3.15 went to pay for a small room at 823
W. Johnson St. in Madison. It was August's garret, and
although he didn't actually starve, more often than not his
meals consisted of bananas, bread and milk. He was forced to
seek other income and found it in tutoring University of
Wisconsin students in psychology (without ever having taken
the course), history, English, and fencing, the only sport he'd
been actively interested in during high school.[3]

Despite these many demands on his time, Derleth kept
writing. He and Mark Schorer were both enrolled in a composi-
tion course instructed by Professor Helen C. White. Amused by
Professor White's confusion concerning some of the logistics of
conducting a class, they collaborated on a play for and about
her. She gave them an "A-". The minus, August felt, was for
their audacity in portraying a venerable, internationally
honored instructor and author as a dreamy, not-quite-with-it
teacher. Besides being a specialist in 16th and 17th century
literature, she was the first woman to be elected president of
the American Association of University Professors, recipient of
23 honorary degrees, and holder of over 10 important national
and international posts.[4] Professor White's teaching, for all of
Mark's and August's caricaturing of it, undoubtedly had an
influence on both authors' future writing. Derleth maintained a
life-long friendship with her and sent her complimentary copies
of his saga books as they came out.

Mark and August found time to write, direct, and produce a
number of plays for little theater while attending the university.
However, things were not quite the same between them. August

needed to work and stretch every penny while Mark was subsidized by his more affluent family. This changed their situations considerably. They moved in different social circles. Mark, with more time and money on his hands, made new friends. They still worked on fantasy stories together and had access to each other's desks. In addition to his various activities, Derleth had started to jot down notes and ideas and sketches that would provide a skeleton for a major writing project he had long dreamed of doing. He'd confided that dream to Mark when they were in high school. He planned to do a series of historical and biographical novels, short stories and poetry, perhaps 25 to 50 volumes, that would someday became a Sac Prairie saga. One day while thumbing through Mark's manuscripts looking for one of their macabre collaborations, August chanced upon two short stories written by Mark that, August claimed, were written around his notes. Derleth was outraged. Once again, he'd been betrayed. Someone he trusted and loved was stealing his notes and his ideas. The break between them was immediate and complete.[5]

The experience may have been the impetus for August's decision to write his first novel. Surely Mark's betrayal stirred up painful memories. August's experience with "Margery" had drawn heart's blood, churned and fomented inside of him for years. He'd written bits and pieces of the experience before, but now, in the space of a few short weeks, a complete novel gushed out in the rare wine of an idyll of love he would one day name *EVENING IN SPRING*.

"...Mr. Derleth's fine writing and excellent characterization lift this novel above the level of a mere idyll..." wrote one reviewer years later, after publication.

"...A story of first love, told with tenderness and charm..." a New York reviewer observed.

"...It's as though he turned back the pages of an old diary and told with rekindled emotion, of the pangs of pain, and the sharp, clear sweetness of a boy's first love..." a *CHICAGO TRIBUNE* reviewer said.[6]

August's years at the University of Wisconsin were to prove very productive, creatively. Since childhood, he had waited in anticipation for each succeeding adventure of Sherlock Holmes.

When the wait between Sherlock Holmes' last adventures became unusually long, Derleth wrote to Sir Arthur Conan Doyle and asked if he planned to write any more of the mysteries. At his "non committal reply", August jotted down "re: Sherlock Holmes" on his calendar. In no time at all he was carrying on the antics of his two favorite characters under the pseudonyms of Doctor Parker and Solar Pons: "Solar" for light, "Pons" for bridge. He imitated Doyle's characters and style as closely as possible. He felt Sir Arthur had, to a large extent, done the same by closely imitating Edgar Allen Poe's Auguste Dupin.

One reviewer said of Derleth's collection of the pastiches, years later, that *IN RE: SHERLOCK HOLMES – THE ADVENTURES OF SOLAR PONS* had "...something of the feel and atmosphere of Baker St.: fog, hansom cabs, and the clatter of horses hooves on the pavements of old London."

Vincent Starret, Bookman, said Pons was "...not a caricature of Sherlock Holmes...rather a clever impersonation with a twinkle in his eye...."

The first Solar Pons pastiche, "The Adventure of the Black Narcissus", was an instant success. Harold H. Hersey of *DRAGNET* accepted the story and said to send more. He was prepared to take up to $1,500 worth.

August cut classes to write "The Adventures of the Missing Tenants", "The Adventure of the Broken Chessman", and "The Adventure of the Late Mr. Faversham". In one day's writing, he turned out "The Adventure of the Viennese Museum", "The Adventure of the Limping Man", and "The Adventure of the Greshom Old Place", followed by three more during the same week: "The Adventure of the Muttering Man", "The Adventure of the Black Cardinal", and "The Adventure of the Sothesby Salesman".

Writing these pastiches was more a game than an art to August. He picked the titles first, then built the mysteries around them. His ideas were culled from photos in *COUNTRY LIFE MAGAZINE*, some from real life. An article about the Bronze Age stone circle and another of the Rollright stones and the boundary of Oxfordshire and Warwicksberg triggered "The Adventure of the Whispering Knights".

August felt the stories did not measure up to the titles. He was really satisfied with only two of them, "The Adventure of the Purloined Periap" and "The Adventure of the Six Silver Spiders".

With the bright prospect of all those checks for selling pastiches ahead, Derleth did what any spirited young man would do under the circumstances. He celebrated, at a bookstore instead of a bar or fancy restaurant. Before he was through, he'd deposited $100 down and walked out with $500 worth of books, enough to slake his mental thirst for a long, long time. Then he sat down and wrote more pastiche.

His market for them ended when the 1929 market crash in October put Hersey out of business. August had to borrow the $400 to pay the balance of the book bill in 1930. Though a painful experience, he learned early that "...great expectations never take the place of cash in hand...."

The books themselves were another valuable benefit. Proust, Dostoveski, Tolstoi, Thomas Hardy, Turgenave, Frost, Masters, Sherwood Anderson, Sinclair Lewis, Andre Gide, and Oscar Wilde formed a good nucleus for the library of 1,200 volumes he would some day amass. They were also a good way to augment his formal education.

A decade later, August noticed an announcement that Fred Danney, a bibliographer of detective stories, was planning *THE MISADVENTURES OF SHERLOCK HOLMES*. Derleth dug out "The Adventure of the Narcrosse Riddle", revised it, and sent it to Danney. The bibliographer was enthused, and asked for more such stories, enough for a book of them. August had only five he thought good enough. He would need 12. He sat down and wrote seven more. He submitted them and then decided to publish the book himself. This time he used the Mycroft and Moran imprint, "...the deerstalker as colophon and Baskerville, the typeface. All were inevitable and part...of the game...." The book was titled *IN RE: SHERLOCK HOLMES*, the note he'd scribbled on his calendar while in college. In 1957, six years after the first book, he published *THE MEMOIRS OF SOLAR PONS*, containing eleven tales, the same number Doyle had in *MEMOIRS OF THE CANNON*. A grand design of pastiche, an entire sequence of the Sherlock Holmes tales, emerged. By 1965, *THE RETURN OF SOLAR PONS* (1958), *THE REMINISCENCES OF SOLAR PONS* (1961), and *THE CASEBOOK OF SOLAR PONS* (1965) had been written and published. With the design accomplished, August wrote "...I cannot promise to write no more of them...." There were a total of 56 Pontine tales.

Writing the first draft of *PEOPLE* (later called *EVENING IN SPRING*) had undoubtedly served as a catharsis for his unhappy love affair. Derleth was then able to put the experience behind him to a certain extent. Without Mark, he was once again lonely and vulnerable. Perhaps, too, Mark's behavior had made Derleth realize that his bitterness against women in general after Margery failed him, was stupid. It was the individuals who'd been unfaithful, and gender had nothing to do with it.[7] When he fell in love again, it was with a student from England he called "Winifred".[8] The influence of Winifred may have helped August achieve a more authentic flavor in his pastiche, and avoid repeating his earlier mistake of using cockney English in the wrong area of England.[9]

The couple wanted desperately to marry, but marriage was totally out of the question for Derleth. He would have had to quit college. A steady job would be necessary, and jobs in the depression years were almost non-existent. The single biggest drawback to their marrying was that August would have to give up most of his writing. He had come too far for that. He put Winifred reluctantly, but firmly, out of his life,[10] except for a few of his later poems which he dedicated to her memory.[11] By the time he graduated from college, Derleth realized he would have to take a regular paying position, anyhow. Right after graduation, he landed a job as editor of Fawcett Publications.

Minneapolis and the editor's job were both big disappointments to Derleth. Being mired down in the logistics of editing other authors' works cut deeply into his own writing schedule. He soon became impatient with sitting long hours at a desk, day after day. Although very disciplined under his own dictates, he was still the free spirit who, even at five, went where he wished, when he wished.[12]

He shared an office with the editor of *TRUE CONFESSIONS*, and often told students in his writing classes years later how romantically inclined the lady editor was, and how he spent a great deal of time dodging her amorous advances. Another anecdote from his six months sojourn in Minneapolis tells of his experience doubling, now and then, for a Miss Carolyn White, who managed a love-lorn department through a column called "Port of Lonely Hearts". When one reader wrote, complaining about her shabby treatment at the hands of her truck driver boyfriend, Derleth advised her to tell the man to get lost. An infuriated, hefty young truck driver turned up one morning at the Fawcett office looking for the author of the column. Derleth tried to enlist his amorous office mate to pose as the columnist and help the rejected suitor calm down. She refused, and Derleth had to lie saying Carolyn White was out of town.

Minneapolis itself was a far cry from Sauk City. He'd pace the streets at night and on Sundays, but no matter how far or how long he walked in any direction, he could never reach the outskirts of the Twin Cities, never reach grass and trees and rivers and marshes and a skyline unmarred by jagged scars of brick and stone.

He tried to fit in with people in the literary and aesthetic groups but could not relate to their Bohemianism, their trivial concerns, the way they worked at being "smart" and their affected manners.

In only six months he'd had enough of the big city ratrace and was back in Sac Prairie. Never again would he leave it willingly, for that long a time.[64]

SOURCE NOTES
CHAPTER THREE

1 A. D. to J. J. Lankes, March 29, 1957.
2 Rauth, "A listing of pulp stories", SWHS museum archives, Madison, Wisconsin, miscellaneous papers.
3 A. D. to Ian Law, December 15, 1956.
4 "Professor Helen C. White, noted U.W. English teacher, dies", *Capitol Times*, Madison, Wis., obituary page.
5 A. D. to Dr. Louise Phelps Kellog, June 3, 1942.
6 Back inside dust cover panel, August Derleth, Evening in Spring, (Sauk City, Wisconsin).
7 August Derleth, "Afterward, in re: Sherlock Holmes", SWHS museum archives, Madison, Wisconsin, miscellaneous papers, biographer's conclusions.
8 A. D. to Howard Duerr, July 4, 1959.
9 Note 7, conclusion.
10 Note 8, op. cit.
11 August Derleth, Collected Poems, (Prairie City, 1944), no page.
12 Note 8, op. cit.; note 7, conclusion.
13 A. D. to Mary Stiver, Sept. 22, 1960; biographer's notes and observations, auditing and attending A. D. classes.

Chapter Four

"...Sweet, sweet living. That's my life. I want nothing more. I write. How could I keep from writing? How the earth crests the hills in April, how the violets purple the earth in May, how the Spring night soothes with a thousand kindly hands...."[1]

It was good to get home to the snug, cozy white house, with its ever-fragrant kitchen, the huge coal stove, Rosella's piano in the parlor, her singing and playing her favorites – "Redwing, My Pretty Redwing" and "I'll Take You Home Again, Kathleen".

At home, right in the heart of Sauk City, Derleth was once again in touch with the townsfolk. Even as he churned out story after story in the small alcove, he kept enlarging his research into data that would one day go into his most important project – his Sac Prairie Saga. In his long walks, he talked to many of the characters who would later live between the pages of books like *WALDEN WEST, WALDEN WEST REVISITED, THE SHIELD OF THE VALIANT*, etc.[2]

H. P. Lovecraft had touched a responsive chord in August when he wrote: "...A man belongs where he has roots, where the landscape and mileau have some relation to his thoughts and feelings, by virtue of having formed them...."[3]

Everywhere August looked, everywhere he turned, he could see or remember how his thoughts and feelings had been formed. Here, unlike Minneapolis, less than half an hour's walk took him to the outskirts of town, past all the memories of his childhood; past the cemetery with "...Catholics buried on the south, Protestants on the north, and the Freethinkers in between...."

Past the Freethinkers' Park. It was in the shelter of the Freethinkers' Hall that his meetings with Margery had taken place, away from prying eyes. Past Frei Gemiende Hall, where August first heard the philosophies of Professor Max C. Otto, of the University of Wisconsin, and adopted them as his own. The spot had been an intellectual mecca, to which came notables from all over, expounding their views. Trainloads of people were brought in from Milwaukee and Madison to hear them.

Past the harness shop, where Hugh Schwenker still worked with leather, skillfully fashioning the harnesses for the teams of farmers who cultivated the rich loam of Sac Prairie and raised the acres of corn and peas and other produce that kept the canning factory operating. Hugh, who always did the nicest things; his friend, Hugh.

Another short hike from home would take August out to the Spring Slough, over which curved the Long Trestle, the Midmeadow Trestle, the Triangular Land Crossing. In a few minutes or a few hours he could reach Wisconsin Heights, Dead Dog Hole, in the back river; or Ice Slough; or Ehl's Slough, way up along the islands. Everywhere he turned, there were memories; catching panfish in the Millpond four miles west of town with Grandpa Derleth and Uncle Charlie; catfish or carp three-four miles south of town along the Wisconsin, with Karl or Hugh. Derleth always tried to palm off his catch on his friends. He liked to eat fish, but hated cleaning them.[4]

His collection of comics brought back many memories. "Toonerville Folks" about small town people; "Out Our Way" revealed a deep insight into human nature; "Barneygoogle", pure nonsense; and comics in which imagination was combined with fantasy, insight, and nonsense. He enjoyed the scope of those strips, the growth of the artists, and he felt most readers did not realize the strips were about themselves, characters that could be spotted in any walk of life. August's comics were to prove valuable as the years went by, not only as a collector's prize, but as a source of information for his work. When he needed to know the mode of dress, the peculiar slang expressions, even the policies and social problems of a particular period, he could usually find the answers there.[5]

Yes, it was good to be home, crowded as it was with these treasures of Derleth's past. Uncomfortable because even though Derleth's parents had agreed to subsidize his attempt to make a living by his writing alone, Rosella was still not convinced. He wrote, under stress, in a small alcove off the parlor, often to the accompaniment of the radio or interruptions from a group of chatting, giggling ladies in Rosella's card club. August settled down, nevertheless, to make a serious bid for literary independence.[6]

He was still placing titles with Farnsworth Wright, who still offered advice and cryptic criticism and bounced back stories again and again until August revised them to the editor's satisfaction. The pay for these was small, ranging from $18 for "A Cloak for Messeure Lando" to $60 for "Colonel Markesan" (a Schorer collaboration), yet considerably higher than the $10-$18 when he started selling. It was hardly enough to make him independent.[7] He also began placing stories in other fantasy magazines. In 1931, *TRUE MYSTIC MAGAZINE* published "Ghosts Who Return to Reenact Their Crimes", "Doomed by Curses That Last for Centuries", "They Saw Into the Future", "Your Picture Can Be Your Death Warrant", "This Great Lover Won Women by Magic Powers", and "I've Seen the Living Dead of the Black Island". *MIND MAGIC, AT DEAD OF NIGHT, STRANGE TALES, THE FANTASY FAN, THE WESTMIN-STER MAGAZINE. TERROR BY NIGHT* and *MARVEL TALES* also published his fantasy stories during the early thirties. Also several of his weird poems were accepted in this period. "Incubus" appeared in *WEIRD TALES*, "Man and the Cosmos" and "Omega" in *WONDER STORIES*, and "Only the Deserted" in *PANTAGRAPH*.[8]

According to Howard Lovecraft, August's detective and fantasy stories were carelessly written, loose, without rhythm, and even of doubtful grammar. In preparing *PEOPLE* for publication he did his first regional writing. In it, he developed a subtle musical rhythm, tighter writing, more precision and clarity.[9]

He sent the *PEOPLE (EVENING IN SPRING)* manuscript to Lovecraft shortly after he had arrived home from Minneapolis. Lovecraft was visiting in Florida with the Reverend Henry S. Whitehead, Rector of the Dunedin Church of the Good Shepherd, and head of a boy's school there. Whitehead, a fellow *WEIRD TALES* author whose work August greatly admired, had already been corresponding with Derleth for some time. After reading an article of Derleth's, "The Intelligentsia", in *MIDWESTERN*, the minister had applauded the "...simplicity plus adequacy..." of the piece. They often argued through the mails, principally over August's use of the

English language. The Reverend Whitehead constantly preached sound English. He pointed out that there were as many possibilities for beauty, order, direction, movement, and fulfillment inside the restraints of correct grammar as there were in music, with its far more rigid rules. Whitehead wondered if August intended to use English to tell the world what he had to say, or use composition ranging all the way from a dadaist to a contortionist. He said that most writers who get sidetracked that way, if they wanted to get anywhere, went back to clear, idiomatic English. He abhorred one specific weakness of August's writing – frequent omission of the verb, which in his opinion destroyed August's sentences.[10]

Both Whitehead and Lovecraft, however, thought, *PEOPLE (EVENING IN SPRING)* a magnificent achievement and were full of praise.

Lovecraft had been supremely supportive all through Derleth's college years. He had furnished most of the research data for August's thesis on *WEIRD TALES*. He offered to show the *PEOPLE* manuscript to some editor who might use all, or parts of it. Derleth countered by typing some of Lovecraft's material, sending him books, even once persuading Farnsworth Wright to accept "In the Vault", a story of Lovecraft's that Wright had already turned down several times.

H. P. L. never ceased to be amazed at August's ability to turn out both serious and popular writing. He often expressed a wistful envy over the younger author's inexhaustible drive and energy. Derleth, he thought, was fast perfecting an insight and poignancy reminiscent of Proust.[11]

Derleth began to explore the history of Sac Prairie in preparation of his saga. He ferreted out old letters, town records, newspapers, diaries, skeletons, and long buried secrets. As he roamed the streets of his microcosm, gossiping with his neighbors, a whole macrocosm of story material emerged, revealing all the drama, the conflicts, the heartaches and despair, the quirks of character that bedevil the human race everywhere.

There was the tragedy of a widow and her daughter who became imprisoned in their memories, fears of suicide and insanity; the crime of the doctor who had consoled a bereaved sister-in-law too well, delivered their resulting child, placing its dead body in a shoe box to float down the Wisconsin River and the city fathers who simply ordered the young doctor out of town; a young lover who committed suicide when he could not persuade his sweetheart to elope because of her parents' strong disapproval of the match; the poor woman who was committed to an institution and died quietly there, "...erased as casually as a penciled mistake on a piece of paper...." There was the "fly" figure in lavender who met the incoming trains and "serviced" the hawkers. He listened and gathered and noted it all down. He probed relentlessly through the texture of the area and came forth with sketches that, according to Lovecraft, revealed "...curious, brooding characters...proud, grim, old gentlewomen harboring ominous secrets; decadent scions with relentless hereditary taints; patriarchal or matriarchal tyrants dominating individual children or entire households; haughty, destitute aristocrats recalling past glories amidst present squalor..." and on and on.

Pacing the quiet, shady streets and verdant country lanes of his beloved Sac Prairie, Derleth discovered Thoreau's "...quiet desperation of mankind everywhere...." Like Thoreau, he turned to the beauties of nature, keeping accounts in his daily hikes, marking the comings and goings of birds, the blossoming of the flowers, the habits of the fauna, the ebb and flow of the seasons.[12]

As he hiked, he jotted down inspirations for poems in tiny notebooks which would one day number into the hundreds. These scrawled notations, would be expanded, shaped, and after up to as many as 72 rewrites would emerge as poetry.[13]

His Grandfather Adams, of *EVENING IN SPRING*, was the character described by Derleth as a projection of himself; a man with a rugged wisdom and a chuckle-evoking sense of humor. Like Derleth, he expressed almost an obsession in his life, with the rapid flight of time.

"...When you are young, you think you have all the time in the world. When you find out you don't, it's too late...you were licked before you started,...."

Grandfather Grendon also comments on time. "We measure everything by time, whether we are cooking an egg for breakfast or holding the stop watch on a dying man...Take my grandson now. He is obsessed by the sense of time. He is convinced he will never have time enough to do all the things he wants to do. The fact is, most of the things he wants to do are not very important. In some respects they represent an extension of his ego."

Other profound realizations find a voice in that of Grandfather Adams. On conformity:

"...They teach it to you from the time you're old enough to wear diapers...the right things to say...."; "...the loneliness of small, pitiful, self-righteous people: "...In some ways, we're all lonely..."; on Steve: "...That boy thrives on opposition and I guess anybody but his mother would have seen this a long time ago...."[14]

Rosella did not see it, which may have been one of the factors that kept August plugging away at his typewriter during the early thirties rather than running around with other young people in their pursuit of various pleasures. He was driven, too, by the need to write something that he could read over without flinching. August's lack of a steady job was getting him the same reputation as Thoreau's: shiftless, ne'er-do-well, lazy. Rosella, swayed by her neighbors' comments and slurs and her own desire to have August amount to something, kept right on opposing her son's determination to write. August kept right on writing.

She was no match for him. Undoubtedly both she and William Derleth were bewildered at the individuality August not only exhibited to them but flaunted to the whole area. August was marching to the drum of Ralph Waldo Emerson: "...Whosoever would be a man must be a non-conformist...."

Thoreau, too, was the epitome of non-conformity as was Wisconsin's own Frank Lloyd Wright. Wright was a flamboyant individualist in dress, lifestyle, and most of all in his talented architecture. His self-designed home, Taliesen, was only a few miles from Sauk City and he visited the town often. In him young Derleth had an example of what a genius was like. It was only natural August should imitate him, should conform even in an act of non-conformity, in the matter of dress as well as other areas.[15] He did not adopt the dramatic opera cape Wright wore at first. That did not come until twenty years later. August did design on ankle-length robe and had a tailor make it up in black velvet, with a green lining. He also sported a lorgnette, and an alpaca overcoat.

One of the newer Sauk City residents, seeing August stride along Water Street in his flashy, ankle-length overcoat, fur bonnet, swinging a cane, tells people now "...I didn't know who he was then, but it was obvious to me he was somebody...."

Another resident of the village tells the legend of a little boy who, as Derleth passed by, turned to his mother with big eyes and asked, in awed, trembling tones, "Is that Jesus? Or is that God?"[16]

Lovecraft had quite another reaction to Derleth's finery: "...I think you'll outgrow your present satorical amusements...Your lorgnette, robe and alpaca overcoat correspond to my Jesse James whiskers and policeman's badge and cowboy hat of thirty years ago..." he wrote. "Go ahead son, and don't let the old folks spoil your good time....";[17] also Derleth as "...an almost amusing egotist who deliberately cultivated eccentricity in order to irritate the complacent bourgeoisie of his somewhat smug and provincial village. He wore a monacle and flaring-tailed overcoat that almost touched the ground, went outdoors (and once to an ice cream social) in a dressing gown and had himself snapshotted in all sorts of asinine poses..."[18]

August never did outgrow the luxurious robe, but had new ones made up in the same pattern with different colors: a deep blue chiffon velvet robe lined with dark gray frost crepe and one of wine velvet.[19]

It is doubtful that Derleth was playing some sort of childish, make-believe game. More likely by that time he was becoming more aware of his own stature and potential. Things were happening to indicate that others were also beginning to sit up and take notice of the Wisconsin author; others outside of Sac Prairie, that is.

SOURCE NOTES
CHAPTER FOUR

[1] August Derleth, Place of Hawks, (N.Y., 1935), p. 91.
[2] August Derleth, Walden West, (N.Y., 1961) pp. 202, 207, 220.
[3] Lovecraft to A. D., Oct. 16, 1929; biographer viewed VCR tape courtesy of Florida Atlantic University library, Boca Raton, and SWHS museum archives, Madison, Wisconsin.
[4] August Derleth, Countryman's Journal, (N.Y., 1963), throughout book; Karl Ganzlin tape, August Derleth Room, Sauk City Library, Sauk City, Wisconsin and SWHS Museum archives, Madison, Wisconsin.
[5] August Derleth, "On Collecting Comics", unpublished manuscript, SWHS museum archives, Madison, Wisconsin.
[6] A. D. to Ian Law, Jan. 7, 1958.
[7] Farnsworth Wright to A. D., Oct. 21, 1928 and May 28, 1929.
[8] Jerald E. Rauth, "A list of pulp stories", SWHS museum archives, Madison, Wis.
[9] Lovecraft letter to Vernon Shea, Oct. 27, 1932.
[10] Henry S. White to A. D., Dec. 6 and 16th, 1931.
[11] Note 3, hoc. sic.
[12] Note 2.
[13] Biographer research, paging through 200+ notebooks at the SWHS museum archives.
[14] August Derleth, Evening in Spring, (Sauk City, Wisconsin, 1937), pp. 3-ff, 106 and 107.
[15] Biographer's conclusions.
[16] Interview with Sibyl Tarnitzer, Prairie du Sac, Wisconsin, July, 1979.
[17] Note 3, op. cit.
[18] Ibid.
[19] See Chapter Five.

Chapter Five

"...I am luckier than most for I still have about me all the familiar scene...and some of the loved people...of my childhood and youth....Moreover, I have incorporated them into print so that I have them not only in mind and heart, but tangibly at hand all the time..."[1]

Derleth, determined to make a living writing even in the face of the depression, branched out into several other directions besides the macabre and the pastiche. He began to submit the stories and sketches that went into his *EVENING IN SPRING*, and others he'd been collecting for his saga to editors and they began to sell to *MIDLAND* and other small magazines. Their quality was recognized when twelve of his short stories received an O'Brien Honor Award in 1933. One of the twelve – "Old Huckleberry" earned their Roll of Honor Award.[2]

He also contracted with Christine Campbell Thompson, Lt., international literary agents, to sell reprints of his material overseas. The *LONDON DAILY EXPRESS* took "Hawk on the Blue" and paid their top price – eight guineas. Christine Campbell, herself, favored August's "Muggeridge's Aunt" and couldn't understand why it was "...rather a stickler..." in the states, because people in England loved it. These were among the first of a long list of Derleth's writings published in England.[3]

He began a new book-length original mystery series, with Judge Ephraim Peck as the central sleuth and the Sac Prairie area and characters woven into the plots. Like the Solar Pons pastiche, his first volume, *MURDER STALKS THE WAKELY FAMILY*, was an instant success. The publishers, Loren and Mussey, were so impressed with Derleth's work they set about trying to corner the Derleth market by promising to bring out four of his books a year: two Judge Peck novels under August's own name and two Solar Pons under a pseudonym. They also offered to publish a fifth book, providing it was a serious novel under Derleth's own name. In June of 1934, he signed a contract with them for six Solar Pons novels to be published under the name of Mason Talliaferre (later changed to Tally Mason).

Derleth had been thinking for a long time about the books in his saga, which he planned would span a period of 125 years. Although he had abundant research material at hand, he did not have a serious book manuscript ready to submit to Loren and Mussey for the fifth publication they'd promised. He went through his material and picked four sketches which he could develop into four separate novellas and combine into a book. Tragedy would be the element that linked the four tales together. He offered them in place of a full length novel. With the country under the heavy financial gloom of the depression, Loren and Mussey were reluctant to take a chance on the inter-related stories of four doomed Sac Prairie families. Shrewdly, Derleth volunteered to waive the royalties on *PLACE OF HAWKS* until it paid out, if they would publish it. His offer convinced them that Derleth had consideration for publishers and was the kind of a man with whom they would be happy to work, so they accepted it. *PLACE OF HAWKS* became Derleth's first published book in the saga. Loren and Mussey published *MURDER STALKS THE WAKELY FAMILY* and *THE MAN ON ALL FOURS* in 1934; *SIGN OF FEAR, THREE WHO DIED*, and *PLACE OF HAWKS* in 1935.[4]

Determined not to be caught short again, should someone offer to publish another of his saga novels, Derleth set to work on his most ambitious book so far, *STILL IS THE SUMMER NIGHT*. It was his first historical novel. When he submitted several chapters and an outline to Charles Scribner's Sons, he became another in a long line of successful authors nurtured by Scribners' prestigious Maxwell Perkins. Wolfe, Fitzgerald, and Hemingway had all worked with Perkins.

The new relationship did not jell without considerable struggle, however. Flushed with the achievement of five books published in two years, Derleth was high-handed at first and attempted to dictate financial terms and contract conditions to Perkins. Perkins was unhappy with the ending of the first draft of the manuscript which, like *PLACE OF HAWKS*, was tragic. He was also doubtful Derleth could do a credible writing job on the book in view of his many other commitments. The writing that he, and many others at that time, regarded as Derleth's hack work, gave little assurance of the young author's ability to separate the two activities, to keep the hack writing from spilling into the more serious work. He rejected August's first hasty draft. August rewrote with more care and Perkins relented a bit on his refusal to go along with any of Derleth's demands agreeing to give an advance. The book was published in 1937. It marked the beginning of a profitable literary relationship.[5]

Maxwell Perkins had good reason to doubt Derleth's ability to produce an ambitious, serious work in so short a time, for August was branching out into several new writing ventures.

A series of short stories emerged at this time built around a bucolic farm couple, Great Aunt Lou and Uncle Joe Stoll (modeled on Derleth's Great Aunt and Uncle Gelhause) and their chuckle-provoking neighbor, the unforgettable Gus Elker. Elker wore an old straw hat perched on the back of his head, had a corn-colored mustache that drooped around the corners of his mouth, and generally wore a lugubrious expression. Five of these stories were published in 1935 and 1936: "Now Is the Time for All Good Men" – a story of Gus's political revenge; "The Old Lady Has Her Day" – describing Aunt Lou's shrewd tactics in saving a neighbors farm from the money-lenders; and "The Lady Turns the Other Cheek" – telling how she outsharked the card sharks. Scribners published all of these. "The Moon Rises Twice" – revealing Aunt Lou's strategy in mending cousin Kathy's broken love affair, and "Expedition to the North" – Gus's determined hunt for a hawk, only to release the trapped bird once he caught it, appeared in *HOUSEHOLDER MAGAZINE*. The Gus Elker story, "The Alphabet Begins with AAA" hit the prestigious *ATLANTIC MONTHLY* in December, 1935. It was all about Gus's elaborate maneuvers to save his pet pig from the government's heartless ax. The editor, F. Sedgewick, tempered August's triumph, however, with her disapproving comment that the magazine did not usually publish such "burlesque". In time, Derleth was to write fifty of these exploits of Gus and the Stolls.

After Derleth's death, when it was quite obvious he was the most important author of the 20th century and the reprints of August's books were planned, these episodes of their neighbors,

Stolls and Gus, *COUNTRY MATTERS* was chosen the first book in a series of 30 Derleth reprints and unpublished material planned for publication within five years.[6]

Other tales resulting from Derleth's methodical prying into the ancient stories and ongoing drama of Sac Prairie were published; one of them – "The No-Sayers" – in the *BROOKLYN EAGLE*. The no-sayers were people who constantly said "no" to life and consequently never really lived.[7]

Another of Derleth's projects at this time was a series of nature pieces contracted by *OUTDOOR MAGAZINE*. Most of these were descriptive passages or vignettes geared to the months in which they appeared, as evidenced by their titles: "Night in October", "January Thaw", "February Pussy Willows", etc...

August's ability to utilize every phase of his daily life experiences in his literary output, is evident in these pieces. He incorporated in each, along with the appropriate mood and climate of the period: 1.) His trips to visit a fishing camp of Hugo Schwenker and Peter Blankenheim, describing their humorous reactions to various situations; 2.) His descriptive prose re the flora and fauna that rivals his own poetry for beauty and vivid illustration of the prairie, the hills, and the marshes of his beloved Sac Prairie; and 3.) His underlying, deeper, profounder philosophical beliefs, such as, for example, the following note from "Night in October".

> *"...I thought of the growing consciousness of quiet as a symbol of man's lifelong isolation even from others of his kind, and it came to me as it has come often before and since that the outdoorsman, the naturalist, the man close to the soil, the man who knows the aspects of earth and its creatures in all their changes is by virtue of this magic knowledge, less alone than that vast army who remain in ignorance of these many-faceted secrets and are thus without the solace to be found in knowledge of earth lore...."*[8]

As usual, on these jaunts, nothing was too small to escape Derleth's eye. One of the articles he wrote for *OUTDOORS* was almost entirely concerned with Hugh and Augie's study of black ants, herding their herds of 25-60 common plant lice – like so many cows – into a clump of tender green willow twigs, forcing them to feed on the willows, then eating the drops of transparent white secretion they produced. If a louse stopped feeding, a guarding ant immediately forced its head back into the willow twig and kept it there until it resumed its gorging.[9]

The build-up of confidence and self esteem that accompanied all these sales was substantiated by the actual cash build-up of Derleth's income. The big magazine stories went for $150 each, a windfall in comparison to the average $25 received for the sixteen pulp stories of the macabre placed during 1934 and 1935.

A break-down of his income during the two year period shows approximately $574 for book royalties, $400 royalty advance, and $1,631 in magazine sales, making a total of $2,605, without incidental sales and fees for lecturing and teaching at various educational events and seminars.[10]

A man could live on $1,500 a year in 1935, not royally, but as good as most. With the rapid turnout of more books to bring in more royalties, and with increased teaching and lecturing fees, he could even begin to dream about building a house big enough to hold his ever expanding library (already containing more volumes than the Sauk City Library), his thousands of comic strips (bulging out of two closets in his parents' home), his records (numbering close to a thousand), the growing piles of magazines in which he was published, his dime-novel collection, the twenty-five to fifty volume Sac Prairie saga he planned to write, and people – lots of people – without the agonizing, cramping, and falling over each other's feet that was becoming a daily hazard in the house August still loved, but had long outgrown. He wanted a large, comfortable, informal house, with a place for everything. Most important of all, a house in which he could say "yes" to life.

August's decision to forgo marrying Winifred had stemmed from his practical, common sense side. The emotional August, however, had sustained still another painful blow. The hunger for someone to love, and reciprocate that love, was back again. He was still suffering over Winifred, wanting someone to fill the void.

He simply could not afford to get involved in any serious relationship. He buckled down to his writing and for a while, seemed successful in pushing any thought of looking for someone new out of his conscious mind. This did not, however, prevent him from noticing the more attractive ladies and the pretty young students in the area.

One of the Sac Prairie ladies Derleth came in contact with at this time was unusually beautiful.[11] "Maris" was married, however. Her husband was held in high esteem in Sac Prairie for his professional expertise. Consequently, he was an extremely busy man. He lacked social graces, according to a doctor's wife who was one of the Sac Prairie elite. She felt he was not a very suitable mate for Maris. She described him as being rather uncouth; as fond of the company of bawdy type women and in the habit of telling off-color jokes, etc. She indicated that according to a town gossip, one of the floozies he associated with, was his mistress. Maris, in contrast, was cultured, intelligent, a good, steady, capable person who had had a successful career of her own before marrying and bearing children.[12]

As the years passed, Derleth's casual acquaintance with Maris grew into a warm friendship, and finally, a love affair. They were both vulnerable, lonely, needing someone who cared. It was spring. Sac Prairie was bursting with the promise of a lush, green summer in Dane County, which seems touched by a magic wand of nature that makes it one of the most beautiful spots in Wisconsin.

Derleth's enchantment with Maris, like so many of his romances, was woven into the lovely Sac Prairie countryside. He picked mulberries and fed them to her on the eastern slope across the Wisconsin River. Years later, walking the same paths they had strolled together, he found his memories of her very pleasant. Ferry Bluff, at the bend in the Yellow Banks Road, one of Derleth's favorite spots, visited for innumerable moonlight strolls with friends, etc., would ever after remind him of a memorable night in July when he was there alone with Maris.[13]

Somewhere along the way they must have met, too, in a small room. In the poem titled "Valse Jubilee", August mourns the absence of Maris, two years and a springtime later,

"...I have never since that time gone there into that room but that lilac fragrance was in the air from the place it rose out of your hair...."[14]

Derleth felt he had to break with Maris when she began talking about marrying him. He was still in no condition financially to marry anyone. Although he seemed to bear little guilt for having started the affair in the first place, with the wife of a man he knew and respected, he could not break up a marriage and a family or deprive Maris's children of their natural father. Maris was heartbroken, but could do nothing to change his mind.[15]

August's guilt came later, and was expressed in another poem named "Of Grief":

> *"...What have I brought her of love but grief?*
> *of love her heart full, of grief twice over,*
> *sorrow and pain, gave love and took*
> *her love in vain.*
> *What have I given her but love:*
> *and love and the slow the lasting grief?....*[16]

Maris remained a staunch friend of Derleth's throughout his life. An interview with her after his death disclosed her life-long devotion to him and his memory, and gave the interviewer a distinct impression her love had lasted, too.[17]

Derleth gave certain clues to the affair in his writing. Some of the short stories based on the romance, which he "...purposely beclouded..." were published in England and not permitted publication in the States. These were the "Joan" stories.[18]

Derleth's respect and affection for Maris lasted long after both the passion and the agony were but nostalgic memories, spurred, now and then by his poetry – like sprigs of faded, dried lilacs, pressed between the pages of a book.

Despite the sad experience, Derleth clung to his determination to enjoy life, to experience as much as he could as long as he didn't hurt other lives or destroy anyone else's happiness. To accomplish this and pursue his own particular lifestyle, Derleth wanted his own home; a house far enough away from others to afford him peace and privacy when he desired it, large enough for people when he needed them, and near enough to enable him to regularly take, in an hour's hike, the heart beat and pulse of Sac Prairie.

In the process of researching for his saga historicals, he found the ideal spot, ten acres of land on the west outskirts of

Sauk City, across from the cemetery. It was a part of the Lueders' estate, the same Frederich Lueders who appears in *RESTLESS IS THE RIVER*, one of his later saga books. Lueders had been a German student at the Hamburg Botanical Academy before migrating to Wisconsin. The windbreak and the cedars and the conifers on Derleth's newly acquired property had been planted by the botanist.

Leo Weissenborn, whom August had met at the Freethinkers' Hall, and who had studied in Paris, would design the house. William Derleth would help to build it. The proposed layout was: "...A simple T-shape with short stem, long bar; full basement 64' long, 41' deep at the stem through the cross bar; north-wing basement room housing comic, weird book, detective, and phonograph record collections; south-wing first floor 20' x 30' living room; second floor, gabled studio, same size. West-wing twin bedrooms, bath and cedar closet first floor, with a bath, personal closet, and a larger bedroom and closet upstairs."

The official descriptions gave no hint of some of the unorthodox features that were later incorporated into the dwelling: an unusual thatched roof from India; secret sliding panels to hide his bookshelves, built three-deep so they could accommodate his immense library; kitchen cupboards attached to the ceiling in such a way that they could be used as separators and moved about to make various sized rooms.[19] At one time he even contemplated building a secret room by submerging the living room. Ed Klein, a correspondent to whom August described his plan, wondered at the purpose of an "elevator" room, and why it would be accessible only through the living room. Would that be the only entrance, or would it open into a room upstairs?[20] Twenty years later, Hugh Schwenker, when asked whether he heard of such a secret room said "No".[21] Perhaps Derleth, intending to keep the room a secret, would not have told even his best friend about it. August's father claimed it couldn't be accomplished.[22] August, however, was not one who gave up easily. He'd had enough experience in his literary career so far to know that if he wanted something badly enough, there were ways to get it. Years later, a visitor at the Place of Hawks, (William Dutch, who had been so charmed with

Derleth's writings about Sauk City and Sac Prairie, moved into the area nearby after his retirement from his position as Supervisor of Education in Chicago), was puzzled to see a beautiful young woman seated in one of the two easy chairs in August's studio. He'd spent half an hour talking to Derleth, had not noticed her there when he walked into the studio and had no inkling anyone besides himself had entered the room. Other such strange incidents cropped up during the years, indicating that there might actually be, if not a room, a hidden stairway, perhaps, connecting the two massive fireplaces from the living room downstairs to August's studio.[23] Derleth was startled awake at one a.m. by someone knocking at his bedroom window. It was Marty, Augie's young male lover, taken after Derleth moved into the Place of Hawks. He had climbed up to the balcony. Derleth was puzzled until he realized a group of students was below. They had come to finish off their evening with a few hours dancing in his recreation room. Nothing unusual, except that Marty never entered the studio that way, although he spent many nights in August's bed. How did he manage that without others knowing he was there? A secret stairway, perhaps – from one fireplace to the other, with the parlor entry downstairs containing an outside exit also?[24]

Though increasingly busy, Derleth was nudged into public service at this time. He was young, under 30, but had already criticized the School Board's decisions on several occasions when they did not coincide with his opinions. When Jo Merk, Sauk City librarian, told him she had cancer, that she was dying, and could no longer serve on the board, she turned to him and asked, "Why don't you run?"

If he could criticize, he should be willing to step in and work for the improvements he wanted, she argued, pointing out that if responsible people didn't run, irresponsible ones would be elected. She touched a chord there and August was hooked.[25]

August announced his decision to run for the school board to a neighbor, Effie Bachhuber, board president. He had introduced Effie to the world of literature when he enlisted her aide in the proofing of his book galleys, a chore he detested. She became a valuable assistant, a never failing source of comfort and help and congenial companionship, not to mention the

51

creative genius behind a mountain of baked goodies August enjoyed almost daily as he stopped to say hello on his trips to the library. Her husband, Dr. Harold Bachhuber, served as August's personal physician as well as good friend. He was also a valuable consultant for the medical technicalities utilized in Derleth's murder mysteries and other fiction.[26]

After Maris, August tried to veer away from any serious romantic involvements. Something in him, however, could not refrain from going out of his way to shock the Sac Prairie populace and supply it with ample fuel for the gossip mongers. As a member of the school board, he became friendly with many of the teenagers in the area. He made sure he was seen strolling through the countryside, dancing at the school hops, etc., with some of the more attractive girls, keeping the gossiping tongues clucking constantly. When he escorted John Stanton's younger sister to the junior prom, the party lines were jammed with comments such as: "He's more than twice her age."; "A disgrace to the school board."; "Such gall."; etc., much to Derleth's amusement.

The author, with his usual concern and sensitivity in the multitude of special, unheralded favors he did for others, did not bother to enlighten the town gossips about the real reason he had escorted the young lady to the prom. She had been invited by some cruel prankster to attend, gone through all the usual fuss and expense of a new gown, a more elaborate and sophisticated hairdo, etc., only to realize after an hour's wait, that she had been stood up. Derleth offered to escort her there himself. He was on his way to the high school to help chaperone the gala event. She could enjoy the music and dancing. She worried about what people might say, seeing a member of the school board showing up with a student, but he talked her into going with him. He not only danced with her himself, giving her the special experience of dancing with the best dancer in Sauk City, he filled her card with the names of students who frequented Place of Hawks and would be polishing off the evening with an after prom party there later, and arranged to have one of them take her along. For the first time in her young life, she had a ball. Derleth, fearful of what he might do to the young punk, asked her not to let him know who it was that made her a bid to the Junior Prom.[27]

One of the young high school students Derleth called "Cassandra", was especially appealing. Derleth had noticed her several times and was somehow drawn to her. She was a graceful dancer, as was August. When she danced with him at the prom, the other dancers stopped to watch them.[28]

He also squired various visiting schoolmates of his who provided, not only pleasant company, but brought back nostalgic memories of his school days. They helped substantiate his growing reputation as a "ladies' man".

One of these, referred to as "Lona", was married and lived out of town, but came home alone frequently to spend time with her family. Up to Lona, Derleth had managed not to get involved in any more than casual, friendly reunions, still avoiding any danger of ending up married. He should have known better than to let things get out of hand with Lona, having experienced the agony of causing Maris and Winifred both so much pain, as well as himself, agony and guilt. Only when he realized her husband could easily get wind of their involvement, with the whole town aware of it, did he back away. It was not fear of what an enraged cuckold husband might do that scared him off so much as the fear that Lona had already chosen August to replace her spouse, and might even confess their affair to him.[29]

He escaped, again, the tender trap, but went through, again, the inevitable sense of pain and loss and wrote:

"...still feeling your arms and your mouth
and body's warmth
the long slow dying
the clandestine day ending in the night
dry leaves rattling at the window panes
and love growing mute with tears
under the covers...."[30]

SOURCE NOTES
CHAPTER FIVE

[1] A. D. letter to Dorothy Unseld, June, 1960.
[2] Evelyn Schroth, The Derleth Saga, (Appleton, Wisconsin, 1979), p. 39.
[3] Christine Campbell to A. D., Oct. 24, Nov. 5 and 12, Dec. 8, 1934.
[4] Loren and Mussey to A. D., Dec. 8, 1933 and Jan. 20, 1934.
[5] T. V. Olsen, Derleth's Historical Novels, "Still is a summer night", unpublished manuscript copy before publication, given to biographer.
[6] E. Sedgewick to A. D., March 13, 1935.
[7] A. D. letter to Ian Law, Aug. 4, 1958.
[8] August Derleth, "Night in October"; "Pike Country"; "July Night"; "February Pussywillows"; "January Thaw"; etc., Outdoor Magazine, 1935.
[9] Ibid., "Late Spring."
[10] A. D. Journal, sales list, Jan. 1, 1934-Feb. 1936 (incomplete), SWHS Museum archives, Madison, Wisconsin.
[11] Interview with "Maris", 1973, and viewing a portrait of her taken at the time of her relationship with Derleth, Sauk City, Wisconsin.
[12] Esther Trautman tape, sent to biographer, 1983, after she went blind.
[13] Note 10, 13, March 5 and 12, May, 1, 18, 22, 24, 26, and 14, 1937.
[14] August Derleth, Collected Poems, 1937 TO 1967, (Sauk City, Wis., 1967) "To Maris", pp. 81-ff.
[15] Note 13, op. cit.
[16] Note 14, op. cit., pp. 81ff., "Of grief..."
[17] Note 11, op. cit., interview.
[18] Romily Devon, "Notes on August Derleth", Dam Courier, Vol. III, No. 4, October, 1942, p. 4.
[19] Herbert Jacobs, "Home of August Derleth, the house that books built, last word in bachelor quarters", Capital Times, 1940.
[20] Ed Klein to A.D., no date.

[21] Interview with Hugo Schwenker, August 5, 1995, old harness shop, Water St., Sauk City, Wisconsin.

[22] Note 20, op. cit.

[23] Interview with William Dutch, Firehouse Restaurant, Prairie du Sac, Wis., 1971.

[24] A. D. Journal, 30 May, 1941, p. 82.

[25] Ibid.

[26] Note 12, op. cit.; C. W. Muelburger to Dr. Harold Bachhuber; May, 1935.

[27] A. D. Journal, 12 July, 1937.

[28] Ibid., 19 April, 1941.

[29] Ibid., 3rd September, 24 August, 1942.

[30] Note 14, to Lu.

Derleth at age 25, from a print appearing on the cover of a 1934 issue of <u>The Writers Review</u> featuring his prodigious 10,000-word daily output on a novel he was writing.

Chapter Six

"...Success of any kind always breeds envy in little people, and the overwhelming majority of people are little people, always will be...."[1]

August had begun work on the second historical novel in his saga. *WIND OVER WISCONSIN* was woven around the life of one of the first settlers in the area, with the fictitious name of Chalfonte Pierneau. It would investigate one of the most important early occupations in Wisconsin – fur trading – and include data about the Black Hawk War, waged and lost in the area by the Rock Island Sacs. He submitted a few chapters to Perkins, who urged completion of the novel in time for Scribners' spring list.[2]

The architecture of a much larger book, *RESTLESS IS THE RIVER*, was also beginning to take shape in Derleth's mind.[3] Faced with Perkins' deadline and the mountains of research involved in the two books, Derleth appealed to a former high school classmate for help. Alice Conger, a petite young brunette, had sharp eyes that literally snapped with spirit. Although she had already established herself as a rural school teacher when Derleth approached her, she agreed to help in her spare time.[4]

In the spring of 1937, August was saddened by the news of the death of H. P. Lovecraft. In the midst of all his projects he couldn't settle down to any serious writing.

He went for solace into the marshes day after day. It was spring, his most longed-for time of the year. He had always welcomed each new bud, the return of every bird, the welling of life in each leaf and blade of grass, and when spring finally burst out all over in May, Derleth abandoned his desk for the entire month to comb the hills for morels. He carried them in a wicker basket so the spores would drop through and reseed the area as he picked. It was a practice that lasted all through his days. No matter how busy, no matter what complications he may be facing, come May, he took to the hills for his mushrooms. He collected something else, too, in the process: something that would inspire his poems, and weave its way through the pages of his books like the breath of spring itself. In his day by day entries in his journal, along with a record of his daily activities, the chronicling of local events, a funny joke or story he'd heard, the deaths in the area, he wrote page after page of explicit nature descriptions.

In one of his strolls through the marshes, he noted the whippoorwills were crying for the soul of a dead or dying man according to an ancient belief. Something inside of August had been crying for a dead man's soul too, ever since March. Three months was long enough for grieving, he decided. It was time, now, to begin investigating some sort of H. P. L. memorial project, like a collection of his stories or letters, or plans for a biography.[5]

Donald Wandrei, one of the friends he had made while working in Minneapolis and one of the H. P. L. "grandsons", had been thinking of a Lovecraft short story collection, too. He suggested they combine their efforts, the two of them backing the first volume financially.[6]

J. Vernon Shea also thought the undertaking a good idea. He gave suggestions for specific stories of Lovecraft's that should, he believed, be included in such a memorial volume. Shea (like most of H. P. L.'s correspondents) had kept every letter received from Lovecraft and offered the use of them to Derleth and Wandrei.[7]

When H. P. L.'s will had named Robert H. Barlow his literary executor, Barlow wanted to publish a volume of Lovecraft's work, all by himself. Derleth was upset. Wandrei did not trust Barlow and Derleth didn't think he could create a book as fitting as the one they'd planned. Whatever they did, they realized it would be wise to have Barlow's cooperation. Derleth invited Barlow to Sauk City to visit.[8] Barlow couldn't make it, but agreed that Derleth take over. Barlow would send all the Lovecraft material he had to Derleth. In a letter to Mrs. Gamwell, H. P. L.'s aunt, Barlow said that concerning Lovecraft's material, she could make whatever arrangement she pleased with Derleth and Wandrei.[9] According to August, she signed over any possible profits from the venture, and years later, claimed Mrs. Gamwell had willed Lovecraft's rights to them, also.[10] Some of Lovecraft's fans have questioned Derleth's claim over the years.

They met the nucleus of the "family" of Lovecraft in New York when Wandrei and Derleth attended a meeting of the Kalem Club at Frank Belnap Long's. Assembled in the *WEIRD TALES*' author's apartment, amidst a fascinating motley assortment of furniture and wall decorations and collections, were: "...Herman Keonig – a tall, tow-headed young man in his early thirties, a quiet, assured person...venerable Dr. James F. Morton – white-headed and white of mustache, stout of body and very thoroughly a gentleman...Rheinhardt Kleiner – a thin, thin-faced, big-eared and big-eyed man of middle age...Arthur Leeds – an aging man, betraying all the marks of faded gentility...Clair Beck – a red-headed youth, a little raw, coatless and somewhat shy with the general air of a knight of the road...Kenneth Sterling – of obviously marked intelligence... reserved with an air of listening...Miss Sylvester – slight, dark-eyed, who professed her eagerness to do what she could to perpetuate H. P. L.'s memory by typing his letters as we edited them....Donald Wolleim – a quiet attendant...Samuel Loveman – wide-eyed, eager for debate, always ready for discussion about anything...." Derleth and Wandrei shared their progress on the H. P. L. memorial project and collection of his letters.[11]

Only a few months later after two publishers rejected *OUTSIDER AND OTHERS*, the memorial collection of Howard Lovecraft's work, Barlow, Wandrei, and Mrs. Gamwell backed Derleth to establish Arkham House Publishing Company and the book finally had a publisher. The partners speculated the book would gross a possible $2,270, three hundred of which they would pay in royalties to Mrs. Gamwell, and the remainder would be just about enough for printing costs. Wandrei suggested he and Derleth underwrite the project by promising in writing to purchase any leftover copies and thus help pay any outstanding costs. August also planned to set aside money for a second and third volume.[12]

Gradually, the initial pain of losing Lovecraft subsided. There were other things to occupy his attention. The manuscript Perkins was waiting for, for one.

He helped go over the summer kitchen in his parents' home for Grandmother Volk's moving into it. She'd been ill, was semi-invalid, and it would be easier for Rosella to care for her if she were in the house. When she was settled, he bought her a small radio and taught her how to use it so she could listen to the barn dances and the German music she loved. He talked to her about the old days, gathering material for still another book he hoped to write someday. It would be centered around the Civil War period and show the effect the war had on the natives of Sauk City.

She repeated the story of how she had saved her baby brother Arnold from freezing to death. The fire in the house had died down and she was too small to reach the firewood. Their mother was in the barn, milking. A terrific snowstorm made it impossible for the child to get to the barn, and drowned out her calls for help. August's grandmother wrapped the baby in a quilt and laid him on the warm stones around the fireplace. If she had not done so, he might have frozen to death before their mother could get back from the barn.

As she talked about Great-grandfather Gelhouse (Stoll) fighting in German provinces and his coming to America in the 1850's and then joining the Civil War, August could see the story unfold. He could see Westley teaching the daughter of the woman he loved, see him glancing through the window across the meadow and the brook-fed marsh, see the other characters – Arnold, Maddi, etc.

He would name the book *THE STARS WORE WESTWARD*, he decided. Though he mentioned the manuscript and the story several times throughout the years, it was unpublished at the time of his death.[13]

Derleth and Alice drove to Portage to do research for the background of *WIND OVER WISCONSIN*. Alice had a car. August didn't. He had not yet learned to drive. Neither of them realized their initial arrangement would develop into a working relationship that would last even beyond Derleth's death; that before long Alice would give up her teaching position to work exclusively for Derleth. He could not have made a wiser choice. Although at the time, Alice was a slow typist she was accurate. Derleth soon enlisted her aid in typing his manuscripts as well as researching for them. She drove Derleth to social engagements, to his lecture appointments, and on other business trips.

They found many useful bits of information for the book: how the bedsprings of the period were made of corded rope, how furniture was held together by wooden pegs and split-board lathes instead of nails, how the quilts were woven in the still popular "Grandmother's Flower Garden" design, etc....[14]

There were books for Derleth to review. Back in 1936, Derleth had made several comments on an Archibald McLeish volume and had reviewed Carl Sandburg's new book for *VOICES*. Now the editor, Howard Vinal, wanted him to review Edgar Lee Masters' *BIOGRAPHY OF WALT WHITMAN*. He also reviewed Clyde Fisher's *EXPLORING THE HEAVENS* and Fisher wrote from the American Museum of Natural History, thanking him for his kind words. Although he was not, at this time, an established book reviewer, August had strong opinions about books as well as about everything else, and needed to express them. He made sure the authors knew those opinions by carefully clipping his published reviews and sending them to the authors. The courtesy often proved a good opening wedge in establishing correspondence with people like McLeish, Sandburg and Masters.[15]

Ever so often a visit from one of Lovecraft's "family" would prime the well of sorrow within, bringing his grief sharply into focus again. Donald Wandrei came first to discuss plans for the memorial. Alfred Galpin, H. P. L.'s favorite "grandson" came, too, from Appleton, Wisconsin. They walked the marshes, re-reading Lovecraft's letters, sharing their grief.[16]

In November, the Wisconsin Education Association invited Sinclair Lewis to speak before 13,000 teachers at its annual conference, held at the Schroeder Hotel in Milwaukee. Lewis came with copies of Mark Schorer's novel, *A HOUSE TOO OLD*, and Derleth's *STILL IS THE SUMMER NIGHT* in his suitcase. When he arrived, he called August, suggesting the author visit the hotel the day before the conference. Derleth agreed and spent the afternoon with Lewis. He noted that Lewis was a tall paunchy man, with sharp, appraising eyes. Derleth thought Lewis still essentially a small town man. Lewis compared August's *STILL IS THE SUMMER NIGHT* to Mark Schorer's book, saying Schorer didn't have a sympathetic character in his, that Derleth's was "...'a far better book, far and away....' "

Lewis insisted August stay to dinner and wouldn't allow him to leave until nine p.m., a longer stretch of socializing than Derleth was inclined to suffer, usually. Their conversation covered a large range of topics. They talked about Wisconsin writers North, Schorer, Green, Gale and others. August brought to Lewis's attention a Milwaukee author, Edward Harris Heth, whose work was unknown to Lewis. Though Lewis commented favorably on Derleth's *STILL IS THE SUMMER NIGHT*, he also told him not to "botanize" so much; said he should cut the book about 5,000 words; advised him to write less – 100,000 words a year instead of 500,000; suggested he cut out wasting time writing book reviews; applauded his decision to stick to Sauk City; and expressed the opinion that it was healthy for August to have an ego. Lewis wanted August to hear the lecture the next day as he meant to weave in a few comments about Derleth. Derleth declined the invitation. He was too busy. When he departed, he left a copy of the manuscript, *WIND OVER WISCONSIN*.[17]

Lewis, the next day, centered much of his talk on August, singling him out as headed for national literary fame and calling him a personal friend after the previous day's visit and the reading of *WIND OVER WISCONSIN*.[18] Lewis's enchantment with Derleth's work made even Sauk City sit up and take notice. Eight years later, Sinclair Lewis still sang Derleth's praises in an article written for *ESQUIRE*, calling the Sac Prairie Saga a giant's notion, lauding August's industry, labeling him '...a champion of and a justification for regionalism...."[19]

So much praise from someone who was also a literary giant made publishers and editors all over the country sit up and take notice. Derleth himself, however, wrote to Lewis after the *ESQUIRE* article came out, denying that, as Lewis had assumed, Derleth could write a really great book. He wrote for other reasons, he told Lewis. He wanted to say or to remember something. He wanted to make certain experiments in writing. He wanted to make money so he could go his own way. He also accused Lewis of writing an appraisal of his work without having read his better books including *VILLAGE YEAR* and

SHIELD OF THE VALIANT. Derleth, having heard Lewis was going to do the article, had offered to send the books but Lewis claimed there wasn't time to read them before the article deadline.[20] (It was difficult for August to understand that, since he often devoured two or three books a day between all his other activities.)

Sinclair Lewis wasn't the only one who thought Derleth "special". Edgar Lee Masters, author of *SPOON RIVER ANTHOLOGY*, and a world renowned poet, had been corresponding regularly with Derleth for several months. Derleth had sent Masters a copy of *STILL IS THE SUMMER NIGHT* and Masters, like Lewis, was impressed. He was even more enthusiastic about Derleth's poetry. The tautness of the poems Derleth sent him, the fresh imagery, and Derleth's own special kind of music delighted Masters. No matter how successful August's novels might become, Masters felt poetry was Derleth's forte. He was complimentary about Derleth's *MAN TRACK HERE*, when it came out later. The two poets continued corresponding until Masters' death, mostly about the poetry each was writing, and other poets and authors. One of his letters of criticism of a later volume of Derleth's poetry, *HERE ON A DARKLING PLAIN*, pointed out several weaknesses as well as strengths. Masters did not see eye to eye with August on Sherwood Anderson, did not think he merited a place in the roster of significant regional writers.

Edgar Lee Masters' opinion of Derleth's writing was so high, he decided he would like Derleth to do his biography. Kimball Flaccus was attempting a biography of the poet at the time, but Masters thought Derleth more in key with his material than Flaccus, who was an Easterner.

Masters' letters included fatherly advice as their personal relationship developed. He warned Derleth against getting tangled in financial matters, a complication of every writer's life. August should stay out of debt. He should avoid writing too much. He should live simply and avoid worshiping the flesh, which was both too expensive and too distracting for a serious poet. He believed that in time Derleth could become the greatest nature poet America would produce. He was not in favor of marriage for writers, although he had been married twice himself.[21]

Derleth, much as he revered Masters' work and relished his praise, turned a deaf ear to his counsel. Determined to build his house and equally determined to build a fitting, lasting memorial to Howard P. Lovecraft, he was already committed to the financial treadmill; he certainly never avoided over-writing nor worship of the flesh.

Grandmother Volk had known August was "special" since he was a child. She told him so again when he sat with her on February 7, 1938. Her health was failing rapidly. On March 22nd, her faith in her grandson was affirmed when an airmail announcement arrived with the good news that August had been granted a Guggenheim Fellowship of two thousand dollars for creative work in the field of the novel.

"...'To think I would live to see this day.' Grandmother Volk wept. 'I always knew something great would come of him!'...." She spread her pride to all the others in the family.

Helene Constance White, Sinclair Lewis, Edgar Lee Masters, Maxwell Perkins, The Knights of the Golden Quill and the Milwaukee Press Club had all sponsored August for the fellowship that August had been determined to win for years.[22]

Derleth rejected the advice of the Guggenheim people, and decided against touring Europe with his Fellowship funds. Since most of his writing was rooted in Sac Prairie and the Wisconsin area, there was no need to go to Europe. Besides, he was too embroiled at the moment in his research for *REST-LESS IS THE RIVER* among other things.

In 1938, August had been contacted by Mr. F. R. Bigelow, suggesting he write a novel based on the life of Hercules Dousman. Derleth wrote back saying the project was inviting but he could not undertake it at the time without an assured income, nor would he consider doing such a book unless he could incorporate it into his saga and be permitted to use poetic license rather than sticking closely to each historical fact. Bigelow offered $1,800, to be paid in monthly installments of $150 each.

Thus Hercules Dousman, who figured briefly in Derleth's earlier novel, *RESTLESS IS THE RIVER*, because the central character of his first biographical novel, *BRIGHT JOURNEY*, published by Scribners in 1941. Dousman, an early Wisconsin millionaire, an entrepreneur in fur trading, farming wheat, constructing railroads, and dealing in real estate, had been a strong political force in the state. His home in Prairie du Chein – the Villa Louise – has become a famous Wisconsin landmark under the auspices of the State of Wisconsin Historical Society. It still attracts many visitors every year.

In June, August had made a trip to the Villa Louis at Prairie du Chein. Mrs. Bigelow was most obliging, offering notes and anecdotes about her grandfather, Hercules Dousman, as well as Jane Fisher Rolette, the house itself, many things that would facilitate the writing of the book. The finished novel, which would be published by Charles Scribner & Sons in 1939, and dedicated to Sinclair Lewis, tells the story of Count Augustin Haraszthy (titled Count Augustine Brogmar for the novel). It includes many interesting stories about the primitive conditions under which the Wisconsin legislature was formed during Governor Doty's tenure. The capitol building itself served as a shelter for pigs, and was called "Doty's Washbowl". On one occasion, a murder occurred during the legislative session which caused swift adjournment. Charles Ardnt, Brown County representative, was blasted with a double-barreled pistol by James Vinyard, over rejection of the nomination of Enos S. Baker, Esquire, as sheriff of Grant County. The trial of Vinyard, as later described by Derleth, was a disgusting affair with the defense lawyer drinking copious amounts of whiskey during his harangue of many hours, and unbelievably getting his client off while getting himself thoroughly intoxicated.

Some of Derleth's own disgust with government affairs crept into the conversation of his characters:

" '...What does Clay do now that he's broken with Tyler?' asked Chalfonte casually in one scene.

"...'Oh, he's found himself a fence and has begun to straddle it assiduously, hoping that if he makes enough noise doing it, he'll be chosen as the party candidate in 1844. This blathering seems to be a firmly established part of our national traditions; it begins approximately two years before each election and lasts until the nominations have been made.' Dousman answered...."

The book has a sequel, *THE HOUSE ON THE MOUND*, published in 1958. *BRIGHT JOURNEY* covers Dousman's life to a year before his marriage to his partner's widow; the sequel covers the last half of Dousman's life.

It wasn't until after *BRIGHT JOURNEY* was published that Derleth discovered Dousman had had two children by his first wife. August had given her only one in the book. He'd already described Mrs. Dousman's death so he had to invent another woman to bear Dousman's second child. He used the preface of *HOUSE ON THE MOUND* to plead poetic license for the error.[23]

Derleth with his careful researcher, Alice Conger, his efficient organization, and his photographic memory, seldom made mistakes. His penchant toward perfection and his instant recall, were admired and appreciated by people who benefited from his response to inquiries on myriad subjects. It was also a source of irritation when a difference of opinion arose and Derleth almost invariably proved to be right.[24]

Donald Wandrei made another visit to Sauk City in June and they discussed Lovecraft's material as they strolled in the bottoms, where they watched night hawks and listened to the music of vesper sparrows and wood thrush. Wandrei and Derleth were discovering other mutual interests beside Lovecraft which they had in common: the love of gourmet food, an appreciation of good music, and a passion for collecting morels.[25]

Derleth was also involved in writing a pageant for the Sauk City Centennial. He would help direct it and assist in ironing out little problems in the production of the event.

August master-minded the centennial celebration itself, even thwarting an attempt of the Legionnaire's Band to take the place of the high school band as leaders of the parade. He'd promised the high school band could lead and he would brook no interference from anybody on that score. He greeted the governor, Phillip LaFollette, who joked about politics and said some very complimentary things about *HAWK ON THE WIND*, Derleth's latest poetry volume. He was everywhere, overseeing the pageant presentation.

The Governor's remarks on the poetry book were topped by a review that arrived after the parade. The reviewer, Percy Hutchinson, said *HAWK ON THE WIND* proved August was a young poet with a brilliant future.[26]

It was enough praise to swell anyone's head, but as always, the praise heaped upon the author from learned critics who knew him chiefly through his writings, was tempered by the antagonism of many Sac Prairie residents who knew August as a neighbor and a native of the area. Malicious gossip, criticism, antagonism, jealousy, ridicule, even hatred, were all part of his daily experience, and the hurt went deep, as deep as his love for the whole area, and its people.

On August 23rd, he received the following letter from an anonymous "friend" who resented his high-handed manner:

"...'August (Dictator) you surely are the biggest bag of Wind that gives You aught to have called your book BAG OF WIND OVER SAUK CITY. You surely have more guts than anybody. It is just a joke the way you act, everybody is laughing behind your back. Some even said they aught to take you to Mondeta (Mendota, a Wisconsin institution for the mentally ill). But for one thing keep your Mouth shut nobody can understand you are all tongue. at the School meeting nobody understood a word about scopper now-lay-low committee of Sauk and Prairie'...."

August realized his anonymous "friend" was a member of the committee in question, and decided to irk the lady still further by demanding three times as much effort from her.[27]

67

SOURCE NOTES
CHAPTER SIX

[1] A. D. to Mary Stiver, May 5, 1960.
[2] August Derleth, <u>Wind Over Wisconsin</u>, (N.Y., 1938); Maxwell Perkins to A. D., no date.
[3] A. D. Journal, 18 March, 1937, pp. 47-ff.
[4] Interview with Alice Conger, Sauk City, Wisconsin, 1968.
[5] Note 3, 24 July, 1937.
[6] Donald Wandrei to A. D., Mar. 23 and 26, 1937; Oct. 30, 1938; Feb. 27 and Nov. 26, 1939.
[7] J. Vernon Shea to A. D., April 12, 1937.
[8] A. D. to Robert Barlow, Mar. 28, 1939.
[9] Robert Barlow to A. D., Mar. 30, 1939.
[10] A. D. Journal, 8 August 1938, box 9, folder 6, p. 91.
[11] Ibid., 12 September, 1938, box 91, folder 5, p. 421.
[12] A. D. to Donald Wandrei, no date.
[13] Note 6, op. cit.
[14] A. D. to Donald Wandrei, 26 June, 1937, p. 114.
[15] A. D. Journal, 9 November, 1937, pp. 211; biographer's opinion.
[16] A. D. Journal.
[17] A. D. Journal, 4 November, 1937, pp. 211-ff.
[18] Ibid.
[19] Sinclair Lewis, Esquire article in August Derleth Society newsletter, Vol. 4, #2, pp. 1-ff.
[20] A. D. to Sinclair Lewis.
[21] Edgar Lee Masters to A. D.
[22] A. D. Journal, 22 March, 1938.
[23] August Derleth, <u>Bright Journey</u>, (N.Y., 1941), T. V. Olsen, pre-publication manuscript given to biographer.
[24] Biographer's conclusion.
[25] A. D. Journal.
[26] Ibid.
[27] Ibid.

Chapter Seven

"I can be as vicious as a snake and I never have the slightest twinge of conscience when I am because I never am unless driven to it...."[142]

With a friend, Donald Laughnan, driving, Derleth set off in September for New York. They detoured to Greenup, Kentucky, to see Jesse Stuart. A picnic was in progress when they arrived. Jesse was not as big a man as August had expected. He was husky, strong-looking, taller than August, but only 184 pounds to August's 204. His face was hearty and sincere. But his expression was bland and in no way revealed the person August knew through the poetry and letters Stuart had written. Jesse introduced the guests to his brother James.

The visit was much shorter than Jesse would have liked. They stayed only a few hours. It must have been a bit hectic, also. An altercation took place at the picnic while they were there. Stuart shrugged it off later in a letter, saying that someone had "assassination in mind", but Derleth shouldn't worry about it. He and James, his brother, could take care of the matter. The experience had been an interesting glimpse into the Kentucky hill background Stuart portrayed so well in his novels. After Derleth departed Jesse jotted down a poem on the back of a calendar, titled "August Derleth, Harried By Time". Unfortunately, when he wanted to send a copy of it to Derleth, Jesse discovered his housekeeper had discarded the calendar and the lines were forever lost to posterity.[2]

He had a four-thirty appointment with Balmer, the *REDBOOK* editor, who told him they were buying "Gina Bleye". Balmer said it was a good story and complimented August on the strength of his women characters, as well as their unique and engrossing mental processes.[3] Others through the years noted in August a sensitivity and anima spirit that was so evident in his poetry and other writing.[4] Before he departed, the editor told Derleth *REDBOOK* wanted anything he could give them.

Derleth took advantage of being in New York to visit Edgar Lee Masters for three hours. They discussed the poetry of Edna St. Vincent Millay, Robert Frost, and August Derleth. Masters told August he was wise to stay in the Midwest. " '...You've got it all – grass, earth, air, sun and moonlight, the birds and the clouds, and running water, brooks and rivers, hills and prairie – and it all comes out in everything you write.' "[5]

Donald Wandrei accompanied Derleth and Donald Laughnan to Lovecraft's beloved Providence the following day. As they approached the city they noted the spires and old turrets set against a background of masses of greenery in the tree-shaded city and they thought of H. P. L., who had so often enjoyed the same lovely view from the slopes. Mrs. Gamwell was obviously a genteel woman. She was very pleasant, and remarkably well-preserved for 75. She smiled readily, but her smile did not disguise the mute grief in her eyes as she stood waiting for them before number 66.

Don Laughnan took pictures of the study. August sat at Lovecraft's desk, selecting from H. P. L.'s papers those he felt might enhance their work, and Wandrei went through the files.

August chose Lovecraft's copy of Machen's *HILL OF DREAMS* as a personal memento. He also purchased H. P. L.'s planisphere. The planisphere would later give him many hours of pleasure.[6] (He willed it to his dearest and oldest friend, Hugo Schwenker. He and "Hugh" had spent many evenings together back of Schwenker's shop, watching the stars and the heavens. Hugo, in turn, presented it to the August Derleth Society in Sauk City in 1993.)[7] They toured the house, saw Lovecraft's statuettes, photographs, star books and the mammoth, neatly filed collection of clippings, starting with architecture and ending with things weird. They strolled, too, in the yard where H. P. L.'s cats had frolicked. August and Don Laughnan went with Mrs. Gamwell along the same path Lovecraft loved to stroll. They walked along College Street slowly, saw the shunned house of Lovecraft's writings, then proceeded to the banks of the Seekonk River and the beauty of Swan Point Cemetery. They paused there for a respectful moment at Howard's grave.

From Providence they traveled to Boston, arrived on the 14th at Walden Pond, as secluded at 8:30 a.m. as it was in

Thoreau's day. They saw the fish pond, the same railroad Thoreau mentioned in his writings, heard only the train whistles, and the "...eternal pulses of infinity in the voice of bird and animal...."[8]

It was a fitting finale to his trip. They headed back home again to the daily routine and an ever-increasing load of writing.[9]

In early 1939, Derleth's work on RESTLESS IS THE RIVER progressed swiftly, as many as 10,000 words a day.[10]

"The Return of Hastur" – his first Lovecraft imitation – was voted best story in the March issue of WEIRD TALES, which was not too encouraging after Derleth missed that honor with eighty stories of his own style.[11]

In April, he offered to do the Zona Gale biography during a conversation with her husband, W. L. Breeze. Breeze was considering Glen Frank, president of the University of Wisconsin, as a possible biographer, which horrified Derleth and prompted his own offer. Although August admired Zona for her loyalty to Frank when everyone else was condemning Frank's switch from liberalism to the right, he thought it ill advised for Frank to do the biography. Zona had started an autobiography, but as Derleth feared it was too short and underdeveloped to make a book, so he simply added it to his own. He signed a contract with Appleton Century for the 1940 publication.[12]

A letter from Chabrun, his agent, in March, 1939, disclosed that Balmer meant to take "The Intercessors" for REDBOOK, but the editor wanted Lillian legitimized, which would remove most of her motivation. In the story, Lillian's mother is determined that Lillian be spared the heartache and disgrace of being deserted and left to raise an illegitimate child, as she had been.

August cut and revised, nevertheless, thinking the story was not much good anyway, and as always he was pressed for money. He advised later in his writing classes that students should compromise if they had to, but they should never tie up material so that they would be unable to go back to their original version if they wished to someday.[13]

The story was filmed and aired in the United States under the title "Summer Night", a few years later. Forty years after REDBOOK accepted "The Intercessors", two international film makers, Halit Refig, a Turkish TV director, and Badia Bahman, an Egyptian photography director, filmed the original version of the story. Refig picked this work for filming because he felt Derleth was a chronicler of Wisconsin. He used the 1856 Madison house of Phillip and Ann Fox for interior shots, the Sac Prairie area for outside scenes. Halit Refrig, who had European connections said the film would be aired in Turkey, Germany, France, and Italy, where Derleth at this point, was better known for his work in the macabre genre rather than for his serious writing.[14] The film moves slowly and sticks fairly close to August's original story. The film, keeping the somber, brooding mood of the story, is of a mother and a would be suitor of the daughter breaking up her ill-favored romance with a deceitful married man.

Although most of Sac Prairie resisted acknowledging Derleth's growing literary stature, some of the less obtuse inhabitants sought him out because of it. Among them, a young high school student, John Stanton, came to interview August in October, 1939, for his freshman class paper. The author was highly impressed with the young man's intelligence and enthusiasm about writing. They became good friends as Stanton returned again and again for advice and help. About a year later, he hired Stanton to help wrap and mail out books and do odd jobs about the grounds of the Farm (Place of Hawks). Stanton earned more than money in return for labor. August guided his reading; took him to church regularly, and took him to Taliesin – the famous home of Frank Lloyd Wright. He also treated Stanton to plays, films, concerts and gourmet dinners in Madison, along with hikes through the marshes. The boy briefly served as Derleth's photographer. The picture of August on the inside dust jacket of *EVENING IN SPRING* was taken by John Stanton.[15]

Although there had been only 150 prepaid orders for Lovecraft's *THE OUTSIDER AND OTHERS* by publication, the buyers were very enthusiastic. To help raise more funds August placed an advertisement in *WEIRD TALES*, "Calling All Fantasy Fans". In it he proposed a whole new concept, an Arkham House Fantasy Library at two dollars per copy, paid in advance. It would include the best stories of Smith, Merrit,

Quinn, Howard, Bloch, Kuttner, Whitehead, and others. Fans would have to accept every book offered, not just their favorites. The first book published was by one of the "others", *SOMEONE IN THE DARK*, sixteen selected weird tales written by August himself. The book was scheduled to appear October 1, 1945.[16]

The book was such a success that Derleth published these others: Clark Ashton Smith's *OUT OF SPACE AND TIME*, in 1942; Lovecraft's *BEYOND THE WALL OF SLEEP*, in 1943; Whitehead's *MUMBEE AND OTHER UNCANNY TALES*, Clark Ashton Smith's *LOST WORLDS*, Lovecraft's *MARGINALIA*, and Wandrei's *THE EYE AND THE FINGER*, in 1944; Derleth's *SOMETHING NEAR*, Robert Block's *THE OPENER OF THE WAY*, Evangeline Walton's *WITCH HOUSE*, J. Sheridan L. Fanu's *GREEN TEA AND OTHER GHOST STORIES*, and a tale suggested by Lovecraft's notes and finished by Derleth, *THE LURKER ON THE THRESHOLD*, in 1934. The George Banta Co., Menasha, Wisconsin, did most of the printing and binding of the Arkham House books. Frank Uptadel, Menominee, Wisconsin, and Ronald Clyhed, New York City, were the chief jacket artists.

Later, Arkham House stocked and sold certain non Arkham House books in the macabre genre, and published three subsidized volumes in addition to many selected volumes. All of these ventures were fitting work for the new publishing house. Arkham, Lovecraft's fictional name for Salem, Massachusetts, had become a great tribute to the memory of Lovecraft and the genre he loved to write.[17]

Earlier in March of 1939, Derleth had signed the agreement with Scribners for *RESTLESS IS THE RIVER*, and received an advance of $600, money sorely needed for the two financial ventures: establishing the publishing firm and building his dream house. The loan from a local bank for the house would be substantial, but with printing bills and the other expenses of the publishing firm, he needed every cent he could muster. Wandrei contributed some, but they still did not have enough.

A fortune teller August visited while working in Minneapolis had told the author his superior business acumen was being wasted on writing. That business sense surfaced now as August realized he could make a house loan work twice for him. There would be an element of risk, of course, but no more than the average business venture entailed. Besides, the market for his own work had increased sharply with the two widely publicized stamps of approval: Sinclair Lewis's praise and the Guggenheim award. So, in spite of Masters' advice, Derleth plunged deeply into debt.

August's profound reverence for growing things was demonstrated by his decision to hold off laying the cornerstone of his house until autumn because he didn't want to disturb the flowers growing at the site during the summer.[18] The cornerstone, complete with a lock box, (the key was later deposited in the State Wisconsin Historical Museum Archives along with Derleth's papers), was laid in the southeast corner of the house area on October 1, 1939. August celebrated the occasion with a party. The Bachhuber family, Leo Weissenborn, and other friends came bearing nonsense items to be placed in the box – among them a bottle of wine. Derleth had the group photographed and used the picture for personal postcards to commemorate the event.[19]

Bartlett Boder, president of a Missouri Valley Trust Company, sent August a salmon colored brick recovered from the foundation of Jesse James' house, suggesting that Derleth find a niche in his garden wall for the curio.[20]

It wasn't until about fourteen years later, noting that hawks did indeed frequent his woods and the tall trees along his front garden, that August adopted the name "Place of Hawks". Before that, it was simply called "The Farm". Derleth had long utilized the concept of the hawk in his work and in his own thinking. As time went by, his admiration and respect for the bird had grown, and he identified more and more with it.

When the Second World War commenced in Europe, Derleth's comment, in spite of his total aversion to anything military, was: "...So the conflict has begun at last and all thinking men and women will urgently hope that soon Hitler and his supporters may be wiped out, brushed from the face of the earth, for it is not even fitting that mad men be confined and so saved for some hellish spawning later...."[21]

The war in Europe, though followed with interest, had no effect on Derleth's busy daily schedule, as yet. He had taken on the instruction of a regional literature class at the University of Wisconsin, having already gained the reputation of expert in the field because of his own regional writing and his extensive library of regional books. This added income was welcomed gratefully in the face of mounting house and publishing costs, both of which exceeded original estimates. It was however, still another inroad on his precious time.

He made trips to Portage with Alice Conger to research Zona Gale's biography. He wrote to Sherwood Anderson, asking whether he might see letters from Zona, and for any insights Anderson might have to offer for the book. Derleth also asked if he might dedicate one of his Sac Prairie saga novels to him. Sherwood Anderson wrote that he would be proud to have one of Derleth's books dedicated to him. Although he had not kept Zona's letters, he was able to supply several pertinent bits of information that added insight into Zona's character.[22]

Lincoln Kirstein, of the Hound & Horn, Inc., who had rejected August's memoirs and confessions eight years earlier on the protest that his analyzing sensations was endless and of interest only to the analyzer, had accused Derleth of being diffusely and formlessly influenced by Anderson. August himself, often listed Sherwood as one of the writers who most influenced his work.[23]

The letters that followed between the two regional writers were read and commented upon in Derleth's University of Wisconsin regional literature class. In them, the two authors lamented the attitude of critics who labeled their work pessimistic because they described life as it was, or dirty-minded because they realized sex had a terrific impact on everyone. They exchanged philosophies: Anderson happy to have lived pretty much as he wanted to live; August stating his desire to win the belief of people he believed in, to be considered by some as a mentor. August felt he had never been favored with the ability to be an outstanding teacher, but his teaching efforts had succeeded in raising literary awareness in his home town.[24]

August was still very active on the School Board, in the Ranger Club for Young People, the Chamber of Commerce, and the Men's Club he had helped to found. He also served as a parole officer, and was a continuing integral force in the social and political patterns of his area. He was anything but reticent about expressing his opinion about Sac Prairie and Washington politics that did not suit him. He was an avid letter-to-the-editor writer. When the local editor demurred or delayed in airing August's views, he would have flyers printed up and distributed about town at his own expense. In 1937, for instance, he had set out to put the voters of Sauk City straight on the men who were serving on the village board. He called them "little tinhorn gods" and scoffed at their presumption that they ran Sauk City. He revealed that one of the board members sold oil to the village, one managed to see that his associates in the business world did most of the city's building and repair jobs, and another managed to secure the use of village property for private purposes and then had the audacity to present the village with a bill. He challenged the town to make these men give an accounting of where and for what they spent the town's money.[25]

It was not only the older folks that stirred Derleth. In his walks along Water Street close to the Wisconsin River he was well aware of the many inhabitants that had drowned in its rapids and strong currents. Wanting to do something about it instead of taking his swims with his friends he would gather up several young children for an outing along the river. He pointed out to them the safest swimming holes and warned them about the swift currents, the dangerous depths and the rapids. He also taught them to swim, and after each session marched them down to their favorite ice-cream parlor for cones. Given his financial situation and his desire to conserve his time for writing, these events showed a softer, caring, generous side of the man that endeared him to many, despite his usual egotistical, arrogant, and sometimes aggressive manner.

(One of those swimming children wrote a letter in 1995 to the August Derleth Society News Letter remembering those happy days.)[26]

[1] A. D. to Inez Weaver, Jan. 31, 1952.

[2] Jessie Stuart to A. D., Sept. 4, 1938.

[3] A. D. Journal, 12 September, 1938, box 91, folder 5, p. 418.

[4] A student in a class on Derleth at the Rhinelander School of Arts commented on the contrasts in Derleth's poetry. Some poems were extremely forceful, others were delicate, gentle, soft, as though from a feminine viewpoint; Biographer attended class.

[5] Note 3, p. 419.

[6] Ibid., September, 1938, box 91, folder 5, pp. 420-ff.

[7] Interview with Hugo Schwenker at his woodworking shop on Water Street, Sauk City, Wisconsin, July, 1993.

[8] Note 3, 14 Sept., 1938, p. 11.

[9] A. D. to Sherwood Anderson, June 29, 1939.

[10] Writer's Digest cover story, "Novels at 10,000 words a day".

[11] Note 3, 26 April, 1939, box 91, folder 6, p. 77.

[12] Copy of contract, miscellaneous file, State of Wisconsin Historical Society archives, Madison, Wisconsin.

[13] Balmer to A. D., March, 1939; biographer's notes taken while attending classes conducted by Derleth at the Rhinelander School of Arts.

[14] Miller, "Derleth on T.V. for the world", Capital Times; "Derleth film draws notable director", Baraboo News Republic, March 23, 1977; biographer viewed the film some years later on a VCR while visiting the home of Iraj Amir Arjumand in Tehran, Iran.

[15] A. D. Journal, 24 March, 1939, box 91, folder 6, p. 36; Evening in Spring, back panel of book's dust cover was taken by John Stanton.

[16] August Derleth, "Calling all fantasy fans" ad in Weird Tales; miscellaneous papers, SWHS archives.

[17] Ibid., book list; biographer's opinion.

[18] Biographer's conclusions; A. D. to Leo Weisenborn, May 16, 1939.

19 A. D. to Ian Law, Nov. 20, 1959; postcard, memorabilia accumulated by biographer on her numerous trips to Sauk City.
20 Bartlett Boder to A. D., Nov. 29, 1939.
21 See Note 18, A. D. to Leo Weisenborn.
22 A. D. to Sherwood Anderson, June 29, 1939.
23 Lincoln Kirstein to A. D., July 21 and Nov. 4 and 5, 1931.
24 SWHS Museum Archives, Madison, Wis.
25 August Derleth flyer, "To the Voters of Sauk City".
26 Letters to the editor's column, August Derleth Society Newsletter.

Chapter Eight

"There is something satisfying about putting books and papers and note-cards in their proper place, in cleaning out drawers and shelves, so that it is possible to start from scratch, so to speak – letters all written, the past years accounts balanced, the books clear for the work to come...."[1]

The house was far from complete when John Stanton came to work for Derleth. The north wing with stone walls 13' high, was up, but the work on the west wing had only just started. Carpenters, urged on by William Derleth, were laying the initial flooring. William with the help of Chris Anderson, did the paneling and finishing of the interior.[2]

Outside of the area August's literary reputation was spreading, helped along by such publicity as having his picture on the cover of *WRITER'S REVIEW*, and an article inside entitled, "Novels, at 10,000 Words a Day".[3]

In December, August went again to New York with Donald Wandrei.

He visited the svelte Fannie Hurst, and was struck by her black hair and dark complexion. The actress was quite emotional as she related stories about Zona Gale. August was in her apartment only a short time when George Jessel came to call. Jessel was a much quieter person than August expected from his performances.

Jessel asked what Derleth did. August told him about the Gale biography, and the one he hoped to do on McCay. Jessel, who had taken him for a football player or a prize fighter, was quite amazed to learn that he was going to write about a cartoonist.[4]

If the visit with two such famous stars and many important New York editors inflated Derleth's ego a bit, the missile he received a few days later back at Sauk City probably took some of the wind out of his sails.

"...Say August, you surely are the biggest Fool running in Sauk City. Why don't you go somewhere and

learn Manners, the way you carriet on in the Church the other nite was a disgrase...at least dress up once, you look like animal big guts like you got hair all over you...." in similar affectionate vein.[5]

August's latest stunt to irritate the locals had been to have 20,000 stamps printed up with his picture on them, which he distributed around town to the merchants and their associates to use on their outgoing mail during the holidays. One of the villagers had even used one of August's stamps in place of a real postage stamp. The irritation went beyond the Sac Prairie area, precipitating a ridiculing article by Betty Cass, a columnist for the *MADISON CAPITAL TIMES*. Cass compared Derleth to one of three pigs who blew himself up and tooted his own horn. Once before the only way he managed to get mentioned in *TIME MAGAZINE*, was to have a special article in Madison papers on the cornerstone laying for his new house, and now to dream up this latest ego trip – the personal stamps.[6]

August had only just begun. There would come a day, not too many years later, when Derleth managed to have three different postcards for sale in the local pharmacy, one showed him leaning against his huge fireplace, one at his desk, and one of the Place of Hawks. Cigarettes sold at the local drugstore were accompanied by matchbooks with Arkham House embossed on the covers.[7]

While August was in New York, Tom Coward of Coward McCann had okayed the use of Frank Utpatel's projected wood-cut illustrations for August's Journal. When Utpatel visited Derleth on the 29th of December, they decided he'd do about thirty cuts to send with the Journal manuscript in fall. Derleth and Frank were old friends, but the relationship of author and illustrator was not always smooth. Once, receiving a woodcut he had asked for, Derleth sent it back with a picture of a whippoorwill. Whatever Utpatel had used for a model for his woodcut, it was definitely not a whippoorwill. More than once, author and illustrator almost came to blows over disagreements about the cuts. The attempted fisticuffs were possibly initiated by the artist, who had been a former semi-professional boxer. Utpatel had studied under John Stuart Curry, the artist-in-residence at the University of Wisconsin. When Utpatel accepted Derleth's challenge to try woodcutting, he also carved out a new vocation for himself. He provided most of the illustrations thereafter for Arkham House and for a good many of August's books. He completed approximately 249 pieces before his death in 1980.

Derleth celebrated New Year's Eve by visiting the Farm (Place of Hawks) with Madison friends to check on the progress of the building. When the Bachhubers joined them later, they had a party.[8]

It had been a productive year, with the forming of Arkham House, the publication of H. P. L.'s *OUTSIDER AND OTHERS*, two biographies researched, *ATMOSPHERE OF HOUSES, MAN TRACK HERE, SENTENCE DEFERRED, and REST-LESS IS THE RIVER* published along with his usual flood of short stories. His dream house was now near completion.

True, Lovecraft's *OUTSIDER* was not moving as fast as they'd hoped. The Farm had already eaten up enough of the loan so Derleth had to apply his own earnings toward Arkham House printing bills, but his financial prospects were good with two biographies, *COUNTRY GROWTH* (his journal), and another book of poetry, *HERE ON A DARKLING PLAIN* (to be dedicated to Zona Gale), and the *NARRACONG RIDDLE* planned for 1940 release.[9]

The first draft of Zona's biography – 70,000 words – was completed by March 5th. He had trouble finding a title for it; went, finally to the Bible and picked several: "Stranger in the Land", "Not By Bread Alone", "Many Waters", "One Light Burning", and "Still Small Voice", only to find that *STILL SMALL VOICE* was the only one that hadn't been used in the past two years. D. Appleton Century Company advised the author that they wanted the book published in October.[10]

In September, August helped the local Parent Teacher Association produce a play that had been performed on Broadway, "The Nights of January". When a local woman went about criticizing the play as "vile" and berating the teachers who were going to take part in it, August delivered another of his scathing flyer broadsides. Luckily his diatribe "On Malicious Gossip" did not actually name the lady in question or he might have been sued for calling her everything from "evil-minded" to "cowardly". In Sauk City, there was no need to name her.[11]

Derleth made his third trip to New York in December of 1940. He learned at the Appleton Century office that *STILL SMALL VOICE* had already sold a thousand copies without the library orders, which would come in after the first of the year. Williams told him the Windsor McCay biography would be a risk, but August stubbornly insisted he wanted to try it.

He had lunch with the current editor of *WEIRD TALES*, and visited briefly with a dozen or more other editors and publishers. He visited also with Stephen Vincent Benet, Edgar Lee Masters, and Sherwood Anderson; attended another meeting of the Kalem Club with Donald Wandrei; escorted Wandrei's sister-in-law Connie (Mrs. Howard Wandrei) to his favorite opera, "Rosekavalier", playing at the Metropolitan. He thought Rise Stevens' performance was fine but List's, who played the Baron Ochs, was better.

The author was amused by the effect his wool opera cape and ascot had upon the "full dressed stuffed shirts" that surrounded him. The earlier fetish for flamboyant costumes had narrowed to the velvet lounging robes, and much later, this opera cape and a few luxurious smoking jackets. As for the rest of his apparel, August had settled into what would become a lifelong clothes preference that was in itself a slap in the face of conventionality. He dressed, not for the occasion, nor to impress others, but in the clothes most comfortable to him: casual slacks, T-shirts or pullover sweaters, and sandals.[12] His apparel never ceased to irritate his contemporaries. As early as 1940, they publicly chastised him for his appearance via an item in the Madison newspaper. It reported that August had attended a "Farm and Home Week" banquet attired in a white sweater and that Verner Nuhn, the husband of Ruth Suckow, a Cedar Falls, Iowa writer, was heard to tell friends he thought he'd have John Stuart Curry paint a tie on it.[13]

In later years, whenever August responded to requests for lectures to various teachers' groups, women's clubs, librarians, writers, etc. he quoted a graduating fee scale: so much for a dress shirt, so much extra for a coat, the highest fee that which included a tie. At one session of the Rhinelander School of Arts, he appeared in what seemed to be the same burgundy T-Shirt day after day. Some of those attending whispered that he was probably too tight to buy more than one shirt, others sympathized, picturing him – the typical bachelor – washing out the shirt every night, draping it over the bathroom towel rack or shower rod to dry. None of them realized that August's huge closet at home contained more than a hundred T-shirts, and because he was especially fond of burgundy, most of them were that shade.[14] One of the exceptions to his dress pattern was the donning of a tailed frock coat and high stovepipe hat to preside at Freethinkers' funerals. He was the one usually asked to give the eulogy on those occasions, since the Freethinkers did not have a resident pastor. Also probably because he knew almost everyone in the Sac Prairie area.

Derleth, even as he kept the day-by-day accounts of the natural phenomena of Sac Prairie, also noted the demise of area residents, mourning their departure with almost as much sorrow as he did the destruction of a tree. His journal is sprinkled with comments on each loss, and to many of the people especially dear to him or connected to some nostalgic pleasure, he composed poems.

The maple sugar camp, background for one of his short stories, was one of August's favorite places. When Mrs. J. P. Kindrich died, he wrote:

IN MEMORIAM

No more the sugar camp will know
Her footsteps passing to and fro,
No more shall Baxter's murmuring stream
Encroach upon her spring day's dream
With soothing words of quiet peace
That hold the Hollow. Now release
Is hers, no more the common things she loved,
For on the splendid wings of death,
Majestically numb, with grief,
A greater peace has come.

When Elky died and August read the obituary, the cold words gave no hint of Elky's eternal search for God, said nothing really about Elky, the town character, racing against inexorable time. It never mentioned that he was one of the old men who congregated at the barber shop, a breed Derleth grieved to see die out.

Later in the marshes that night, August wrote a short poem to Elky's memory, about his eternally questioning "Why?"[15]

The day after he returned to Sauk City, he made his usual trip to the harness shop, watching Hugo work as he listened to Nick Knectges play warm and mellow music on his violin. The smell of recently washed leather assailed his nostrils once again. He also walked to the post office and noted on the way that Croenan Brothers' Restaurant was advertising a "Hitler Sundae – Half Nuts" for 13 cents.[16]

On New Year's Eve he gave the first of the many celebrations he would hold in the Place of Hawks, to welcome the new year. Three of the younger boys became very ill when someone spiked their soda pop with whiskey. At three a.m., August vacuumed. He couldn't rest in a room that wasn't clean and orderly.

One of the local residents described the event as follows: "...Open-house pot-lucks they were and the women vied with each other to produce the tastiest dish. At midnight, a local doctor's wife (Effie Bachhuber) mixed eggnog, the old-fashioned kind with real eggs and a regular ceremony, mixing them. Those who wished played bridge in one room. The old men played Sheephead in another. The children sought out his comic collection area, while the college students congregated in his study with his fabulous book collections and his mammoth bed (long before king-sized beds were on the market, Derleth had his father fashion a bed frame large enough to accommodate two full bed-sized mattresses, side by side). Others simply sat and talked on a long sofa before the living room fireplace. Women with small babies retired to a bedroom where they could nurse their infants in private. Each guest was asked to bring food for himself and a friend. Any liquid beverages other than eggnog were furnished by those who wanted to drink them. After the eggnog, most of the older folks went home and the house was turned over to the young people. They danced in the recreation room until four a.m., and if anyone wished to drink a coke, August only charged them ten cents a bottle..."[17]

These affairs cost Derleth as little as $40.00. He usually had enough food left over to last several days, and several additions to his liquor cabinet, as well. It was the only way he could afford such large parties, and even if he had been able to furnish everything himself, there was no way he could buy the array of delicious food provided by the expert cooks all over the Sac Prairie area.

While the young people of Sac Prairie were dancing the early morning hours of 1941 away, Derleth was in his study, going over the year's accounts, settling old business, clearing a way for the new. It was a mental housecleaning as well; a way by which Derleth could get a more cohesive picture of his accomplishments thus far, so he could sketch out a tentative schedule of goals for the year ahead. The practice persisted throughout his lifetime. His planning was the greatest reason for the great volume of work he accomplished through the years. Only a carefully planned work program would allow him to abandon his typewriter for daily treks downtown and hikes into the countryside, for on-the-spur-of-the-moment indulgences in a concert, movie, or gourmet dinner.[18]

Max Perkins of Charles Scribner's Sons, was becoming increasingly impressed with August's "...amount of work in so many lines...." Perkins was very complimentary about the *BRIGHT JOURNEY* manuscript, writing "...It promises to be the best of the novels...." He was pleased and complimentary about the reviews *COUNTRY GROWTH* was getting. "...They show a true appreciation of your remarkable talent for truly important fiction. Stories don't often get much attention..." he wrote.[19] By the end of January, 1941, *EVENING IN SPRING* was ready for the publishers. Portions of it, however, had been published as early as 1932 in *THE MIDLAND*, and *THE PRAIRIE SCHOONER*. Other bits appeared in *SPACE*, 1934, *LITERARY AMERICA*, 1935, *STORY, (RIVER AND AMERICAN PREFACES* [University of Iowa]), 1937, *THE STORY WORKSHOP*, 1938, *ATMOSPHERE OF HOUSES*, 1939, *COUNTRY GROWTH*, 1940, and the *CORONET*, 1941. The completed book was published by Scribners in 1941.

"...Up to date, it is without a question my best novel... nostalgically auto-biographical.... Among my forty books, it is the only one I can take up and read through with unalloyed pleasure and uninhibited laughter...." He wrote in the forward to a later edition in 1945.

The book was dedicated to "...all the young, all the lovers, blind to the hawk of time that hovers, hangs with no haste, no hour lost...." It chronicles the budding, flowering, and bitter fading of a first love, and mourns the passing of springtime, itself. As the story begins,

"...The street lights came on, flowing softly into the spring night, like great moths among the trees and along the lands. The afterglow was crimson...beneath a wash of amethyst and lemon deepening into copper, and trees were darker still, thickened buds and new leaves swollen with Spring. Robins with their breasts turned toward the west caroled a bright song against the gathering dark...."

And then the book ends:

"...All around me the night whispered, rustling leaves, and owl crying, limbs rubbing against each other and village sounds. The wind blew, the street light swung to and fro and the leaves whirled and raced in the yellow glow on the street below. There is a loneliness about streetlights and trees at night: lemon lights, dark trees, far sky and stars: and wind that blows all the earth, a wanderer, too, ..."[20]

Many years after the real story ended, Derleth retained his fascination for those yellow arc lights and when the village tore them down, he asked to have several to use in front of his home on Lueders Road, in the hope he could enjoy them a few more years.

The young people who trooped through the Farm (Place of Hawks) daily were so grateful for the opportunity to browse through his comic collection, dance in the recreation room far into the night to the music of his extensive record collection, and read from his rapidly expanding library. They rewarded his hospitality by helping to keep everything clean and ship shape in and out of the house. At the same time he could study the antics of the younger crowd and use them in the novel he would call *SHIELD OF THE VALIANT*.

The reactions of the Sac Prairie populace to Derleth's youth open houses were mixed. A few loyal followers praised him for establishing a sort of club house for the students. Others were relieved to know where their teenagers were, especially in the hours after shops, ice cream parlors, movies, were closed and ball games were over. The hard core telescope gossipers were overly suspicious that something wicked was happening up there on the "king's" hill.[21]

1 A. D. Journal, 1 January, 1940, box 92, folder 1, p. 80.
2 Ibid.
3 August Derleth, "Novels at 1,000 words a day", Writer's Review, January, 1934, p. 3.
4 Note 1, 11 December, 1939, box 91, folder 8, p. 11.
5 Ibid., 28 December, 1939, box 91, p. 22.
6 Beverly Cass, Capital Times, February, 1940; A. D. Journal, 11 December, 1939, box 91, folder 8, p. 11.
7 Memorabilia collected on biographer's many trips to Sauk City.
8 Note 1, 18 February, 1941, folder 1, p. 8.
9 Ibid., 19 February, 1940, box 91, folder 8, p. 63.
10 D. Appelton Century Co. to A. D., March, 1940.
11 August Derleth, flyer, "On Malicious Gossip", SWHS museum archives, Madison, Wisconsin.
12 Note 1, 3, 4, 5, 6 and 7 Dec., 1941, box 92, folder 1, pp. 67-ff.
13 Ibid., 1 Jan., 1941, box 92, folder 1, p. 80; "Paint a tie on that", Capital Times photo, Jan. 31, 1940.
14 Biographer's observations and experiences as she served as accountant, treasurer, and consultant at the Rhinelander School of Arts.
15 Note 1,
16 Ibid.
17 Esther Trautman tape to biographer, no date.
18 Biographer's conclusions.
19 Max Perkins to A. D.,
20 August Derleth, Evening in Spring, (Sauk City, Wisconsin, 1945), beginning and ending.
21 Note 1,

Chapter Nine

*"...I shudder to think of any decision in the nation of life
or death to be left to the military..."*[1]

Donald Wandrei and Derleth had been continuing their
efforts to sell Lovecraft stories, and in June, 1941, the
WEIRD TALES' editor, Dorothy McIlwraith, offered to take
"Shadow Over Innsmouth" if it could be cut from 20,000 to
15,000 words in time to catch the anticipated fall circulation
comeback of the magazine.[2]

Derleth added another ongoing chore to his writing and
publishing commitments in 1941. At his own suggestion to
William T. Evjue, editor and publisher of the *CAPITAL TIMES*,
and in direct opposition to the advice of Sinclair Lewis that he
stop doing book reviews, he became literary editor and book
reviewer of the paper. At first, Derleth wrote the reviews with
no compensation except the complimentary copies of books sent
by the publishers.[3]

In September, he wrote the first draft of his first juvenile,
OLIVER THE WAYWARD OWL. It took him half an hour. The
book was slanted to the pixilated old as well as the very young.
Clare Dwiggins was the illustrator. It was published in 1945.
Dwiggins and Derleth later collaborated on four additional juve-
nile picture books: *BILL'S DIARY, A BOY'S WAY, IT'S A BOY'S
WORLD*, and *WILBER, THE TRUSTING WHIPPOORWILL*.[4]

Up to October, 1941, August had worried little about being
called upon to serve his country in the armed forces, assuring
friends that his three health problems – hernia, bad teeth, and
hypertension – would classify him unfit for military service.
Then a headline in the *CAPITAL TIMES* brought the war right
into the lap of Sac Prairie. "Powder Plant to be Built Near
Merimac", it announced.[5] Derleth was upset and displeased at
the news and had many questions about the wisdom of the project.

His concern increased as farmers were pushed out of their
homes in the upper Sac Prairie region. One of the homesteads
dated back to President Polk, who had signed the sheepskin

deed to Swain Mather's property. Charles Kunze had just built a new home and was finishing the woodwork when he was forced to vacate. Mrs. Dahnke had been born on her land and had a book with the names of 250 people buried in a cemetery nearby. Farmers were torn between spreading their lime and planting their corn, in case they didn't have to leave, and not wasting the time, supplies and energy, in case they did.[6]

August after attending a protest meeting, sent a letter to President Roosevelt, whom he greatly admired, reminding him that "...one of the most treasured aspects of a democratic life is the right to protest; if such protests are ignored, the democratic process is being ignored...."[7] (Such a letter and Derleth's vehement fight against the powder plant, took courage. He was, after all, of German descent and all over the county Germans were having difficulty proving their loyalty to the United States.)[8] He pointed out that only 75 miles north, in Adams County, there were 18,000 acres of land not suitable for farming.[9] He wrote an open letter stating the arguments against "booming" the town and had it printed up in flyer form and distributed. His distress grew as he witnessed the effect on the twin cities: real estate changed hands rapidly; fast deals were made foolishly; townsfolk turned reckless with the prospect of big money; even the Men's Club acted without common sense when it donated $25 to the Red Cross, Derleth thought. Their expenses were $225 a year already and their income was $150. He knew what havoc the plant would bring. How it could multiply the population and destroy the peace and quiet of his beloved Sac Prairie.[10]

In spite of Derleth's all-out war against it, the Badger Ordinance Plant (now known as Badger Ammunition) was built on Highway 12, close to the slope of the Baraboo range, displacing 60 fertile farms and consuming 7,400 acres of land. The Northwestern Railroad had exerted greater pressure than August and other Sac Prairie dissenters were able to counter. The local residents were given the flimsy excuse that the site was necessary because the hills obscured the area from above, in case of Japanese air attacks. Conservationists in the area were distressed over the pollution that was poured into the Wisconsin River by the factory. Ice skaters who regularly used the river to skate for miles, found their natural skating rink melted away in the vicinity of the plant.[11]

The news about the powder plant brought August's draft status into more alarming focus. Not about to waste a moment when he went to Milwaukee for his physical, he brought along a manuscript for revision during the bus ride and the long waits in one queue or another that were according to Derleth,

"...a sight to behold: short, squat men; tall, skinny, round-shouldered men; men whose average age was 35 or better, most of them terrible in build, incredibly bad in posture, so that I thought one could not blame most women for going to live communally together by themselves...though, no doubt any like number of women would come off as badly, anything in mass being bad...."

August weighed in at 214 pounds, his waist measured 26 inches, and he was barrel-chested. His blood pressure was 170/110, his pulse 110 at the time of the physical. He had to make two trips for medical examinations before the final classification was made. August had been right about his hernia and his hypertension making him unfit for military service.

He received his 4F classification two years before his friend Karl Ganzlin enlisted in the Voluntary Officers' Corps in August, 1942.[12]

He also received another poison pen letter calling him the biggest "scooper" in town, berating him for getting out of the draft and asking him to please get a clean sweater or let the U.S. put a suit on him.[13]

In addition to his deeply ingrained hatred of guns and violence, he could not face the thought of having his life topple about him just as he was about to realize his dreams. There was no way he could hang onto his house and the publishing company should he be inducted into the service. Arkham House had only recently lost the active help of Donald Wandrei to the military, leaving Derleth solely responsible. Above that, August knew very well he was not cut out to follow orders. If he could not have the top position, running the show, he would probably be court marshaled in a hurry for extreme insubordination.[14]

Instead he offered his services to the Civilian Defense Headquarters in Washington, and was included in a talent pool in the Office of Facts and Figures, and also filled in a long form for doing work for the Coordinator of Information Department.

The Writers' War Board named projects they wanted Derleth to do: "...a 500-700 word narrative for a daily short-wave radio program to the A. E. F...should be upbeat; filler service to a newspaper syndicate, up to 100 words, inspiration, factual, or humorous, pertaining to some phase of the war; and 1-2 minute speeches dramatizing the importance of the civil-ians' individual day-by-day activities demonstrating graphically and simply, how seemingly dull routine efforts contribute to Victory...."[15]

August also wrote a radio play, *SILENCE TO THE HARBORERS OF PAST ILLUSIONS*, based on his poem of the same name, which had appeared in *THE NEW WORKERS MAGAZINE*, Oct. 11, 1941. It demonstrated how the Nazis shoot those who will not discard ideas of the past, like those of Thomas Paine. It was placed on file for possible use in propa-ganda broadcasts.[16]

There is reason to believe that the whole question of the draft was also the source of considerable conflict between the many paradoxes within Derleth. He abhorred what Hitler was doing to Germany and the world. He hated and mistrusted the military. He was so very German himself, he must have wanted to demonstrate in a substantial way his own belief in the need to rid the world of the Nazi scourge. Yet, his own mind was relieved that he was exempt from military time.[17]

In spite of Derleth's anger over the powder plant, he and the twin cities survived the years of "boom". He also managed to write a play – *HERE WE GO AGAIN GRANDMA* – before Karl Ganzlin left for the service, and to survive the production of it although he found nothing in it he could praise, due to the play-wright's terrible lines, and incredible scenes. The play was pro-duced by a little theater group he'd started with the help of Ganzlin in July of 1939. Twenty-five people had turned out for their first meeting, some local, some Madison students. Under the guidance of August and Karl, the group produced plays shown in many communities in the area.

Harried more and more by the lack of time, Derleth was forced to give up two of his favorite pastimes during this period.

He couldn't fish and hike, much less play chess, and he much preferred hiking.[18]

Shortly before Ganzlin left for the service, he had accompanied August and John Stuart Curry, artist-in-residence at the University of Wisconsin, on a leisurely three-day canoe trip down the river. The jaunt was in preparation for the writing of *WISCONSIN, RIVER OF A THOUSAND ISLES*.

Curry sketched the illustrations for the book and Derleth researched as they went along. The entourage accompanying them included, among others, his two employees, Alice Conger and John Stanton. They were packed into two canoes and a motorboat (in case they ran into trouble). The trip was well covered by the press, with *WISCONSIN, STATE JOURNAL, CAPITAL TIMES* and the *MILWAUKEE JOURNAL* reporters present. A group of about 25 people gathered to wish them 'bon voyage' in spite of the early hour and all along the route, clusters of Derleth's friends and fans waved them on. It was a good publicity stunt and Derleth milked every inch of it. He took notes on points of interest and significance: the hole with no bottom, which legend claimed had never been plumbed; Ferry Bluff, significant during the Civil War for ferrying would-be soldiers closer to Milwaukee so they could enlist quicker than if they'd taken the longer route around Sac Prairie; Law's Landing; Goode Island, Snake Island, Blue Mound Arena, lead mining country, the hill of Taliesin, etc., down to Prairie due Chein.[19]

The finished book included much of the history of the river, from its discovery by Pierre Esprit Radison and Me'dart Chouart Sieur de Groselliers. It is replete with vivid descriptions of the birds and foliage along the banks; filled also with August's nostalgic memories of "...an intimate...pastoral river, a canoeist's stream, an angler's river, a swimmer's paradise...quiet now, aging, seldom rising to the flood stages of early years, pastoral and beautiful where it flows slowly down between the hills that enclose its valley to give itself through the Mississippi to the sea...." In the book are many other evidences of Derleth's life-long love affair with the "Oisconsin".

The nature trip and history lesson of the book are leavened with interesting anecdotes, such as his account of the twin city rivalry in the battle to secure the county seat. Sauk City had enlisted the aid of nearby Baraboo to help protest when they thought they might be losing it to Prairie du Sac. The upshot of their protesting was that the county seat was awarded to Baraboo, and the twin cities were stuck with holding the bag, empty now!

The fight over where to locate the post office, which ended with both villages getting their own (more service than the area warranted) is also included in the book. Bridges came into the battle next, then schools, etc. Their eternal conflict ranged from fights between groups of boys to battles about where the railway station would be located. The irony in their long dissension is that they are united finally in their common sewer system, causing one native to observe "...The only way upper and lower Sac could get together was underground...."

The book touches on the agriculture of the region, on its folklore, on fur trading, on politics, on river rats, and on lumberjacks "...addicted to Booze, Bawds, Batter and Ballads...."

Derleth included a plug for his new business venture, mentioning Arkham House, a publishing firm in Sauk City, which was unique because it was devoted solely to the collection of uncanny stories. Later, he mentioned August Derleth as one of the reasons that Sauk City had more prestige than Prairie du Sac.

The book was published by Farrar and Rhinehart, Inc., New York. It was edited by Stephen Vincent Benet and Carl Cramer; dedicated to Dr. Louise Phelps Kellog, "...pre-eminent among historians of the old northwest...."[20]

August had sent the manuscript to Dr. Kellog before publication, asking her to check it for errors. Some time after the book was published, Dr. Kellog came to him considerably upset. She relayed a conversation she'd had with Mark Schorer about the book. Schorer had told her August said he slapped together a book, then got Dr. Kellog to re-write, or polish it. August denied the accusation, and that he ever "slapped together" anything. Instead, he claimed to have told Schorer that he turned to Dr. Kellog whenever he had a problem because he considered her the ultimate authority. He maintained that Schorer had told a deliberate lie in order to arouse Dr. Kellog's ire against him.

He then proceeded to enlighten the Professor concerning the reasons Schorer might want to cast aspersions on Derleth. He repeated alleged plagiarism of two short story plots in college, and claimed, also, that Schorer drew upon his notes for *A HOUSE TOO OLD*, Mark's first novel. Mark had known August planned to use those notes for his own Sac Prairie saga. The reason Schorer got his book written first, August claimed, was because August had to live in part on his earnings and Mark was supported by his parents in such a fashion he did not need to work while in college.[21]

Schorer's *A HOUSE TOO OLD* prefaced each chapter with a short historical summary of Sauk City for the period or mood covered by the chapter, and these did indeed resemble some of the colorful Sauk City and Prairie du Sac happenings recorded in Derleth's daily journal and later incorporated into *WALDEN WEST*. Schorer's account of two school teacher sisters who reportedly had gone "insane", and been institutionalized with the help of a prominent villager who had been unsuccessful in his attempt to purchase their property, did not contain Derleth's "punch" to the story – that the women wrote and managed to get published a booklet telling how they'd been railroaded into the asylum. As a result of a news reporter reading the pamphlet and agitating for their release, they were freed. No firm conclusion can be reached concerning the supposed theft of August's ideas until all the papers of both men are open to public scrutiny.[22]

SOURCE NOTES
CHAPTER NINE

1 A. D. to Edward Uhlan, Feb. 3, 1960.
2 Dorothy McIlwraith to A. D., June 15, 1948.
3 A. D. to Wm. Evjue.
4 Erhart A. Mueller, Only in Sumpton, (Steven Point, 1977).
5 "Powder plant to be built near Merimac", Capital Times, October, 1941.
6 A. D. to Sprague De Camp, Oct. 20, 1962.
7 A. D. to President Roosevelt, no date.
8 Biographer's knowledge and opinion.
9 Note 7, op. cit.
10 August Derleth, flyer, SWHS Museum archives, Madison, Wisconsin.
11 Note 7, op. cit.
12 A. D. Journal, n.d.
13 Ibid., anonymous letter.
14 Biographer's conclusions and opinion.
15 A. D. to Victor Kilefbeck, Jan. 2, 1942.
16 A. D. to Inez Weaver, Feb. 2, 1967.
17 Biographer's opinion.
18 Note 15, op. cit.
19 "Artist, author plan canoe trip on river", Milwaukee Journal, March 2, 1941, caption beneath photograph of Derleth and John Stuart Curry; Note 11, July 1941, pp. 129-ff.
20 August Derleth, The Wisconsin River of a Thousand Isles (New York, 1967).
21 A. D. to Dr. Louise Phelps Kellog, April 28 and June 3, 1942.
22 Mark Schorer, A House Too Old, (New York, 1935).

Chapter Ten

"...I bear too many scars from the wars of love...."[1]

In July of 1943, Derleth attended a writers' banquet in Chicago. He was pleased to learn that Meridel la Suer would get a Rockefeller grant, as he had suggested her for the honor. Other writers he knew, or whose names he was familiar with, were there. He thought Vincent Starret, well-known bookman, as handsome and delightful as his books. Marcia Masters, a quiet, attractive young woman, was also there.

It was the first time he'd seen the daughter of his revered Masters. She told him how anxious she had been to meet him because every time she went to visit her father in New York, August was all he talked about. She had soft brown eyes and a frank, friendly smile.

He learned she had been married in her teens to a man 17 years her senior, was widowed and had an 11-year-old daughter. She wrote for the *CHICAGO SUN*, had a juvenile out, and was currently working on a book of poetry.

August, charmed, demanded they sit together, to the annoyance of conference chairman, who had to juggle carefully planned seating arrangements.

Masters' daughter seemed interested, not so much in August Derleth, the man, as August Derleth, the phenomenon. Again, like the too eager little boy leaping upon his grandfather's back, Derleth phoned her the next day, and arranged a rendezvous for the following afternoon.

Marcia arrived, beautifully dressed in white from head to toe. Though frankly curious rather than shy, she said little.

Fifteen days later August stood waiting at the Northwestern station for the streamliner that was bringing Marcia to him. She looked very chic and seemed to be excited about being in Sauk City.

They strolled leisurely along Lower Hill Road and later over the railroad bridge. They walked again the next day. August showed her through the canning factory. He read some of her projected poetry book. They spent six days together, walking in the marshes and the hills, lunching at Karberg's, swimming for hours in the Wisconsin River, necking casually in the sand. As usual, the news traveled fast and August soon noticed that some of the townspeople had fetched binoculars to watch them.

They shopped, one evening, for a friendship ring. Zienke's store had nothing they liked except an open-work wedding ring. They purchased it, chuckling as they speculated what the town would have to say at that.

August felt a sense of loss when Marcia returned to Chicago on the 23rd. He wrote a poem of goodbye:
"A Peewee at Dawn"
"...Will you who are going
Know the way back?..."

Marcia's letter arrived on the 27th, assuring him that she was coming back and would never leave again.[2] Her father wrote, too, saying he would send his blessings when the betrothal was settled. When Masters wrote again, his blessings included the offer of a house he owned in Chicago for a wedding present. He thought August and Marcia were fortunate to have found each other, in spite of his former advice to Derleth against marriage at all.[3]

Marcia came back in less than a week, accompanied by her daughter, Andrea, a delightful thirteen-year-old with a certain grace and air of complete ease, according to their host.

Marcia's father had bestowed the nickname "dear grandma" because she reminded him of Marcia's mother. August, Marcia and dear grandma spent many pleasant hours swimming, picnicking, sight-seeing on foot and in Alice's car, and soaking in the lush Indian Summer beauty and abundant harvest of Sac Prairie. Dear grandma, along with her poise and good manners, displayed a sensitivity toward the starry-eyed lovers, giving them space by spending hours at the beach alone and finding other things to do without them, allowing Augie and Marcia privacy, and long hours to spend in each other's arms in the studio, or one of Derleth's secluded nature nooks. Alice Conger played her usual role of chauffeur on these occasions.

When the three were together, hiking, swimming, picnicking, shopping, or out on the town for dinner and the movies in

Madison and surrounding areas, she was also enchanted with everything. There was no evidence that she suffered the pain of seeing her mom completely enraptured with a total stranger. Nor was there any indications that she worried about the quite obvious plans Marcia was making to marry this giant of a man, who would then become her stepfather. There were signs indicating that the young, impressionable teenager had herself fallen under his aura of charm, and his love of people and life, itself. As a mature woman 20 years later, she urged Marcia to make advances to August, with a plan to snare him before someone else did; if Marcia did not aggressively pursue him, dear grandma vowed to go after him for herself!

When the time came for parting again, Marcia was distressed and August didn't want her to go. He cheered her up by telling her she could announce their engagement and set the date for their wedding.

Six days later, Derleth was in Chicago, visiting the minister of Marcia's church. He met relatives of the Masters and announced the engagement at a dinner at the Key Club. He also wrote several announcements for the newspapers.[4]

An article by Judith Cass in the *Chicago Daily Tribune's* "Events in Society" column, September 17, announced that the engagement was of special interest to the literary scene, with Marcia herself a writer, working on various newspapers and the author of a juvenile – *GRANDPARP FLEW IN* – and of a projected poetry volume – *THE GUNNER ON THE MERCHANT SHIP*.[5]

Sauk City was stunned by the news.[6]

Ewald (Ewie) Blum, a friend in the service, wrote that his sister Irene had sent him a clipping, and he was bowled over.[7]

As usual, the time, energy, and mental cloud nine August stumbled around in when engrossed in his more serious love affairs, cut into his rigid production schedule. Even the death and funeral of his grandfather were pushed aside rather hastily.[8]

August had time only for love; but he could not entirely ignore his Muse. The afternoon of his granddad's funeral, his feeling for Marcia poured out in two poems: "The Solitary" and "Humbly In the Dark – A Prayer":

"...lips, eyes,
  something forever in the pulse,
the cell of memory gives out its
ghosts..." he wrote; and *"...As daylong*
cradling in his mind
the girl somewhere
dark hair, brown eyes warm,
the girl a bird
the girl an April rain
the girl a star, the word of
love...."[9]

When Marcia returned to the Place of Hawks early in October, she was tired. There was a chip on her shoulder, August thought, over a disagreement they'd had about the poetry of Shelley. A few days of being together, picnicking in the hills, strolling in the marshes through the breath – taking beauty of a Wisconsin Indian Summer, even dancing one magic moonlit night in the cemetery across from the Place of Hawks, and again, the lovers could not bear to part. She cried, and when she had gone, August couldn't work.

He was pleased to see her so affected by the parting, which was even harder than the earlier ones because Marcia had to make a trip to the West Coast. She didn't want to go, but had no choice.

She sent a wire from California, telling him how much she missed him, and signing it "Sprite". Earl Broderick, the wireless operator, was confused, "...Say, how many women have you got on the string, anyway?..." he asked Derleth.

Marcia could not get back until after the holidays. She seemed more content with being in California than she was at the thought of going. August brooded, and conveyed his fears to Marcia's father, who advised him first to go after her, then advised him not to, saying it might only cause August more pain.[10] Though her things arrived in Sauk City on the 20th of November, August was apprehensive enough four days later to type a passionate, four-page, single-spaced letter, declaring his love and entreating her to come back to him.

"...Whatever happens between us now and hereafter, I am very proud to have been loved by you even for a little while. No other person had ever made me so happy in my entire life – so happy, indeed, that I would willingly pay ten times over in pain for that happiness and know that I had been incredibly enriched...in some respects being loved by you and loving you has altered my course of existence; and the memory of the days...spent with you will always, inevitably live sharply within me, sometimes ineffably sweet, sometimes with terrible pain...I am...essentially a monogamous person; when I give myself I do so completely. I am and always will be a one-woman man, and it takes me a long time to recover from separation...once I have made the submission to love. I am helpless before it...."

He accused her of having two major selves, obvious to him from that first evening; one the real woman – a sprite with magic and beauty and creative spirit – the other, mostly defense constructed by social credos, conventions, restraints, concepts and beliefs that have no place in the creative artist's life.

He cried out in pain at her misunderstanding his offer to teach her to jitterbug...She had compared it to offering instructions of the foxtrot to Nijinski. He chided her for being vain, for being so casual about his love.

"...You are just at heart a lovely hurt little girl who wants to run into shelter but who resents the need of giving herself that shelter...I am not ashamed to confess that I need you with absolute desperation...When I told you that I would sacrifice my career for yours, I was being utterly sincere...."

He reminded her of the many changes he had already made for her, would make for her, going so far as to clean the house if he couldn't afford to hire a maid, yet she wrote, "incredibly" asking if there was anything about her August was not intending to change.

"...Please stop fighting me and start loving me," he pleaded.

"...It is Thanksgiving Day today, and I thank God for you – I thank Him for your soft, warm eyes, for your mouth which is like a wild poppy;...I thank Him for your wonderful youth, for your loveliness of spirit, for all the magic and sparks; I thank Him for the lovely being who sits and gazes at the brook, who goes into the hills and marshes and the fields with me: I thank Him because I may love you, and perhaps, if He is willing, because someday I may be your husband...."[11]

August accused Marcia of pride, but his own pride was stronger than his passionate need for her love. He did not send the letter that might have changed the course of both their lives. He waited a few days, wrote Marcia a sonnet. An opportunity to go to California after Marcia without seeming to be following her had presented itself a few weeks before when the McCormick Agency of Beverly Hills proposed August come west for a session of screen writing. August took Masters advice this time, and rejected the offer.[12]

Marcia, away from the magic of Sac Prairie, the marshes, the mounds and the moonlight, had already taken a second look at the situation. She was more than a little frightened of this genius, this bigger-than-life phenomenon, this multi-man. How would she be able to cope with him? Perhaps, being the daughter of a legendary poet, and an author and poet herself, she knew more than most about the ego, the intense introspection, the agonizing, the sacrificing everything and everyone else to the whims of the Muse. She had her own pride. Sauk City was separated by not-so-many miles from Chicago on the map, but their two environments were worlds apart. How would her chic, her sophistication, her social background blend into the simple, old-fashioned, old-shoe existence of Sauk City, where time, itself, seemed almost to stand still? Her doubts and fears built up, away from the reassurance of August's presence, his love.[13]

Right before Christmas, Marcia suggested that she might not come back in February. They had set the wedding date for February 24th, August's birthday.

Again, instead of sending the passionate Thanksgiving letter, Derleth delivered a blunt ultimatum: Marcia should either come back in February or break their engagement.

Marcia broke the engagement.

In the absence of anyone in Sauk City having an abortion, an illegitimate child, or running off with someone else's spouse, the broken engagement had the local gossips interested throughout the day.[14]

The response of his friends was varied. Ewie Blum, who sensed August's blue mood when Marcia was slipping away, had a sympathetic note. Ewie knew full well how August felt, so refrained from offering advice.[15]

August, much as he loved Marcia and wanted her to be his wife, was in a sense relieved. Deep down he knew what he wrote to a correspondent years later: "...It would have been a tragedy if I had married, even Marcia Masters."[16]

He hid the wounds of still another disastrous plunge down life's romantic stairway with caustic remarks about what a "pain" Marcia was. His own pain is evident in his telling virtual strangers, and pen pals he'd never met, that he was the one responsible for breaking off the affair.[17] Yet, paradoxically, he bragged about having been loved by Marcia. As late as 1969, Derleth was disappointed when Marcia did not show up for a writers' conference in Chicago, as expected. He had planned to flaunt a beautiful young woman in Marcia's face, and introduce her as his wife.[18]

SOURCE NOTES
CHAPTER TEN

1 A. D. to Mary Stiver, Sept. 22, 1960.
2 A. D. Journal, 31 July and 17, 21, 23 August, 1943.
3 Edgar Lee Masters to A. D., 26 August and 7, 17, September, 1943.
4 Note 2, 6 September, 1943.
5 Judith Cass, "Events in society" (column) Chicago Tribune; August Derleth, "Sauk City author is engaged to Marcia Masters Jennings", Capital Times, Sept. 17, 1943.
6 Note 2, 18 December, 1943.
7 Ewald Blum to A. D., Nov. 2, 1943.
8 August Derleth, "Poetry, A Magazine of Verse.", May, 1944, pp 7 ff
9 A. D. Journal, 1, Oct.
10 Note 3, Nov. 22, 1943.
11 A. D. to Marcia Masters Schmidt, unsent 1st draft of letters on back of A. D. Journal entries, this one written on Thanksgiving, November, 1942.
12 Note 2, December, 1943.
13 Marcia Masters Schmidt to biographer, Nov. 22 and Oct. 4, 1979.
14 Note 2, 17 December, 1943.
15 Ewie Blum to A. D., no date.
16 A. D. to Dorothy Unsell, July 20, 1960.

Chapter Eleven

"...I am too soft for my own good...."[1]

Marty's brief experience with dating different girls ended when he became acquainted with "Cassandra". In Derleth's earlier years of service on the Sauk City School Board, he had defended her when the jealousy of some of her classmates broke out in a rash of rumors that had no real foundation, but could have resulted in her being expelled had not Derleth intervened. Cassandra had "...gray-green eyes edged with intense blue, stubborn mouth, sensuous lower lip, little hollows in fair cheeks, slender arms, lithe fingers, slim body, enchanting grace of a restless spirit...." August loved to dance with her, and often strolled about the high school grounds with her when attending school hops and other student gatherings there. He had grown quite fond of her over the years. He felt somehow very comfortable and at ease when he was with her. She made him feel good.

Marty and Cassandra eventually became engaged. Derleth heartily approved of the match. He was happy for both of them. They were young but probably wouldn't marry until after Marty graduated from college. He might not have smiled so benignly on the young lovers if their romance meant that his relationship with Marty was over. Marty still came back to August's arms after escorting Cassandra home for the evening.

Groups of young people who'd been converging on the farm almost nightly, still came by. Through his work on the school board, his help with school dramatics, and his involvement with juveniles in the boys' club and as probation officer, he had collected quite a swarm of young friends: Dr. and Effie Bachhuber's boys, David and Richard; Thomas and Milton Trautman, sons of Dr. and Esther Trautman; John Stanton's girl friend – Myra Lee Poad – and her twin sister, Mary; Henry Meyer; Schimmel; and a score of others who dropped in, uninvited to page through his comics, play records, dance, browse in his growing library, wrestle on his huge bed, or otherwise amuse themselves in the big house. Derleth's door was always open. He joined in their jitterbugging, and didn't even protest too much when they came out late at night and rousted him out of bed to help polish off their evening festivities. About the only time he could count on a night without interruption was when there was a high school football game. Derleth not only didn't play football, he didn't watch it either if he could help it.[2]

It wasn't until 1944 that the war began to exert a more decided effect on Derleth's life. August was doing his bit on the home front, serving as Sauk City representative on the Wisconsin Committee for Russian War Relief (for which he received a citation from the United States Government) and keeping up a constant correspondence with those serving. John Stanton, Ewie Blum, Karl Ganzlin, W. ("Shimmel") Kroenen, and others received letters and books regularly. He consulted with Donald Wandrei concerning Arkham House and the H. P. L. letter collection.[3]

His ambitious publishing schedule for Arkham House hit a snag when the government decreed that no firm could consume more than five tons of paper a year for commercial book printing. The restrictions threatened to reduce the market for Derleth's own writing as well as curtail Arkham House books and cause headaches for his printers with problems such as Banta's difficulty in reducing the picture sizes of Lovecraft's *MARGINALIA* to conserve paper.[4]

After a few months, the paper allotment changed, easing publishing, but other changes close to home emerged. As August had predicted, two men were killed in an explosion at the powder plant. The plant had absorbed many workers from the area, and the canning company had to import a group of German prisoners of war to take their places.[5] His very good friend, Jesse Stuart, enlisted in the army.[6] His right hand in his publishing ventures, John Stanton was drafted. August pulled all the strings he could to get him exempt from the draft, but got nowhere. Stanton would just have to serve his "hitch".[7]

He continued with his collections; his record collection, especially, at this time. He had acquired a taste for classical music in college. His main passion for music in this period was for jazz. He was partial to the blues: "Joe Turner Blues", "Mood

Indigo", "Jazz Me Blues", etc.

Everything that went on around Derleth was grist for his creative mill. His musical interest and activities of his young guests gave impetus to what Derleth would call one of his better books. *SHIELD OF THE VALIANT* utilized an old theme, that of a boy falling in love with a girl from the wrong side of the tracks. It is unique, nevertheless, in the portraits of Sac Prairie characters woven through the romance of an aspiring musician and his singing girlfriend. The novel was an important addition to his Sac Prairie Saga.

Here again, August projected himself into the book; this time under the name of Steve Grendon, a younger version of *EVENING IN SPRING'S* Grandfather Adams, who also counsels the other characters in the book. Steve suffers the death of Miss Merken, the librarian. He writes to the President protesting the powder plant, and experiences many of the things Derleth was experiencing during this period.[8]

August had given up his position on the school board in 1940, having become increasingly disillusioned with the post. As director, he'd received $13.20 a year, for which he was subjected to libel and detraction. The villagers accused him of being a publicity hound and a self-appointed Sauk City crusader in a *MADISON CAPITOL TIMES'* article when he attacked the selling of liquor to minors by several Mazomanie taverns. He felt the attack was merely performing his duty as Director of the Board of Education since several Sauk City High School students were securing liquor in Mazomanie bars.[9]

He had always hovered over young people under his charge like a mother hen. Yet, paradoxically, when it came to his sexual life-style, he was not the protector but rather the victimizer of those he cared the most about, like Marty and Cassandra.

When Marty was drafted, Cassandra was devastated. She was lonely, despondent, miserable, and pleaded with Derleth for help. August tried to console Cassandra as best he could. He succeeded too well. The awareness between them over the years, her warmth, accelerated and burst forth in a flame neither one could control. Even as Derleth was faithfully writing to Marty, sending him gifts, he was betraying his young lover by stealing the heart of the girl Marty was pledged to marry.

August later described his feelings for Cassandra as some-what the same kind of love a man has for his favorite pet. He felt comfortable with her. She made no demands on him but that of filling the void left when Marty went to war. She had a tremendous need for affection, and sex. Derleth was only too happy to provide both, for he too, needed someone to take Marty's place.[10]

Cassandra graduated and entered a school outside of the Sac Prairie area, she sent amusing little notes, sad ones, too, full of her missing him. August, in turn, sent her copies of his new books, candy, flowers, cute stationery, etc. She came home now and then on weekends, and they'd take to the hills and the marshes for intimate hours.[11]

As discreet as they were about their relationship, the inevitable rumors, speculations and slanderous gossip followed their movements from the first. By the time Marty was released from the army, he had already heard some of the gossip. When he confronted Derleth and demanded the truth, Derleth con-fessed. Instead of fighting over what had happened the two men sat down and discussed the situation like two rational adults looking for a solution. Both of them evidently felt confident of the young woman's affection when they finally agreed to let Cassandra choose between them. The lucky one would marry her. The loser would step aside gracefully. If August married her, however, Marty vowed he would break off his romantic and sexual relationship with Derleth. When Cassandra arrived home for her next visit, the two would-be husbands advised her of their decision. Cassandra had a confession of her own to make. She was pregnant and didn't know for sure whether it Augie or a young man from school who was responsible. The two suitors graciously offered to marry her anyhow. Cassandra, in her charming manner, refused both offers and married the other young man, leaving August and Marty holding both ends of an empty bag in somewhat of a parallel to Prairie du Sac and Sauk City's loss of the county seat.

Though Derleth did not get to marry Cassandra, he was still so upset over Marty's threat to leave him, he put an end to their affair, also.[12]

Sales of *WIND OVER WISCONSIN* had reached the 10,000

mark by March and *SWEET GENEVIEVE*, 2,000. His agent sold "McCrary's Wife" to *GOOD HOUSEKEEPING* for $1,000. Here, too, Derleth was forced to change the ending to what he called "pathetic hogwash" in order to comply with the upbeat of the magazine.[13] Stanley Rinehart offered a fairly good contract for *SLEEP NO MORE*, which he accepted.[14]

During this period, Derleth added the Mycroft & Moran imprint to his publishing house. It would specialize in what he called "off-trail sleuthing stories". Mycroft was derived from the name of Sherlock Holmes' brother and Moran from the Colonel Sebastian Moran, the most dangerous man in London. Derleth finished his first collection of pastiche and Vincent Starret kept his promise to do a complimentary introduction.[15]

SHADOW OF THE NIGHT was chosen by the Cardinal Hayes Literary Committee as one of the best Catholic books in 1943, and his overseas sales began to expand.[16]

August was welcomed into the prestigious Fortean Society, whose list of members included Booth Tarkington, Alexander Woolcott, Oliver Wendall Homes and Clarence Darrow.[17] He also became a member of the American Folklore Society.[18]

One of Derleth's new ventures – an anthology of horror stories titled *SLEEP NO MORE* (illustrated by Lee Brown Coye) was published by Farrar & Rinehart in 1944, with a fairly good contract. Derleth followed it with *WHO KNOCKS?* In 1946, *DARK OF THE MOON* (poems of fantasy and the macabre), *THE SLEEPING AND THE DEAD* and *THE NIGHT SIDE* (horror stories) in 1947, and *STRANGE PORTS OF CALL* (science fiction) in 1948.[19]

In publishing these anthologies, he not only increased his own income slightly, but helped many other fantasy authors achieve increased exposure of their writings. Most of them had been published in what was known as "pulp magazines" and sold at five, ten and twenty-five cents. Putting them in hardcover not only rescued them from wastebasket oblivion, but helped many authors get a good hold up the ladder of success. Isaac Asimov, Ray Bradbury, Robert Bloch, and many others achieved fame in their genre. Little did Derleth realize how far some of these authors would go. All together they form a nucleus of the thriving macabre and science fiction market of today.[20]

Derleth and Marty remained friends through the years. Marty married later and raised a family. As for Cassandra, their interlude together had not sated August's desire for her, nor her desire for him.[21]

In many ways, the romance was an echo of his idyllic experience with Margery, of *EVENING IN SPRING*, except that the high school romance had not included any real sexual relationship in spite of the town gossips. At one point, Derleth compared his entanglement with Cassandra to that of Somerset Maugham's Phillip Carey and his entrapment by a trollop in *OF HUMAN BONDAGE*.

Derleth wrote a novel about the whole experience with Marty and Cassandra, *DROUGHTS OF MARCH*, which remained unpublished because the heroine would easily be recognized by area residents and, also, because Capp Pearce of Duell Sloan & Pearce thought the story a personal affair; that, no matter what name August might publish it under in order to protect Cassandra and others involved, people would recognize Derleth, take the story as actual autobiography, which would not do him much good. Pearce believed *DROUGHT OF MARCH* was an act of atonement on August's part. He said that certain psychological, uncharacteristic Derleth faults of the work were his main reason for rejecting the novel. Yet, he didn't dislike it as much as others who read it did. The book had sultry episodes, but merely cutting them would not remedy the faults. In spite of them, Pearce found the book fascinating, since he knew Derleth personally.[22]

Another account of the affair was written from a different viewpoint in *THE FORTS OF REASON*, based on a Sauk City scandal; it was also unpublishable because its principal characters were alive and easily recognizable. The title was taken from Act IV of *HAMLET*:

> *"...So oft it chances in particular men that for some vicious mole of nature in them (As in their birth) – wherein they are not guilty, since nature cannot choose his origin; By the o'ergrowth of some complexion, of breaking down the pales and forts of reason."*[23]

The contrast between Derleth's relationship with Marcia and Cassandra seemed to have strengthened his resolve to never marry an intelligent woman. He shied away from a romance with any of the intelligent, successful women who would welcome a relationship (some of whom openly pursued him) up until the last three years of his life.[24]

Derleth's poetic tribute to his "pet", *HABITATS OF DUSK – A GARLAND FOR CASSANDRA,* was published some time after they broke up.[25]

SOURCE NOTES
CHAPTER ELEVEN

[1] A. D. to Gerald Klein, Oct. 29, 1964.

[2] A. D. Journal, 19, 30 August, 18, 23 September, 17 October, 6 December, 1944; 12, 13 January, 1945, etc.

[3] John Caddy to A. D., Feb. 16, 1943.

[4] Banta Publishing Co. to A. D., no date.

[5] A. D. to Ewie Blum, Nov. 25, 1943.

[6] Jessie Stuart to A. D., Dec. 29, 1964.

[7] Robert M. LaFollette to A. D., Aug. 10, Sept. 7, Oct. 2 and 10, 1945.

[8] August Derleth, Shield of the Valiant, (New York, 1946), brief synopsis.

[9] A. D. to Judge Henry Bone, n.d.

[10] Biographer's conclusion. A. D. to Inez Weaver.

[11] Cassandra to A. D., no dates.

[12] Marty to A. D., Aug. 26 and Sept. 6, 1946.

[13] Note 2.

[14] Biographer's notes taken in Derleth's classes while she was a student, and when she audited the classes for Doctor Robert E. Gard; Stanley Rinehart to A. D., no date.

[15] August Derleth, In re: Afterwords, a speech prepared by Derleth, miscellaneous papers, SWHS Museum archives, Madison, Wisconsin.

[16] Cardinal Hayes Committee, 1944 to A. D.

[17] Wm. Weber to A. D., March 5, 1944.

[18] American Folk Society to A. D.

[19] Rauth, list of pulp stories, SWHS Museum archives, miscellaneous papers, Madison, Wisconsin.

[20] Biographer's observation.

[21] Note 2, 7 March, 1953, box 71, p. 91.

[22] Capp Pearce to A. D.

[23] William Shakespear, Act IV, Hamlet.

[24] Biographer's observations and conclusion.

[25] August Derleth, Habitats of Dusk, a Garland for Cassandra, (Sauk City, Wisconsin, 1946).

Chapter Twelve

"I am always interested in money, provided it can be come by honestly. As for fame, it's a commodity I can do very well without, for it always carries with it too many factors I find increasingly difficult to cope with as I grow older...."[1]

A group of about fifty young people converging upon the Place of Hawks on an evening in mid-October, 1948, included a precocious fourteen-year-old beauty who had made up her mind a year earlier that she was going to marry August Derleth.

Sandra Winters told Derleth that evening of her love for him. He brushed off her crush as "ephemeral" in his own mind, but was careful not to damage the hopes and the spirit of his ardent young admirer by immediate rejection. She would get over her crush in a few weeks or months, he thought.

At first, spurred by village gossip, Sandra's parents forbade her to see Derleth, which only made Sandra all the more determined to see him. Later they went along with Derleth's reasoning that Sandra would recover from her fixation in a little while and no harm would result. Sandra was amusing, and a tremendous lift to Derleth's ego. He was vulnerable without both Cassandra and Marty now, and as always desperately needing someone to fill the void his former lovers had left. Sandra was not only determined, she was an extremely attractive, sexy, young lady, looking and acting older than her years. By the time August realized he'd been wrong about her getting over him, it was too late. He had become hopelessly involved.

Many of the people in the area got the mistaken impression that it was Sandy's mother that August was courting, and tongues wagged once again over his carrying on with a married woman. At first the older woman had made a point to go along with Sandra and August on their dates. Derleth, with his typical Puckish sense of humor, did nothing to set the gossips straight, but instead encouraged their mistaken assumptions. Gradually, it became obvious to Sandy's parents that they could not shake Sandy in her determination to become Mrs. August William Derleth. They stopped trying to and began looking upon the union as desirable. Derleth was the most popular bachelor in the Sac Prairie area. Like many others, they realized that his growing fame, coupled with his beautiful, big home, made him a desirable catch for any single maiden.[2]

August, too, began to consider the union in a different light. Sandra was surprisingly adult company. He took her to concerts, plays, and recommended books for her to read, preparing her for the possibility that she might be his wife. Yet even as he mapped out a program that he hoped would help to mold her into his image of a suitable mate, he expressed again and again the belief that his child love would tire of him long before a marriage took place. Again, he deliberately set tongues wagging by making sure he and Sandra were seen shopping for a diamond long before he'd really made up his mind. He told Sandra he would not marry her before she was eighteen and had finished the twelfth grade; she was too young to know her own mind. As always, August set down his love, his passion, the progression, the affair, and the final denouement of their relationship.[3]

The poet's obsession with time, and his determination to enjoy life to the fullest are highlighted in such lines as:

"...There are not days enough for love
And no moment comes to listen to the
no-sayers of life...";
"...the clocks hasten the hour and the year
pitiless, serene, the clocks lend
to each beginning its predestined end..."

In his poems, Derleth's awareness of the gap between Sandra's fifteen and his forty years is evident:

"Immortal Psyche
you too, in this child's disguise...";
"...to see the countenance of
a little more than child,
that warm impassioned spirit,
lurking deep,
hidden by a child's serene and lovely face...."

Realization of his own helplessness, even as he knew fully well the folly of such an affair, spills out:

"...Call each lover but a fool of love
or God in love or what you will
only he knows how earth moves
stars reel and passion shatters
the forts and battlements of reason...."

Here, again, "...the forts and battlements of reason..." indicating that this poem might have been written for Cassandra, not Sandy, or even another lover he was protecting.

He senses, too, the beginning of the end:

"...oh, once, this was a dream of love
So it began a while ago: and once I have thought you
Juliet to my Romeo,
But now, this enigmatic hour,
the dream's a nightmare,
and to my Hamlet you've become Ophelia...."
"...Is there no pity sitting in the clouds
that sees into the bottom of my grief...?"

PSYCHE, first published in 1953 was greeted by some reviewers as a volume that deserved to be ranked with the finest love poetry on the contemporary scene, and was listed in the Fifty Best Books of the Year for 1953.[4]

In spite of the toll on productivity during August's courtship of Sandy, he still managed the work load of several ordinary men.

Much as Derleth had admired Thoreau, he missed or ignored one of the points made in WALDEN AND CIVIL DISOBEDIENCE, just as he had turned a deaf ear to both Masters' and Sinclair Lewis' advice. From the very first, Derleth was hard pressed to pay for both of his houses – Place of Hawks and Arkham House. In that sense, he was very much like the farmer Thoreau wrote about who had "...endeavored to solve the problem of livelihood by a formula more complicated than the problem itself...with consummate skill he has set his trap with a hairspring to catch comfort and independence and then, as he turned away, got his own leg in it...and when the farmer got the house, he may not be richer but the poorer for it, and it be the house that has got him...."[5]

Struggling with his financial situation, treading the mill, Derleth often neglected his saga work to concentrate on other projects that meant money in the hand; projects like his history of the Milwaukee Road, which he had to rewrite twice because *HOLIDAY* rejected the first two versions. These projects presented an immediate advance and a fairly firm market, which he could not afford to turn down.[6]

"...I have payments to meet the first of every month for the next four months," he wrote to one of his correspondents. "That is why I have to write some trivial lush romances for the slick magazines...."

The payments were for printing bills.[7]

"Shane's Girls" was one of the romances and appeared in *REDBOOK*. It is a triangle story of Shane and his two loves who "...belonged, somehow to the summer nights in Badger Prairie...to the south wind sweet and fresh with the smell of the Wisconsin River flowing by, aromatic with the pungence of herbs along its shores...to the nostalgic crying of the whippoorwills...to roses and day lilies giving their heavy perfume into the summer darkness...to the wine-white moonlight and the shadows along the lanes and streets...."

The story is a fascinating study of how fiction sprouts out of the seeds of fact. In it, Alix, whom Shane marries first, grows miserly with the years. When Shane's aged father falls ill, she agrees to take care of him providing he first signs a paper saying he'll pay her five dollars a day for taking care of him the rest of his life. The arrangement is a factual, right out of Derleth's family experience, and his way of getting back at the greedy relative in question. The romance in the story resembles Derleth's involvement with Psyche and Cassandra.[8]

In addition to the books he was writing, Derleth contracted to do a historical series of sketches on Wisconsin cities for the Pictorial Review section of the *MILWAUKEE SENTINEL* in 1948. The contract called for two pages containing complete stories and illustrations and would appear every Sunday for 49 weeks. The piece done on Prairie du Sac and Sauk City gave a synopsis of the history of Count Augustine Haraszthey, on which the leading character in Derleth's *RESTLESS IS THE RIVER* was based, and mentioned the rivalry between Prairie du Sac Yankees and the Germans of Sauk City. Frank Utpatel's wood engravings were used as illustrations in these articles, along with snapshots of Prairie Pioneers.[9]

The first "Arkham Sampler", an Arkham House organ, came out in 1948. It contained newsy information about Arkham House and August's writing, plus articles, poetry, etc., by Arkham writers and clients.[10]

Derleth hit the news columns of area newspapers himself during this period by writing a letter to Mrs. Eleanor Roosevelt, criticizing Francis Cardinal Spellman for losing his temper in a diatribe against the First Lady's defense of separation of church and state. He called Cardinal Spellman's outburst an example of bigotry. It was narrow-minded and inexcusable and demonstrated that the Cardinal was denying freedom of opinion to others. Derleth wanted to assure the First Lady that not all Catholics, nor all Catholic priests, were like Spellman. He also informed the public, as he saw to it that a copy of his letter was sent to the newspapers.[11] He had often boasted that he had the area newspapers in his hands and indeed he did make good use of them to air his views and keep his name before the public.

Derleth's anthologies made still more inroads on his time as they entailed a substantial correspondence with the authors of the selections. He wrote, for instance, at least 21 letters to L. Sprague De Camp, whose "Git Along" appeared in *THE OUTER REACHES*, and his "The Ordeal of Professor Klein" in *BEACHHEADS IN SPACE*. Moreover, Derleth was forced not only to read many stories before arriving at each selection, but sometimes to page through years of magazines when authors failed to send copies of their stories. There were other chores, too, that developed out of his correspondence, like Sprague's request for a list of Derleth's fantasy works published in magazine form from 1926 through 1952. With 3,000 or more pieces of Derleth's work published, compliance with De Camp's request was no simple task. However, the exchange of materials between the two authors was mutually beneficial, with both men swapping Lovecraft information and leads to Lovecraft's letters. Derleth also offered material re: the Conan series and Robert Howard (fantasy author and one of H. P. L.'s "grandsons") which De Camp could use for his projected biography of H. P. L., someday. (Little did either man realize at the time, that almost 40 years later, the Conan series would give impetus to a multi-million dollar movie and a comic strip, *CONAN, THE BARBARIAN*.) Also, when L. Sprague De Camp was preparing a collection of verse for publication, he turned to August for advice.[12]

In May of 1951, Derleth was in the middle of writing a book on murders committed in Wisconsin when he got a telegram from Mrs. Lillian J. Bragdon of Aladdin Books asking him to call her. She told him that Aladdin wanted a series of Junior historical novels on a sixth grade level, with a "punch and gusto" for the *AMERICAN HERITAGE SERIES* and wanted to know if August would be interested in writing them. By June, he'd sent in the first chapter of the story of a pioneer family in Sac Prairie and the friendship between a white boy and a Winnebago youth. Their adventures rose out of the common experiences in cultivating land and trapping for furs and meat, and the traumatic separation of the friends when the Winnebago tribe was moved down the river by the U. S. Government. He wrote that he hoped to be able to have the book finished early in August.

Mr. Merrimer, president, was enthusiastic about August's first chapter. Before June was over, August had two more suggestions for novels; one on the youth of Hercules Dousman; the other about fur in Wisconsin. He went on to publish six junior historical novels with the Aladdin imprint: *THE COUNTRY OF THE HAWK*; *THE CAPTIVE ISLAND*; *LAND OF GRAY GOLD*; *EMPIRE OF FUR*; *LAND, OF SKY-BLUE WATERS*; and *SWEET LAND OF MICHIGAN*.

Although he was not exactly satisfied with the writing caliber of the books, he still felt good that he was able to participate in what he considered one of the most worthwhile ideas in American letters developed in many years. Derleth credited juveniles with being more critical than most readers in America.[13]

Derleth's time, worth more than money, was in constant demand by others, and – precious as it was – he usually gave it unstintingly. No request was too insignificant or too difficult to elicit a generous response in spite of his tight schedule. The requests came from near and far, from all walks of life.

When Clifford L. Lord, Director of the State of Wisconsin

Historical Society, planned to complete a *DICTIONARY OF BIOGRAPHY*, started by the Federal Writers' Project in the 1940's, he asked if August would serve on the Board of Advisors for re-checking and completing the biographies listed.[14]

Robert Livingston Schuler, editor of *DICTIONARY OF WISCONSIN BIOGRAPHY*, also requested that August prepare a biographical article of 1,500 words on Zona Gale for a new supplement in the process of preparation.[15]

August was constantly being asked to appear as speaker or honored guest at such events as science fiction conferences, meetings of the Mystery Writers of America, teachers' conventions, library events, book fairs, writers' conferences, etc. Also, his talents as critic and judge were constantly being tapped. He received numerous requests to judge contests like those for The Actor Meets the Critic Award,[16] The Society of Midland Author's Award,[17] The National Amateur Press Association Contest, etc.[18] He spent an entire day in Madison on July 22, 1947, reading over 100 essays to pick the three best, six second best, and nine third best. He felt the inferior quality of writing made the job depressing. That was only one of the ten years he served as judge in the Scholastic Writing Contests.[19] The total list of these duties he performed is unbelievable. Some of them paid a fee, and again, August was almost forced to oblige for the sake of Arkham House.

There were other intrusions on Derleth's time, triggered by his own concern and need for involvement in the affairs of his friends, his community, his country, and the world at large.

When one of the sons of Dr. Milton Trautman found his father less than happy about the boy's desire to marry a "foreign" girl (before Hawaii became a state), Derleth helped persuade the Doctor to listen to reason.[20] When one of the sons of Dr. Harold Bachhuber ran into parking violation trouble with a local traffic officer, and both father and son landed in jail as a result, Derleth interceded to help establish police harassment as the real culprit.[21]

He kept a constant vigil over legislative procedures in his community and was quick to step in and put a stop to any political shenanigans, a good way to make enemies, which could be one of the reasons for his defeat when he tried to get back on the Board of Education. Another reason would be his very defiant and often controversial ideas on education. Back in college, while writing the initial draft of *EVENING IN SPRING*, he cut many of his classes, and especially those in education, to do so. He was called in by Dean Sellery who said August might be required to take examinations in the courses he had cut to make sure he knew what had been covered. August thought writing his first novel was more important than attending education classes, with the kind of 'garbage' being taught there and he told the Dean so. Instead of being shocked or angry, the Dean told August that in his day they had not been required to spend time on those kind of foolish courses. However, he was careful to get up and close his office door before making the confession. August sailed through both his high school and his college years with all A's.

In one of Derleth's *MADISON CAPITAL TIMES* "Minority Report" columns, he quoted George Sampson, Cambridge University Press, as having expressed the crux of the education problem in one of Sampson's "Seven Essays". Sampson believed a student who does not want to learn cannot be taught; that equal opportunities and higher education for all is impossible. He suggested a better lower education especially in speech and language, and maintained that many people are not educable.[22]

In Derleth's annual report to the Sauk City School Board, the night he retired as director, he had warned educators to "...guard against the insidious poisoning of textbooks on one hand and attacks against textbooks on the other...." He also warned that what went on in his school district and in public education as a whole was still one of his primary concerns and he would step on toes when necessary, whether he was a member of the school board or not.[23]

One of the battles he waged for his country was seething inside of him years before Leroy Gore came to town in 1952. Gore made Miles McMillon's Madison speech against Senator Joe McCarthy, self-appointed crusader against Communism, a front-page story in the first edition of the *Sauk City Star*. Back in 1950, noting that the *MADISON CAPITOL TIMES'* editorials were riding McCarthy, Derleth wrote "...If I had my way, I'd shoot the swine, for he's a greater enemy of our country than the Communists, for we know what the Communists are about, but we never know what seeds of disruption, lost faith and discontent a troublemaking jackass like McCarthy will cause. He's a first class liar and a scoundrel...."[24]

In 1952, he answered Inez Weaver's defense of the Senator by pointing out that McCarthy had not come up with a single Communist. Hiss, according to Derleth, had been unmasked even before McCarthy had entered a senate race. When Hiss was convicted, it was for perjury, not for his Communistic activities.[25]

On March 18, 1954, Gore's editorial asking responsible Wisconsin citizens to help in a recall effort, was flanked by a sample petition.[26] On the 27th, Gore and several other Sauk City residents, including Derleth, called a meeting to recall McCarthy. CBS, NBC, and many other press cameras were present at the packed meeting. Gore started a "Joe Must Go" fund and collected $500 there. August Derleth was the first to sign the petition.[27]

Wide publicity over the nation bought requests for 10,000 petitions and donations of $12,000 in a few days. Many of the signatures didn't count because they had not been notarized as per regulation, so the final count fell short of the 403,000 signatures needed in the sixty days allowed by the statutes.

By July, Derleth and Gore were working on the "Joe Must Go" manuscript which would hopefully create public sentiment for a second petition drive. Congress, itself, by this time had become aware of McCarthy's menace and shortly thereafter started the investigation that led to his downfall.[28]

Not all of Sauk Prairie backed the "Joe Must Go" movement. According to Peter Blankenheim, hair stylist in one of the barbershop battlegrounds of Sauk City, the town's super patriots objected vigorously to Gore's efforts. One of those patriots managed to have one of the donkeys in the local parade adorned with a blanket that said "Augie" on one side, "Gore" on the other. A week or so later, the local drama being produced by Derleth sported an actor dressed in red, white, and blue pants, riding a scooter and waving a flag through every scene. Derleth didn't need a name to identify the character being portrayed. Everyone knew.[29]

When Gore sold *THE STAR* and founded *WISCONSIN TALES AND TRAILS* magazine in 1959, the first issure contained a spread on Derleth.[30]

One of August's worldwide concerns was the population explosion. His 1939 letter in the *NEW REPUBLIC*, supporting the use of sterilization to prevent the birth of defective children, caught the eye of Dorothy Walton, founder of the Wisconsin Race Conservation Committee and she appealed to Derleth for help on a sterilization bill her organization was trying to get passed. When Derleth replied "...I am perfectly willing that you use my name in support of your bill..." Mrs. Walton put his name on her committee's letterhead. However, it stayed there for only one printing. When she learned August was Catholic, she had instant regrets, pointing out that due to an encyclical of December, 1929, all tampering with the human body in order to prevent childbirth was forbidden by the Pope. Anyone doing so would automatically cease to be a Catholic.

"...Go shinny back up into your ivy tower and forget all about how I tried to lead you astray..." she told him.[31]

The encyclical apparently had little effect on Derleth, for in the summer of 1953, an advertisement entitled "Population Explosion Nullifies Foreign Aid" was signed by 62 leading Americans and appeared in several newspapers as well as being reprinted in the *READER'S DIGEST* as a news story. It was signed by 61 other leading Americans and August Derleth.[32]

In 1964, he was asked to sign a similar statement calling the President's attention to the fact that population explosion was a basic cause of poverty.[33]

For Derleth, there was no ivy tower. He was always right down in the pit of each and every fray that passed his way and, as often as not, served as one of the instigators.

SOURCE NOTES
CHAPTER TWELVE

[1] A. D. to Edward Brian February 13, 1960.

[2] A. D. Journal.

[3] A. D. to Inez Weaver, 11 June, 17 and 19 May, 2 December.

[4] "August Derleth reads Psyche", blurb for a recording August made, SWHS Museum archives, Madison, Wisconsin.

[5] Henry David Thoreau, Walden Civil Disobedience, (26th printing, New York, 1960), p. 27.

[6] A. D. to Mary Stiver, 5th May, 1960.

[7] A. D. to Jessie Stuart, Feb. 5, 1954.

[8] Note 2.

[9] August Derleth, "History passed this way", Milwaukee Sentinel, January 18 and February, 1948, courtesy of Sauk City Public Library, Sauk City, Wisconsin.

[10] Biographer owns a copy, courtesy of a friend.

[11] A. D. to Mrs. Eleanor Roosevelt, February, 1948.

[12] A. D. to L. Sprague DeCamp, November 19, 1951, March 29 and Sept. 11, 1964; Biographer's personal viewing of two films and the comic strip.

[13] Note 2; Lillian Bragdon to A. D., May 8, 1951; A. D. to Lillian Brogdon, May 24, 1951; Lillian Bragdon to A. D., June 18, 1951; A. D. to Lillian Bragdon, June 30 and November 30, 1951.

[14] Clifford L. Lord to A. D., July 21, 1950.

[15] Robert L. Schuyler to A. D., April 12, 1955.

[16] Les Cole to A. D., March 20, 1954.

[17] W. D. Brannon to A. D., May 19, 1949.

[18] Martin Stone to A. D., January 26, 1951.

[19] Note 2.

[20] Note 2.

[21] A. D. to Judge Bone, May 30, 1953.

[22] Biographer's conclusions; Note 2; A. D. "Minority Report", Madison Capital Times, April 29, 1950.

[23] Ibid.

[24] A. D. to Madison Capital Times, 1957, reprint from Sauk City Star.

[25] Note 3, op. cit.

26 Leroy Gore, editorial and sample petition, <u>Sauk City Star</u>, March 18, 1954.

27 Meeting to recall McCarthy by Gore and others; Gore starts "Joe must go" fund.

28 Pat Peckham, "Leroy Gore's Eulogy", <u>Sauk Prairie Star</u>, April 21, 1977, p. 1.

29 Peter Blankenheim tape recording on A. D., Sauk City Public Library.

30 Note 28, p. 4.

31 Dorothy Walton to A. D., February 12 and 25 and March 2, 1939.

32 Biographer's observation.

33 Hugh More to A. D., 29 January, 1964.

Chapter Thirteen

"...You now show me love enabling me to gather strength to face anew the truth tomorrow to take my destined share, not only love, but also sorrow...."[1]

August Derleth presented Sandra Winters with a diamond engagement ring for Christmas, 1952. He felt he could not go back on his promise to marry her when she was eighteen and had graduated from high school. His deep sense of responsibility had a great deal of influence on his decision to keep that promise. Sandra, during the years since he met her, had not dated young men near her own age, had instead devoted her time exclusively to the man she hoped to marry. He realized he was getting on in years. If he ever meant to have children, it was time to get started. Despite his own pessimistic forecast that the marriage could not last more than five years, Derleth planned a wedding for April, 1953.[2]

Though Derleth, in his poetry, sang the praises of his young sweetheart, was romantic, passionate, gentle[3] – in real life, right from the start, he had a cold calculated plan to make her over.

"...She is in a large part the product of her environment," he wrote to Inez Weaver in 1953. "Now she will become the product of mine, by hard, ruthless measures, means of which I have at my control. I will unmake her and do what I can to eradicate the influence of her heredity. It can be done, for I've done it before, though primarily with boys. If and when she leaves me, she will be the better for it, believe me...."[4]

Sandra graduated May 25th, 1952. She got a job in Madison after her graduation. She came back to Sauk City to be with August, but they spent a lot less time together than they had during the previous three years. As the projected wedding date grew nearer, August became more reconciled to the idea of marriage. Given his lifelong enchantment with continuity, he was almost obliged to carry on the proud name of Derleth. Sandy, whom Derleth described as a "healthy, young animal", would certainly bring forth healthy babies.[5]

August was unaware that Sandy was already in a family way. History was about to repeat itself. When Sandy, like Cassandra, confessed she had been intimate with her employer in Madison and was pregnant, Derleth hit the ceiling. He was not as willing this time to assume the expense and burden of what could be someone else's child. He insisted Sandy go to his doctor for paternity tests. Results of the rather inadequate test methods of that era were inconclusive. Dr. Bachhuber couldn't determine the paternity by them, but when he compared the approximate date of conception with the dates of Sandy's visits home, he warned that the child was "probably" Derleth's. "Probably" was not good enough for August. When Sandy's parents phoned asking Derleth to meet them in Sandy's Madison apartment, he learned they had consulted four doctors to see if Sandy's pregnancy could be terminated. The doctors all agreed it was too late. Sandy's pregnancy was too far advanced. Derleth was disappointed as he had demanded she have an abortion. After a closer look at the dates when Sandy had sex with him, he realized the baby could have been conceived by either of her lovers. Still reluctant to accept the realization was valid, he decided to consult Judge Hill for advice. He admitted to the judge that he no longer loved Sandy, that he was fond of her and "...she was, besides, in a most disadvantageous position which, quite frankly, he (sic) could now exploit...She (sic) must now at last be punished...."!!! He met with Sandy and her parents, and advised them of his decision about the marriage. It would take place only on one condition: that Sandy agree to give up the child as soon as it was born. August simply was not going to raise "somebody else's brat...."

Sandy, faced with the alternative of having her five-year dream of becoming Mrs. August William Derleth evaporate into thin air a few short weeks before the appointed wedding date, agreed.[6]

Roberta, Sandy's mother, seemed upset and acted very strangely during the weeks that followed. So irrational was her behavior that Derleth was faced with a terrifying thought. Could Roberta be losing her mind?

August took Sandy's mother to Dr. Bachhuber to pinpoint

the cause of her bizarre behavior. Long before scientists con-
ceded that some mental illnesses were probably hereditary,
August firmly believed the old wives' tale about "bad seed".
There was no way he'd take a chance on fathering Sandy's
future offspring if her blood-line was tainted.

Dr. Bachhuber assured him he need not worry. Roberta's
strange behavior was not due to a mental impairment but
merely a combination of symptoms arising out of her
menopause.[7]

The *MILWAUKEE JOURNAL* article announcing the coming marriage highlighted the difference in the couple's ages
with its headline: "Derleth, 43, and Teen Age Sweetheart to
Wed in April".[8]

News of the event also spurred another poison-pen letter,
claiming to be from a group of Marquette University students
from Milwaukee. It was definitely not a credit to any writing
courses there. By this time August should have been immune to
the poison pen missiles, knowing full well the source, but it
could not have been easy reading the crude remarks on the dis-
parity in age, and the prediction that "...just as soon as she
wakes up, she will fly from a bachelor button to a sweet
William...." The remarks, however crude, were echoes of his own
doubts and fears about the match, as well as a portent of the
future.[9]

August was more sensitive to letters from people like his
friend Robert Marx who recommended August read *THE OLD
GOAT*. Marx, when he realized August's ire was raised because
he thought Marx had referred to the applicability of the title,
hastened to assure the groom-to-be it was the central portion of
the novel about the romance of the forty-year-old sophisticate
and a fifteen-year-old female aggressor Marx wanted August to
read, since it so closely paralleled August's case.[10]

Marx's explanation did not erase the "old goat" image in
Derleth's own mind. Describing his romance seven years later,
he wrote: "...I saw myself as two people, the one watching the
goat cavort so to speak, so that I was both subjectively involved
and objectively entertained, possible only for a creative person
accustomed to existing on more than one plane at a time..."[11]

August had other worries about the coming event. Although

he had managed to buy Sandy a diamond, his finances were still in the red. He could not even afford to buy a television set.[12]

He thought it was nerves that brought on a severe spell of abdominal pain as his marriage approached. His doctor assured him that nerves had not been the source of his malady, but rather a non-functioning gall bladder.[13]

LeRoy Gore, in his Thursday "Stardust" column, quipped that it was difficult for him to swallow the non-functioning gallbladder diagnosis. He wondered if Augie's wedding should not have been included in the referendum along with fluoridation and reapportionment, there'd been so much local discussion pro and con for months about it. Gore was right about the pros and cons. Many of Augie's friends and writing associates were congratulating August, happy for him, and some obviously envying him for getting such a beautiful, young lady for a wife. Roberta was having to deal with the "con" element. They sent her letters, made phone calls, even suggesting Roberta should send her daughter to a convent, rather than ruin her life by marrying Derleth! Gore also informed his readers that, upon careful examination of his invitation to August's wedding, he could discover no price list of Derleth's books printed on the back, as rumored.[14]

The wedding took place on the sixth of April, 1953. August was up at six, after a hectic day before, doing a number of tasks in preparation for the event. He was still dashing about at 9:20 a.m., arranging every phase and last-minute detail at St. Aloysius Church. Guests were already arriving when Sandy's great aunts – Clara and Hazel – spurred him to leave for home and change clothes.

The church was jammed with about 500 people. Richard Bachhuber and some of his other young friends, with their typically sly humor, had stuck signs reading "Reserved: Funeral" in the curb in front of the church. Derleth took no offense at their pranks. They had a right. August had done plenty of outrageous pranks of his own in his time to friends and foes alike.

August took a few minutes to talk to his best man, John Stanton, before the ceremony. David Bachhuber pinned a red rose boutonniere on August's lapel, and Derleth returned the favor.[15]

Contrary to persistent rumors that August was married in a maroon t-shirt, the bridegroom was epicurely resplendent in his banker's grey suit and smokey green tie. Sandy was demure and beautiful in a blush pink bridal gown which had been created by Francine of New York and been chosen by August personally.

Easter lilies bedecked the altar before which the high mass was offered by the Reverend Fr. Sylvester Van Berkel. Jerry Ramsfield, a friend of August's from Chicago, sang the offertory of "Panis Angelicus" in a "deep, moving voice".

A score of cameras – many from the newspapers – greeted the newlyweds as they left the church. Ninety-seven guests dined at Riverview ballroom. Over 400 friends and neighbors attended the reception at the Place of Hawks.[16]

By six o'clock Augie had changed clothes and deserted the reception for the marshes. It was a mild, sunny day, and he headed for the bridge, relieved to be free of the doings. He had always hated weddings and wedding receptions. Still keeping the accounts, even on his wedding day, he noted the songs of: Hyla Piceringii, mourning doves, cardinals, Hyla Grylla, flickers, robins, redwings, meadowlarks, killdeers, bronzed grukles, and song sparrows.

He met Hugh Schwenker at the Spring Slough Trestle and walked with him to the Mid-Meadow Trestle and back to the bridge. Most of the guests were gone by the time August arrived home. As always, unable to rest in an untidy place, he began to clean up with the help of his faithful friend, George Marx.

Shimmel, taking his leave, remarked that it was truly a historic night, "...'It's the first time in a long and sinful life that Derleth has gone to bed legally with a woman....'"[17]

SOURCE NOTES
CHAPTER THIRTEEN

[1] August Derleth, "Derleth reads Psyche", advertisement for a phonograph record, SWHS Museum archives, Madison, Wisconsin, miscellaneous file.

[2] A. D. Journal, Dec. 25, 1952.

[3] Note 1, op. cit.

[4] A. D. to Inez Weaver, 1953.

[5] Note 2.

[6] Ibid.

[7] Ibid.

[8] "Derleth and teen-aged sweetheart to wed in April", Milwaukee Sentinel, p. 1.

[9] Note 2.

[10] Robert Marx to A. D.

[11] Note 2.

[12] Note 2.

[13] Ibid.

[14] Leroy Gore, "Stardust Column", Sauk City Star, Madison State Journal photo caption, April 7, 1963.

[15] Note 2, 6 April, 1963.

[16] Sauk City Star, April 7, 1963.

[17] Note 15, op. cit.

Chapter Fourteen

"...Erased as casually as a pencil mark."[1]

The honeymoon was postponed until June second. August had planned a trip west with John Stanton and David Bachhuber months before he knew for certain the wedding would take place. He saw no reason for a change in his plans, even in view of the advanced stage of Sandy's pregnancy.

The quartet made their first stop at Petersburg, Illinois, where they searched for and found the simple grave of Edgar Lee Masters. Not far away was Anne Rutlege's grave, the marker inscribed with lines Masters had written to her.

August was moved to write a poem to Marcia's father describing the spot "...high above the lovely Sangamon whose praise/ he sang in all his days".[2]

They toured the Texas panhandle, Albuquerque, and Los Angeles, then went to see Claire Wiggins, the comic strip creator, in Pasadena. They found him stretched out on a porch swing of a little cabin cottage, looking sixty, not eighty.

August worked over the first draft of the teleplay script of "Night Light At Vordens", going over it page by page with studio script writers Karl Cramer and Kick Irving. Kick declared it was an excellent first try, but weak in a continuing stream of action, and too wordy in dialogue. August agreed with their suggested changes. Although he didn't comment on the jardiniered fern on the set, he couldn't help but point out that in 1910, the maximum prices for punch and a slice of cake were only five cents and would not reach the ten cents price until 1925 or later.

SUMMER NIGHT was filmed next, and the studio was considering two more scripts, which would increase August's reimbursement to $1,800: Good news, as the trip was expensive.

While Derleth was busy fulfilling his commitment, Sandy, who had been dropped off at the Catholic Hospital, was busy giving birth to a healthy, bouncing baby girl. August and the boys picked Sandy and her newborn baby up from the hospital and took them to the home of August's Aunt Tillie and Uncle

Fred. They stayed there until Derleth had wrapped up the filming of "The Night Light at Verden's" teleplay and had completed working on "Farewell Performance" and "Summer Night".

They discussed doing, also, another teleplay of "Psychophonic Nurse", planned for a future filming.

His classes over, it was time to head home to Sauk City. They took their time, stopping at several places to visit tourist attractions and national landmarks, then on to the house of the woman who had agreed to take the baby. She had rolled out the red carpet for them. Her guest house was stocked with linens, food, and anything else they might need. Both Stanton and Bachhuber were very impressed with the royal treatment at their hostess's hands. When they took their leave the following day, the baby stayed behind. Sandy, true to her word, gave up her first born as her lord and master had demanded. Derleth's journal entry was brief, with no mention of Sandy's feelings, or any type of formal or informal adoption procedures. His later entries over the years contained no mention of the baby. It seems that Sandra's first born, like the unfortunate young Sauk City girl who died in a mental institution (her life, according to Derleth "...erased as casually as a pencil mark...") had the same treatment from the man who might have fathered her. The woman who received the baby was in comfortable financial circumstances at the time. Several letters from her, years later, indicated that her financial situation had changed considerably with the death of her husband. Would August help her out? He sent her $100 on at least two occasions, a considerable amount in those days. With August's own continuing financial bind, his generosity in those instances would seem to indicate that his conscience was bothering him about turning his back completely on Sandy's (and possibly his) child.[3]

The newlyweds and Stanton arrived home September third, after wending their way home to Sauk City. David had taken a plane home, arriving there a week before the others.[4] They found August's father at work on a new two-car garage. The old garage and a chicken coop had been razed in their absence.[5]

As usual, Sauk Prairie gossips had been very busy during their trip, spreading wild rumors and accusations about the bizarre honeymoon. Some suspected the truth – that August had made Sandy give the child away. Others whispered the baby had been born with a horrible physical or mental handicap and was confined to an institution. Some thought the child had miscarried, or died, due to the long rough, tiring journey to California. Others said the trip was planned for the express purpose of causing a miscarriage.[6]

August wasted little time in trying to produce a child he could be dead certain was his own. Sandy bore another beautiful girl a year later. As with the first baby, Derleth was not there. This time, however, it was because the baby came after only 20 minutes notice.[7]

Faced with the additional expense of a family, Derleth was forced to let Alice Conger go, which also enabled him to pay $2,000 more off his debts. It was, however, a costly sacrifice.

Alice Conger had been more than researcher, typist, chauffeur, girl-Friday. She was a friend and companion on jaunts to Madison or into the hills to hunt morels or over to Ferry Bluff to watch the northern lights. She had become almost indispensable to Derleth. It was Alice Conger who, armed with reference books, dictionaries, and magnifying glass, patiently translated Lovecraft's miles of spider web script. Demands on her were often heavy, when a deadline for a manuscript had to be met, and Alice worked far into the night typing.[8]

Alice had a "marvelous" life working for Derleth, met many interesting and famous people, never regretted giving up her teaching career or not marrying and raising a family of her own. Derleth brought glamour, challenges, good times, fellowship, friendship, and a unique purpose into her life; working for him, there was never a dull moment. She was even a confidant and facilitator in the clandestine affairs with Derleth's current paramours (the "straight" ones). She often drove Derleth and his lady-love of the moment to secluded spots in the woods and hills of Sac Prairie, before August learned to drive.

August, according to Alice, liked to "put people on" and hinted that some of the stories he told were embellished by his imagination and his love of shocking less cosmopolitan and liberal minded people. She gave as an example, a story about a party given for 40 high school boyfriends in the studio Mark and August shared. August claimed, according to Alice, that he'd donned a black frock-coat with a hood, sat at a table and wrote furiously with a feather pen as the guests arrived. The studio had been decorated as though for a Halloween bash, with cobwebs, and other scary adornments to create a weird and mysterious background appropriate for the two mystery and macabre authors.

It doesn't seem possible that Alice, working so closely with August for most of her life, could be totally innocent of the author's bisexuality. It may have been that Derleth was "putting her on" as well as other people. A letter from Derleth to a friend many years later, described the same setting and the party he and three of his homosexual pals had arranged for 40 of their male classmates. The purpose of the affair was to introduce those 40 teenagers to the joys and delights of a new sexual experience. It was a sex orgy! Derleth maintained that not one of their guests practiced homosexuality as adults. They all reverted to so-called "normal" heterosexual behavior, strengthening Shakespeare's "Forts of Reason" theory.[9]

Other incidents Derleth described in his journal re: high delight in teasing Alice, and her ability to take his teasing with good humor, are factual, according to Alice. His journal description of one of the things that happened as a group of August's friends and staff members set out in two canoes and one motor boat to research a stretch of the Wisconsin River for one of August's books. As Alice bent to climb into one of the canoes, a huge bee settled on her posterior, depositing his stinger there.

Poor Alice had a very uncomfortable trip trying to balance herself on the half of that posterior not affected by the bee sting. To make it worse, she had to listen to the solicitations and wise cracks of the other members of the entourage, all the way down the river. Her experience that day was not allowed to fade away with the healing of the bee-sting. She was forced to remember the incident over and over again through the years as August and others retold the story and added new wisecracks, etc. to the tale.

One of the reasons, perhaps, that Derleth and the others so often teased Alice was that, as Derleth mentioned, she was such a good sport about their banter.

Alice's importance to Derleth is emphasized by one of his

journal entries about the visit of Jesse Stuart to the Place of Hawks. Alice was not to be found at either her house or Derleth's. She was spending the day at one of the lakes in the area, sailing a boat she kept there. She also had a trailer parked near the dock. When August could not induce Jesse to stay at the Place of Hawks overnight, he insisted Jesse had to meet Alice before he left for Kentucky. The two regional writers spent most of the afternoon waiting at Alice's trailer, while she enjoyed her most treasured pastime – sailing.

She did not get home in time to meet Jesse. August, determined not to have a repeat of the incident, contacted owners of cottages around the lake, and asked for their help in signaling Alice when she was out on the lake. Many of these residents were equipped with horns, bells, or other loud noises-making apparatus they used to call their own inmates. Thereafter, one phone call from Derleth, and the first signal of a special code for Alice would echo all around the lake. When Derleth wanted something, he managed to get it, one way or another. His respect and consideration for Alice was far more than that usually displayed by employers toward their employees. He wanted her to meet all of the unusual people he wrote and talked about, to share his own feelings about them, and the reasons he considered them special.[10] As the years passed, these "special" people came to August's home from all over the country and many foreign countries as well.[11]

Derleth was quick to ask her back after his financial emergency eased somewhat. When she returned to work for Arkham House, she had still another skill to contribute – accounting. As the publishing house grew, this newly acquired expertise was put to good use.[12]

SOURCE NOTES
CHAPTER FOURTEEN

[1] August Derleth, <u>Walden West</u>.

[2] A. D. Journal, 2nd June, 1953, box 95, folder 2; 28 July, 1953; box 95, folder 2, p. 46.

[3] August's benefactor to A. D., no dates.

[4] A. D. Journal, 3 September, 1953.

[5] Ibid.

[6] Ibid.

[7] Note 2, 9 August, 1954.

[8] Interviews with Alice Conger, August, 1972, Sauk City, Wisconsin.

[9] Alice Conger to biographer; A. D. to Ian Law.

[10] Note 2.

[11] Ibid.

[12] Ibid.

Chapter Fifteen

"...Out of 475,000 words written last year, I took pleasure in less than 20,000...!"[1]

Arkham House operated out of the Place of Hawks at first, gaining strength gradually. Derleth, with help from Wandrei, tracked down Lovecraft's letters. Derleth's correspondence increased daily, as many as 100 letters and/or orders in one day. With each he sent out a catalogue of titles available.

He kept buying up the plates of his out-of-print books to swell the Stanton & Lee imprint.[2] He continued his policy of guarding the Lovecraft material with an almost obsessive determination to let nothing and no one sully the sacred memory of H. P. L., not even Sonia, Lovecraft's ex-wife.

After Lovecraft's divorce, or possibly only a separation as there seemed to be some question as to whether the divorce had been finalized, Sonia disappeared. No one knew where she was when Lovecraft died. When Sonia surfaced again, she had married for the third time. She was now Mrs. Sonia Davis. Her interest in Lovecraft had resurfaced, too, with her decision to cash in on her ex-husband's growing fame by writing an expose of *THE PRIVATE LIFE OF H. P. LOVECRAFT*.

Sonia read part of the manuscript to Derleth when he visited her on one of his trips to New York. She had pictured H. P. L. as a Jew-baiter (although his only wife was Jewish) and claimed to have completely supported him for eight years. She expected to sell a million copies of her projected expose, and Derleth laughed at her. His own book, *H. P. L., A MEMOIR*, published two years earlier, had not yet sold 1,000 copies.

Sonia was very startled when August told her he had copies of H. P. L.'s letters containing a detailed description of Sonia's life with Lovecraft. He forbade her to quote H. P. L.'s letters without his and Wandrei's approval.[3] His action was not without an unfortunate reprisal, for subsequently Sonia burned most of Lovecraft's letters to her, another invaluable source of information about his personal and romantic life, destroyed for posterity.

137

A few years later, Derleth received a 181 page paper from Warren Thomas, a university student. It had originally been a thesis, drawn from H. P. L.'s papers at Brown University. Barlow had given Thomas permission to use the material, and now Thomas wanted Derleth's permission to submit the manuscript to publishers.[4]

August, reading the work, was inclined to refuse, saying the study presented a distorted picture, in which Howard emerged as "...sexless, sapless supine, selfish, a mama's boy, a sissy, and pretty much of a heel...."

Barlow and Wandrei agreed with Derleth, as did Block, who qualified his opinion by advising that if Thomas's biographical thesis on Lovecraft were properly documented, it should be given a chance, but if it were prejudiced by Lovecraft's ex-wife, permission should be refused.

Derleth told Thomas to withhold publication until he had a chance to examine all the rest of H. P. L.'s letters, or copies of them, which Derleth intended to deposit at Brown University as soon as the first volume of Lovecraft's letters was off his hands.[5]

In September, 1946, Mycroft & Moran received a letter from a New York law firm on behalf of the estate of Sir Conan Doyle, demanding that the publishers stop using the fictional name and character of Sherlock Holmes or anything connected to the Sherlock Holmes' stories. They stated that they would force Mycroft & Moran to do so.[6]

Since Derleth had not used the name Sherlock Holmes in his pastiche (he used Solar Pons), the Doyle estate had no grounds for suit. Derleth learned this from Frederic Dannay, who did half of the writing collaboration published under the pen name of Ellery Queen.[7] Dannay was writing the introduction for Derleth's second book of pastiche.[8] As a result of Dannay's letter, Derleth stood up to the Doyle lawyers, and nothing happened. Later he discovered that he had nothing to worry about since Doyle's material was all in the public domain.

Derleth appeared to have learned two valuable lessons from the incident. The first, not to back down too easily when threatened. The second, the moment anyone infringes on your territory, threaten to sue.

In 1954, he threatened *Science Fiction Digest* with legal action for publishing "The Rat", by S. Fowler Wright, unless the magazine paid $50 for having used the story. It turned out that the magazine had already paid Wright for use of the story so Derleth threatened to sue Wright if he didn't turn over half the amount, as per contract between Arkham House and the author.[9]

To Groff Conklin, in 1954, he wrote demanding payment for the publishing of Conklin's anthology, and threatened legal action to collect if payment wasn't tendered.[10]

Derleth, like any good general, continually operated on the theory that a good offense is the best defense. This attitude prevailed not only in Arkham House business, but in his personal life and in his own writing, as well. When his long time pen-pal, Eunice McClosky, sent an article about Derleth which she hoped to publish, he advised her that if she published this profile presenting him as insufferable, arrogant, and a bore, he would see to it that his lawyers take immediate action.[11]

When a Sauk City druggist ribbed one of the local men by telling him exaggerated accounts of incidents about his wife, which had appeared in <u>*VILLAGE DAYBOOK*</u>, the author was quick to threaten suit.

"...That's the best news I've had all day," August told him. "That book hasn't been selling very well, and a good suit is just the publicity it needs...."

Derleth needled the now less belligerent, more cautious gentleman deliberately. "...Come now – don't back down. You see your lawyers and I'll see mine, today...."[12]

As Derleth expected that was the last he heard of that particular suit, as is the case with most threatened court cases. Under his formidable Derlethian offense, people usually backed down in a hurry and there was no need for legal action.[13]

In the case of Lovecraft material, like the individual stories in *THE OUTSIDER AND OTHERS*, which were in the public domain, he went right ahead and threatened suit anyway, knowing he didn't have a leg to stand on. Many authors who wanted permission to publish reprints of Arkham House copyrighted material, paid him more out of a feeling of moral obligation than because they thought he had a legal right to refuse that permission. They felt Derleth was largely responsible for the rapidly expanding interest in Lovecraft's writings and had every right to guard H. P. L.'s work from less dedicated, more profit-oriented Lovecraft fans.[14]

Derleth ran a tight ship re: Arkham House. Though he bent backward trying to be fair to authors, he simply had to adhere to rules and regulations that would not short the publishing house, which depended on his personal input of funds as it was; rules like expecting an author who started with Arkham House, to remain there. If an author took his books elsewhere, August would not publish any more of his work. Neither would August sell books to dealers who cut prices below the published price lists.[15]

In 1955, Derleth started a new series of historical juveniles for the Vision Books series – *FATHER MARQUETTE AND THE GREAT RIVER, ST. IGNATIUS AND THE COMPANY OF JESUS*, and *COLUMBUS AND THE NEW WORLD* – for which he received the Papal blessing (indirectly, for Pope John blessed Vision Books' publishers and authors of the series). Derleth had a field day enjoying the outraged reaction of his Sac Prairie neighbors on reading his article in the local paper to highlight the honor.[16]

In writing the books, he had to gloss over St. Ignatius's morbid side. As for Columbus, Derleth claimed he was a slaver, but left that out of the book because he felt he had to make Columbus a good egg for history's sake.

When he finished the first draft of Columbus, he was not at all satisfied with what he considered a quasi-fictional biography. The book, however, was reprinted in England in 1956.[17]

August's bitterness at having to waste time on these juveniles and other assignments instead of his saga and his poetry, became more and more evident, though he seems to have managed to keep his sense of humor about the situation.

When a writer of verse, George M. Cornell, penned a little ditty asking why August preferred Sauk City to, say Sheboygan, Wisconsin, Derleth responded with:

> "In answer to your ditty
> as to why I pick Sauk City-
> This is the town where I was born,

that's half for realism, half for corn.
Here none thinks of me as a writer
because I look more like a fighter
Here we can live a life of ease
and I can loaf just as I please.
The only trouble as I've learned to know –
a writer's is the toughest row to hoe
of books, in order just to stay alive,
I've had to turn out seventy-five!
If only one had been a book-club choice,
I'd have reason to rejoice!
But never a one had sales to soar-
I'll have to write as many more!

Which he did before died: 150 published or edited books and several more that had not, as yet, been published.[18]

Edgar Lee Masters was in the habit of writing out his frustrations and tensions in similar verse, some of which he sent to August from time to time. Masters' wife, Ellen, requested that Derleth refrain from using any of these verses in his lectures or writing after Masters' death as they had been written while the poet was in his "waggish" state.[19]

Some of Derleth's own frustration and tension broke out in a letter he wrote to Jesse Stuart in 1956. Tom Coward of Coward McCann asked him to write a series of three books, centered and connected to the life of one man in Milwaukee. August tried to talk Coward out of the idea with no success. Three books about the same man seemed just too much. He finally picked Alexander Mitchell, a banker, with Coward's approval, hoping later to talk the publisher into settling for Mitchell's son and grandson for the second and third book. He also tried to get Coward to accept some of his saga work for publication instead. Twenty of what he considered his better books were still without publishers at this time.

"...In the past ten years, there have been only three books published in the saga, exclusive of poetry, he lamented to Jesse Stuart. "Out of 475,000 words written last year I took pleasure in less than 20,000...!" His nine junior books had already outsold by far his best adult work.

"...No matter how tired I get," he complained, "I still have to do all this, knowing it is wearing away and thinning my creative energy, and dissipating what small talent I have to keep my family on a day-to-day basis, and I have reduced my debt load from a total of $18,000 in late 1953 to $14,500....When I wrote my *LAND OF THE SKY BLUE WATERS*, I knew it for an inadequate and poor book; ditto my *MARQUETTE* – yet the reviews were 97% favorable...." "...I take little pride in my work now because my good work isn't appearing in book form...."[20]

Coward had rejected his saga material in favor of publishing the novel on Alexander Mitchell and his fight for banking in Wisconsin, which Derleth named *THE POTTER AND THE CLAY*, and referred to as "...perhaps the dullest, most pedestrian thing..." he had ever written.[21]

SOURCE NOTES
CHAPTER FIFTEEN

[1] A. D. to Jesse Stuart, March 30, 1964.

[2] A. D. Journal.

[3] A. D. to Robert Barlow, Oct. 23, 1947; to Ray Bradbury, Nov. 21, 1947.

[4] Paper of Steve Eisner to George T. Wetze, III., "Copyright problems of Lovecraft Literary Estate", no date; James W. Thomas to A. D., Nov. 18, 1949, SWHS Museum archives, Madison, Wisconsin.

[5] A. D. to Robert Barlow, Nov. 18, 1949 and March 24, Aug. 10, 1950; to Robert Block, Aug. 7, 1950 and from Robert Block, Aug. 16, 1950; to James W. Thomas, Aug. 18, 1950.

[6] Fitelsen Meyers and London to Messrs. Mycrof and Moran, Sept. 16, 1945.

[7] Frederick Danney to A. D., September 16, 1945.

[8] "Baker Street from Wisconsin", Milwaukee Journal bookpage, n.d.

[9] A. D. to Science Fiction Digest, Feb. 4, 1954; to A. Fowler Wright, Feb. 17, 1954.

[10] A. D. to Groff Conklin, Feb. 26, 1954.

[11] A. D. to Eunice Loncosky, May 10, 1964.

[12] A. D. Journal.

[13] Biographer's observation.

[14] L. Sprague DeCamp, Lovecraft, a Biography, pp. 428-ff.

[15] A. D. to Leo Weisenborn, May 22 and April 9, 1956.

[16] A. D., Sauk Prairie Star, n.d.

[17] Note 15.

[18] George M. Cornell to A. D., Aug. 29, 1954; from A. D., no date.

[19] Ellen Masters to A. D., no date.

[20] Note 1, hoc. sic.

[21] August Derleth Book Review Column in the Madison State Journal.

Chapter Sixteen

"...I had no alternative but to divorce her for the children's well-being, and for the good of my work...It was either divorce on my terms, to which – fortunately for both of us – she agreed, or arrange a convenient drowning accident, which I'd have done with no more qualms and only a little more distaste than killing a fly. I had it all planned if needed...."[1]

The treadmill was beginning, gradually, to wear him down. Not only was his professional work full of stress, so was his private life.

Sandy's third child was born on the 10th of August. Before the birth of April Rose, August had chosen the name of Walden William, in anticipation of a son. He would later bestow that name on April's 3rd child. As with April Rose, August failed to reach the hospital in time for the birthing.[2]

In these beginning years Sandy was docile enough, but gradually she began to rebel. August was very inflexible about his rules. One evening when they visited the home of Dr. and Mrs. Trautman, Sandy was enjoying the company of the Trautman boys, who had been students with her in high school. When August announced, "It's 10 p.m., time to go home," Sandy didn't want to go.

"Suit yourself," Derleth said as he got up and departed. Dr. Trautman had to drive Sandy home later. The Trautman boys would have gladly escorted her home, but Esther Trautman thought it wiser they didn't, feeling repercussions for Sandy's rebellious behavior would probably have been much worse. Esther Trautman had never been too fond of August because he consistently snubbed the Sac Prairie upper crust gatherings in spite of numerous invitations to these gala events. Esther liked Sandra, however, calling her a basically sweet girl, much too young and full of enthusiasm for life to be stuck with an autocratic old egotist like Derleth.[3]

As August predicted the marriage did not last, and on

March 24, 1959, he was granted a divorce. He had been married a little less than six years. The immediate effect on Derleth was an easing of his hypertension. The judge prevented any news media from prying into the event by impounding the testimony in which Sandra was censured and Derleth given custody of the children.

Sandra did not even appear in court and she did not contest the divorce. She and Derleth tried to keep up appearances until a week before the decree, in order to avoid damaging news coverage, and also to discourage a lawyer from convincing Sandy to countersue.

Sandra, unaware that August's love had cooled, had been astounded when he demanded a divorce. He had given her everything she wanted – clothes, entertainment, even affection, not to mention "servicing his wife" as he called their sexual activities. August felt a more sensitive woman would have realized love was lacking right from the start of the marriage.

"...I had no alternative but to divorce her for the children's well-being, and for the good of my work,..." he wrote to Mary Stiver in 1960. "...It was either to divorce on my terms, to which – fortunately for both of us – she agreed, or arrange a convenient drowning accident, which I'd have done with no more qualms and only a little more distaste than killing a fly. I had it all planned if needed...."[4]

August admitted he was hard to live with. He was a strict disciplinarian, for one thing. Like most writers, he abhorred interruptions. Rose Derleth said she had learned early not to interrupt her son when he worked. Sandra never did learn that, according to her mother-in-law, who agreed that August was a hard task master.[5]

L. Sprague de Camp, who visited Derleth in 1955, was not surprised by the divorce because he said "...it looked like August were trying to run his household on the lines of his German forbearers, with women being relegated to Kirche, Kuche, and Kinder...."[6]

Another guest was puzzled, his curiosity piqued, to hear Sandra using the long outmoded formality of addressing her husband as "Mr. Derleth" instead of "August" or "Augie" (the nickname Derleth asked even total strangers to call him).[7]

Although Derleth had declared he did not want an intellectual equal for his wife, he maintained it was Sandra's "stupidity" above everything else that cemented his resolve to terminate the marriage.

What Derleth failed to note in his journal was that the marriage was a complete sham right from the start, as far as he was concerned. Along with the trauma Sandy must have experienced being forced to choose between her first born child and her husband, she was subjected to psychological abuse beyond belief. Like Margery and Mark, Sandra had made the fatal error of betraying Derleth. Her brief affair in Madison had opened the first wounds in their relationship and brought forth from August his basest nature.[8]

Along with demanding Sandy give up the child as a condition of the marriage, he informed her that she was not to interfere with his relationship with his old flame, Cassandra. Cassandra, still married to the young man she had chosen over Marty and Derleth, mother of several children, sought out Derleth's company more and more. She confided to him that her husband beat her frequently. The two former lovers soon could not be in the same room together without the flame of desire springing up anew. Derleth did nothing to quench that flame. Instead he went out of his way to fan it, often inviting Cassandra out to dine with him and Sandy. He'd sit between the two beautiful, young women, relishing the way they vied for his attention, egging them on. On special occasions, such as Valentine's Day, or Sandy's birthday, he'd take both of them shopping, buy a present for Sandra and an equally expensive one for Cassandra. He was slowly, deliberately, ruthlessly destroying any semblance of love, romance or even apparent respect between himself and his young wife.[9]

Sandy obviously became disenchanted with the whole situation. She become irritable, not at all like her usual sunny self. Her anger surfaced in the handling of April and Walden, according to Derleth. When she spoke sharply to them, August, in turn, treated her like a naughty child. What happened eventually was inevitable. Sandra, like Cassandra, sought consolation elsewhere.[10]

When Derleth accidentally overheard her talking on the

telephone to a man he called "Slimey", he was enraged. Sandy, suppressed and tormented since the day Derleth had discovered her first pregnancy, was vulnerable to anyone who would give her a second glance, even Slimey (according to Derleth, the most notorious womanizer in Sac Prairie). When Sandy confessed she was having an affair with Slimey, she also revealed that she had posed nude for him to photograph. "Such pornography," Derleth raved. Yet, during their courtship, Derleth had taken Sandy to the meadows, disrobed her, and arranged her in "erotic" ("artistic") positions, telling her he meant to use the pictures to illustrate the book of poetry called *PSYCHE*. It is doubtful August was telling Sandra the truth. He must have known no prestigious publisher in those days would allow such pictures. *PSYCHE*, like most of Derleth's work, was illustrated with woodcuts.[11]

Sandra seemed even more anxious than August to be free of the marriage. She moved out of the Place of Hawks, taking a flat in Madison. The transition was very smooth, with Sandra visiting the children every few days at first, then gradually widening the space between visits to once a fortnight or so. She soon married again and began raising a second family.

With August's parents planning to move in, happy at the opportunity to take Sandra's place, the shock would be minimized as far as the children were concerned. Derleth felt that April might be more affected, as Walden William was still very young.[12]

August assured a friend a year later: "...I am far better off, feel satisfied, revel in my old freedoms, still have my children, suffered no great financial loss, put in one of my best production years among the last ten (115 titles as against 74 in 1958 – 430,000 words instead of 250,000; 64 placements instead of 48, and nineteen new markets in place of 6 in the last year of my marriage....)"[13]

After his divorce, August had the kitchen from the old Damn house moved to the Place of Hawks. The family had possessed it for over a century and now the homestead was up for sale and he could not bear to part with that portion of it.

Rose and William Derleth came to make their home with their son a few days later. Though it was a relief for Derleth to be single again, he found still another responsibility added to his already long list, that of being both mother and father to the children. His aging parents were a tremendous help in caring for the house, preparing the meals, and tending to the children. August felt, however, he could not put all the burden of April Rose and Walden William on his parents, so he undertook to care for them upstairs during the night, giving his parents a chance for undisturbed rest. He had to cut out many of his social activities, even those as important as the Governor's open house on December 20, 1959. Walden down with a cold, had coughed all night and Derleth was simply too tired to go to the mansion.[14]

April Rose was less of a problem at this time than Walden. She was older, and of a more placid temperament as a child. Derleth delighted in her company, took her along on his shorter hikes, and on trips to town. Mark Schorer cautioned him against spending more time with April than with Walden. (This was the first indication in Derleth's journal that he was communicating again with his former lover and collaborator.)[15]

Walden was more like his father, livening up life at the Place of Hawks considerably. Only a few months after the divorce, Walden wandered away while August was visiting in town. The whole neighborhood was in an uproar, searching for him. He was found crying lustily before the entrance of a vacant building a few blocks away.

Walden got into one scrape after another: Like locking April Rose in the doghouse, and walking away; or chasing a rooster when his grandfather took him to visit the Paul Risler farm, ending up with a scratched cheek and hole pecked into his side. Although he lost a lot of blood in a hurry during the mishap, he was more frightened than hurt.

Derleth included a graphic description in his journal of the difficulties involved in attempting to write while the children were in the house. Busy with a tender scene between Governor and Kate Dewey for *SHADOW IN THE GLASS*, he wrote: "...'For a few moments the scene held – their lips together, the fire's warmth laving them....' Then his son came running upstairs."

August wrote the next few lines to the blare of a railroad yard record: "...then she drew away a little, still clinging to him, her eyes searching his face...."

"...The story of Nelson Dewey came limping out of my fingers...to the accompaniment of Walden running through the room to throw the apple core out over the balcony, 'for the rabbits Daddy!', detouring to run along the window seat, jump to the bed, cross it cater-cornered to thump to the floor on the other side...It was a little short of a miracle that Governor Dewey ever did learn that he was about to become a father...April sat quietly reading throughout it all...."[16]

To accomplish any creative work at all, August had to rearrange his writing hours, getting up at 4:30 a.m. to put in several hours while the children were asleep, and retiring at 11:00 p.m.

Walden was afraid of thunder and Derleth, during storms, comforted him as a mother would. That the boy had inherited some of his father's imagination is evident in his response to a talking record asking his sister's age.

"...'seven, eight, and nine,' Walden replied...."

"...April, indignant, pointed out that Walden only had one sister...Walden claimed he had three...."

When August asked who the other two were, Walden replied, "...'Debbie and Joanie. I 'magined them.'...."

Derleth's son was very insistent on getting what he set his mind to. (Not unlike August.) He wanted a printing set. Derleth refused to buy it for him. Walden persisted in bringing up the subject repeatedly for two days, finally wearing his father down.[17]

Some 20 years later, one of the proprietors of a popular restaurant in Prairie due Sac – Betty Boss – commented that Walden seemed to be following in his father's footsteps because he had recently written a letter-to-the-editor of the Sac Prairie paper, complaining that the tennis club didn't do enough to help young people. Mrs. Boss said she liked Derleth, who often brought his visitors to the Firehouse Restaurant. She told how he criticized some new make-up she was wearing one night and demanded she take it off. She didn't mind because August made her feel like a "real" lady, she said. The Firehouse Restaurant put a portrait of Derleth on display after his death in spite of the fact that some of its customers objected to the author's being accorded such a tribute.[18]

April, according to her teacher, Sister Rebecca, was "...'a perfect little lady – so well behaved'...." April used bigger words than the other children in her class, attributable, no doubt, to her father's example. She was also very proud of her dad. She had a mind of her own, too, as illustrated when, at seven, she informed August that she had outgrown the nickname he had for her, "Peaner".

August felt April inherited his own characteristics of neatness, demonstrated by the way she put her valentines in order and collected the discarded envelopes for the wastebasket after a Valentine party.[19]

At eight, April was already helping to pack books for shipping. As she grew older, August took great pride in her willingness to learn from Rosella, her ability to perform chores, learning to can pickles and prepare meals when her grandparents were off visiting her Aunt Hildred.[20]

All in all, Derleth had a full, active life even beyond his writing and he tried his best to be there for his children.[21]

SOURCE NOTES
CHAPTER SIXTEEN

[1] A. D. to Mary Stiver, 1960.

[2] A. D. Journal, 9, 10, August, 1951.

[3] Esther Trautman taped letter to biographer.

[4] Note 1, op. sic.

[5] Interview with Rosella Derleth, Maplewood Nursing Home, Prairie du Sac, Wisconsin, 1976.

[6] L. Sprague DeCamp to A. D.

[7] Interview with Professor Ed Kamark, Rhinelander School of Arts, Rhinelander, Wisconsin, while attending his playwriting class.

[8] Biographer's studied opinion.

[9] Note 2, November 1949; A. D. to Inez Weaver, April 16, 1948.

[10] Ibid., 10, 11, February, 1959.

[11] Note 9, (letter), 2 January, 1958.

[12] Note 2, 11 May, 1960, box 97, folder 3, p. 92; 29 June, 1960, box 97, folder 4, p. 9; 24 _____, 1959, folder 1, p. 108; 3 Jan., 1962, box 97, folder 6, p. 100; 11 Nov., 1960, box 94, folder 4, p. 97; 4 March, 1961, box 97, folder 5, p. 42; 14 Feb., 1963, box 98, folder 3, p. 16; Note 1, op. sic.

[13] A. D. to

[14] Note 2, 20 December, 1959.

[15] Mark Schorer to A. D., no date.

[16] Note 2, 11 May, 1960, box 97, folder 3, p. 92; 29 June, 1960, box 97, folder 4, p. 9.

[17] Ibid.

[18] Interview with Betty Boss, at the Firehouse Restaurant, Sauk City, Wisconsin, 1973.

[19] Note 2.

[20] Note 2.

[21] Biographer's opinion.

Chapter Seventeen

"...I have certain principles and I adhere to them...."[1]

Derleth enjoyed his children, took them "trick or treating" on Halloweens, hiking in the marshes, on trips to Wisconsin Dells, and later, to concerts and plays in Madison. Nevertheless, they did impede his rest and his social life. He found it difficult, for instance, to get up to take them to school after celebrating, in July 1962, the publication of his 100th book, *CONCORD REBEL, A LIFE OF HENRY D. THOREAU.*[2]

Derleth, disgusted with *SHADOW IN THE GLASS*, had vowed never again to write another book he didn't want to write. The biography of Thoreau was a book he had wanted to do for a long time. Thoreau's influence on Derleth is evident in that so much of what the biographer wrote, or quoted, could be said of Derleth as well.

"...He went, as always, in wonder, clear-eyed, anxious to mix no detail which might enlarge his horizons or add to his knowledge of nature and his fellow man...."

"...My faults are paradoxes, saying just the opposite...."

"...The records he kept were meticulous...."[3]

August stressed Thoreau's philosophy and love for nature, saying little about his politics. One reader berated Derleth for underplaying Thoreau's anarchy and failing to treat the naturalist as a whole person. August answered by saying "...An entire book could be written about the Thoreau of civil disobedience, but it would not be a biography of Thoreau only an explanation of a portion of his life...."[4]

Derleth was writing of his own experience as well as Thoreau's when he wrote: "...At this point he must have learned that his fellow townsmen looked upon him as eccentric, more or less a loafer, and...as an irresponsible rascal. This is the kind of discovery almost every creative solitary sooner or later makes...."[5]

In July 1960, the boy he had hired to help with book packing and chores around Arkham House quit to work at a grocery store. Derleth was sitting in his favorite captain's chair in the old harness shop, visiting with Hugh, when he chanced to glimpse young Rikki Meng strolling by. He went out to intercept the youth and invited him for a ride to talk about the possibility of Rikki's coming to work for him.

Rikki agreed to give the job a try. He had a quick, inquisitive mind, and was an honor student. By September, he'd mastered the job of packing books. He was also good with the children. He soon learned to drive, a prerequisite for the job. August had his driver's license but hated to drive, especially in winters, and was one of those people who turn into little Hitlers, or speed maniacs, behind the wheel. He was apt to push the gas pedal to the floor and even when others drove, Derleth became involved, demanding they "...Pass that fool ahead! Hurry up! Etc...." He preferred to utilize the time spent in an automobile viewing the scenery or jotting down ideas for poems. His dislike of driving was so intense, it even crept into his dreams. One recurred over and over: August would be driving, park his car someplace, go into a building, and when he came out of the building, the car would be gone. He'd be frantically running through the streets searching for his car. The dream disturbed Derleth so, he went to consult a so-called expert on dreams. The man told him that the dream indicated his reluctance to drive was battling his need to get places.

August's new helper took up typing in the next school year and was later able to defray the costs of college by typing for Arkham House.[6]

Derleth was well pleased with Rikki's work and his intelligence. He also was pleased that Rikki neither smoked or indulged in intoxicating beverages, and handled money carefully. Rikki's presence in the Place of Hawks helped ease the difficult years of child-rearing, of adjusting to Rosella's frequent blowups, and lessened the more tedious tasks connected with the publishing business. Rikki filled in wherever he was needed, and he soon became like one of the family.

George Marx stopped in periodically, to read to the children at bedtime and help out when and where needed. Numerous references to the tasks Marx performed at the Place of Hawks are noted in Derleth's journal. He often drove Derleth to the marshes and other favorite spots around Sac Prairie, to watch the fireflies, star-gaze, or just enjoy the beauty of the night. At Christmas Marx was included on August's gift list and in the family Christmas celebrations. Still, the largest share of caring for April and Walden fell to August, himself. Rosella, with her culinary skill, was a welcome addition to the kitchen, while Derleth's father did maintenance chores around the house and grounds.

It wasn't exactly easy, having his mother in the house, trying to run his life. Derleth, in despair at first, turned his thoughts toward a possible second marriage to someone who would be a good wife and mother. Although several Sac Prairie women aspired to that position, Derleth was afraid to take another chance. Augie did put his foot down on Rosella's "smothering". Her domain was the kitchen and he would tolerate no meddling anywhere else.

When Rosella became ill and developed frequent dizzy spells, Derleth had a new worry. What would he do if he lost Rosella? He himself did not feel well. His blood pressure was not as high as before; but in 1962, he went into St. Mary's hospital at Madison for an adjustment of a bilateral hernia.

When Sister Mary of the Angels saw Derleth garbed in his long velvet robe, she was surprised to learn he was only an author. His robe had suggested at least a prince.

The week's mail awaiting him at home after the hospital stay, numbered over 200 letters. Life resumed its normal frantic work pace, which had increased considerably since the divorce.[7] Derleth was also gaining more recognition every day.

THE MILL CREEK IRREGULARS published in 1959 was a selection of the Junior Literary Guild. In 1960, The Book Club for Poetry chose his collection, *WEST OF THE MORNING,* as one of its selections. (August had revised the collection at least 12 times.) "The Tail of the Dog" was picked as the best short story of 1959, by *SCHOLASTIC MAGAZINE,* which also awarded him $1,000 for the best juvenile of 1959. His picture was on the August, 1961 issue of *WRITER'S REVIEW,* with his article inside about writing novels, and in 1962, he was mentioned in *PLAYBOY.*

A correspondent wrote that she was thrilled to see August's

name flashed on a "thriller" program as author of "The Wig". The program, narrated by Boris Karloff, was frowned upon by the National Association for Better Radio and Television Monitoring, which was quoted in one of Drew Pearson's columns in 1961. Pearson outlined Derleth's plot of "Mr. George" and advised viewers to boycott the sponsors. Derleth was sure Pearson had not viewed the film himself but had taken another person's opinion of it. "Mr. George", according to Derleth, was actually a gentle thriller, and at no time were any of the murders by ghostly relatives of the girl shown on television. They were all indicated. The child in the film never knew those attempts on her life had been made. He also advised that parents should monitor their children's viewing as he did. They could always turn the dial if they deemed the material unfit for children. "The Return of Andrew W. Bentley" was aired on television in 1962.

Doubleday asked if they might use the following lines from August's poem "Dusk over Wisconsin" as caption with the picture of the Dales of St. Croix, Wisconsin in their "Our America", an engagement calendar for 1961:

"...Wisconsin is still a young man – sprawled
in the deep grass of summer afternoon
remembering how Sacs and Foxes and how Chippewas
fell back, and how soon the forests came to end,
dreaming memoried footfalls
soft against the unquiet earth...."

All this attention was gratifying and every now and then a letter would arrive to further bolster his ego, such as the response to his complaint that the SATURDAY REVIEW passed over more good books than it assigned for review. Norman Cousins' answering letter promised a close look would be made at their book-selecting policy, and added some very satisfying words on how much he admired both August and his writing, calling him a writer of stature whose work warranted attention.

Derleth appreciated the success of those he had tried to help and encourage: messages like Robert Block's "...Just a line to let you know that PSYCHO has been bought for the movies...."; and Arkham House Fantasy Library, (hard cover editions of many science fiction and macabre authors) had help increase sales to 96 books per week in 1961.[8]

Not that there weren't frustrations and irritations along the way. The busier Derleth got with Arkham House and his less serious writing, the less time he had to devote to the saga. With a little more money coming in, it was time to think of reducing some of his writing chores. He considered discontinuing his "Minority Report" book review column in the *MADISON CAPITAL TIMES*. He was being swamped with books every week and felt he was letting publishers and authors down when he couldn't give space to their books. The books had been a problem at first, until he hit upon a way of handling them that would benefit the readers of Sac Prairie. He'd unwrap the books right at the Post Office to save himself the trouble of disposing of ten to twenty-five wrappings every day. He'd take the books home and examine them to determine which he wanted to review and which he could discard. He sorted the discards, picking the cream of them for the Sauk City Library. All the rest, except those more lurid novels unsuitable for libraries, he set aside for the Prairie du Sac Library. As a result of over eighteen and a half years of receiving books from Derleth, the Sac Prairie libraries had probably the largest stock of books for their size of any in the state, if not the whole country.[9]

Derleth's books were a mixed blessing to the libraries. He charged a very minimal price for them so the library board could scarcely afford to turn down such bargains. Even at the low price, however, Derleth supplied so many there was never enough money in the treasury to purchase other volumes. Many of the board members most bitterly resented Derleth's high-handed approach depriving them of a freedom of choice, and lost sight entirely of the benefits of the arrangement.[10]

The Sauk City librarians, in subtle, perhaps subconscious, ways, struck back at Derleth. During one annual Wisconsin Week, they dutifully prepared a display containing books by contemporary Wisconsin authors, among them *WISCONSIN LORE*, by Robert E. Gard and L. G. Sorden, and *THE WISCONSIN STORY* by H. Russell Austin. There was no mention of the work of August Derleth, the most prolific regional writer of Wisconsin. A careful search of the library revealed a section of shelves in a tiny, obscure alcove, devoted to Derleth's books, as though the intent were to hide, rather than display, his works.[11]

Seven years after Derleth had started his book reviewing for the *MADISON CAPITAL TIMES*, William Evjue, editor, suggested Derleth accept a $10 stipend, saying his conscience had been bothering him that August was doing all those book reviews and getting no pay for them. By 1960, that amount had swelled to $25 a week, for which August reviewed an average of five to ten books.[12]

Right from the first, he ran into trouble. He felt a review was more effective before the book was published, so he made sure his reviews were sent into the paper well ahead of publication date. The editors of the paper were less concerned about the timeliness of the review than about making space for advertising and/or other features and news items, and often omitted Derleth's reviews, or cut them, with resulting fireworks.

When Evjue sent August a letter addressed to "Voice of the People", complaining about a listing of 16 who-done-its in one issue of August's column, and saying people were griping that top books weren't being reviewed, only books of little known authors, Derleth patiently explained that he could hardly review a book that hadn't been sent to him. Many publishers didn't send August books because he couldn't guarantee the reviews space in the paper. He claimed to have reviewed three books of Pulitzer Prize material out of every five. He gave preference to books by Wisconsin authors and books on Wisconsin; his final choice was outstanding books of unusual merit, irregardless of their classification.[13]

The day the artist-in-residence at Wisconsin University, John Stuart Curry, was buried, a Madison book reviewer came to the Place of Hawks unannounced and uninvited, toting a quart of whiskey, ranting and raving as he consumed the liquor. The intruder's presence prevented August from attending Curry's funeral, as he had planned. Finally, expecting guests for dinner, Derleth requested he leave; instead the man entered one of the bedrooms and proceeded to stretch out on the bed, fully clothed. Derleth, disgusted, kicked him out of the house.

As a result, a long letter from the reviewer appeared in the "Voice of the People" volume, headlined "One Reviewer Castigates Another". In it, the irate reviewer pounced on Derleth for mentioning eight of his own books in his annual listing of the best ten books of 1947. (August said he had listed only one – *VILLAGE DAYBOOK*.) The letter accused Derleth of being Romily S. Devon, the name signed to the *MADISON CAPITAL TIMES* reviews of Derleth's books. The letter writer charged August with denying Wisconsin and midwestern authors favorable reviews, because Derleth's review of a book by the whiskey-toting writer was unfavorable.

Derleth's letter replying to Evjue was a scorcher. Evjue published it in the letter column a few days later, but it was really the editor August was upset with for ever publishing the first letter. He felt it had utilized one of Hitler's techniques – making a lie so big that even if people do not buy all of it, some of the falsehood sticks. The paper, he felt, had done him a discourtesy by not showing him the letter so he could answer it in the same issue. August made it very clear to Evjue that he would not hold still for a lie which attacked his integrity.

Relations between Evjue and Derleth had been anything but smooth almost from the beginning. With Derleth already half inclined to give up the position, Evjue's letter in December of 1939 objecting to a review of Kelly's *TEN EVER-LOVING, BLUE-EYED YEARS WITH POGO* was more a two-by-four than the straw that broke Derleth's patience. He had long before urged Evjue to pick up the Pogo strip, but the editor-publisher ignored him and Pogo landed in the Wisconsin State Journal instead of the *MADISON CAPITAL TIMES*.

Derleth tendered his resignation, effective February 11, 1960. He also sent a letter to the Publisher's Weekly advising them of his resignation.

"...The editor of the *CAPITAL TIMES* is a noble exponent of the school of personal journalism, with noble record of fighting for causes, against what he calls 'scarewords' ...anarchism, radicalism, communism, socialism, and the like; his latest crusade would appear to be against Pogoism..." Derleth wrote.

" '...Come in and we'll talk,' Evjue suggested...."

" '...Not until the Pogo review is run,' Derleth replied..."

159

Evjue did not run the review. He accepted Derleth's resignation instead.

The Pogo review, as threatened, was included in a front page news story by the Wisconsin State Journal saying the Times refused to publish the book review because the Pogo comic strip runs in the Journal.

One publisher wrote, lamenting Derleth's resignation, calling him one of the few reviewers in the country who consistently turned out material worth reading. He felt it was a blow to good writing that Derleth would not be choosing and commenting on books of the current literary scene. He also told August he'd continue sending books he felt the author might enjoy.[14]

The Times must have received its share of protesting letters also, because the break was short-lived. By August, "Minority Report" was back in the paper, and by January, 1961, Derleth was receiving better compensation for his reviews. The column ran until four days after Derleth's death.[15]

SOURCE NOTES
CHAPTER SEVENTEEN

[1] A. D. to Gerald Klein, Oct. 29, 1964.

[2] August Derleth, Concord Rebel, A Life of Henry D. Thoreau, (Chilton, Pennsylvania, 1962).

[3] Note 2, quotes.

[4] Robert Wellen to A. D., Nov. 9, 1962; A. D. to Robert Wellen, Nov. 13, 1962.

[5] Note 2, op. cit.

[6] A. D. to Inez Weaver, Aug. 10, 26, Sept. 1, 7, 22, 28 and Oct. 12, 1960; June 9 and July 2, 6 and 8, 1964.

[7] A. D. Journal.

[8] A. D. to Wm. Evjue, June 16, 1961; Drew Pearson, "Outcries at TV Horror Reach Sponsors", Madison Capital Times, June 16, 1961; A. D. to Joe Slotkins, Sept. 2, 1960; Joe Slotkins to A. D., Sept. 25, 1961; Edna Meudt to A. D., Jan. 6, 1960; John Vetter to A. D., Aug. 14, 1962; Sesta T. Matheson to A. D., Feb. 4, 1962; Norman Cousins to A. D., March 20, 1962; Robert Bloch to A. D., May 22, 1959; Note 7.

[9] A. D. to Simon Friar, Feb. 10, 1960.

[10] Biographer's interview of Sauk City and Prairie du Sac librarians, August, 1973.

[11] Biographer's visual experience, Sauk City Library, 1973.

[12] Wm. Evjue to A. D., April 9, 1949; A. D. to Wm. Evjue, Dec. 18, 1961.

[13] Norma Goodfellow to the editor of "Voice of the people" column, Madison Capital Times; A. D. to Wm. Evjue, Dec. 22, 1947.

[14] A. D. to and from Wm. Evjue, Dec. 21, 1959 to March 8, 1960; David Macdowell, March 15, 1960; A. D. to Wisconsin State Journal, March 8, 1960; Ralph Peterson "One book editor castigates another", Madison Capital Times, Dec. 1947; "Derleth scorches Peterson in reply", Madison Capital Times, Dec. 22, 1947.

[15] "Derleth, Books of the Times", July 8, 1971, p. 12.

Chapter Eighteen

"...a sly old fox..."[1]

W hy did he go back to the Times? It was hardly the money, this time. More likely he missed communion with his contemporaries. Having to read much of what was being published kept him in close touch with both the writing and publishing trends. Since he had always purchased extra copies of the paper and clipped his reviews to send to authors and publishers, he picked up many new correspondents who helped stretch the perimeter of Sauk City. Without the constant input of information, opinions, various viewpoints, his own well of creativity and his objectivity would both have probably suffered. "The Minority Report" was also a constant display window in which August could present his own beliefs and prejudices. A random sampling of Derleth's reviews discloses much information about the author.

His bird watching and religious "keeping of the accounts" are revealed in his review of *SILENT SPRING*, which stated that Derleth had his own yearly records on birds, kept up-to-date for decades. From them he had ascertained a 90% decrease in the bird population which could be blamed on U. S. D. A. officials, town and village boards, city councils' criminal stupidity. His awareness of the need for conservation of natural resources was demonstrated in his labeling Rachel Carson's book one of the most important of his era and advising people to not only read it but to pass it along to others to read.[2]

His complete detachment as a critic was evident in reviews of books by people he knew, like Mark Schorer's biography *SINCLAIR LEWIS, AN AMERICAN LIFE*. That book was picked by Derleth as one of the outstanding works of 1961, although August had never really forgiven Mark for his betrayal.[3]

His effort to separate the critic from the author were intensified in the review of at least two of his own books, *THE HOUSE ON THE MOUND* and *SHADOW IN THE GLASS*. Derleth panned *THE HOUSE ON THE MOUND* saying that aspiring writers could learn what to avoid in novel writing by reading this dull, tiresome book. When Duel, Sloan & Pearce, its publishers, reared up to deny Derleth's words, and called the book a major and engrossing work written by one of the country's highly important and versatile authors, both their letter and the review hit the front page. Charles A. Pearce described Derleth's reviews as "...usually exemplary, concise, informative, fair-minded...Why has Derleth never once in all his writing years acknowledged that the most attractive and lasting qualities of his books derive from his knowledge of the human heart and his love and understanding of humankind of all ages, especially the people of his native Wisconsin?...." Dr. Bachhuber's son, Richard, reading both letter and review, called Derleth a "sly old fox".[4]

If he had planned his books deliberately to obtain an effect, it would not be the first time he'd pulled that kind of stunt. In 1941, he lambasted the author of his own book of verse, *AND YOU, THOREAU*, under his pen name, then – assuming an injured innocence attacked his own criticisms. He kept up a lively pro and con debate for weeks with this device. Quite likely, though, it was his business acumen surfacing again, instead of a trick. August, already disgusted with having to do books like *SHADOW IN THE GLASS* became even more disgusted over how he had done them. In spite of his own evaluation, both books sold quite well.[5]

August's review of Dr. John Rock's *THE TIME HAS COME* agreed that birth control must be accomplished, but disagreed that it must be the church man who should solve the dispute. It should be up to the gynecologists and sociologists, he suggested, with typical foresight.

Derleth said Barry Goldwater's perspectives were from the past in his review of *WHY NOT VICTORY*. He was astonished that Goldwater considered himself presidential material. In Derleth's opinion, the man was woefully unqualified. The reviewer's own prejudice against military men may have had some influence on the resulting unflattering comments. His sister, Hildred, had married a military man, against his strong objections. It was not the man, himself, Derleth objected to, but that his brother-in-law was part of an institution Derleth despised.[6]

August's own supernatural interests and an actual happening from his own life was revealed in his review of *THE PICTORIAL KEY TO THE TAROT*, by Arthur Edward Waite. He hesitated calling reading the Tarot cards a game and explained why. He had read the cards for three ladies of the same family, three times for each. Without his knowledge, they had all asked the same question. The cards predicted disaster for the five persons involved in the question if the family sold their property as planned. They disregarded the predictions, and sold it anyhow. Within five months, one of the five was dead, two were bankrupt, and the last one of the five was divorced because she became involved with a middle-aged sodomite and adulterer.

That Derleth had an eye for the ladies was revealed in his review of a book of one woman's work calling it lively, knowledgeable and interesting, then adding his own totally unrelated observation that she was more photogenic than most poetesses.[7]

A fragment of one of Derleth's longest, most bitter feuds cropped up in his review of three books on Thoreau: "...This is the year which will go down among Thoreauvians as that in which the U. S. Government saw fit to memorialize on postage stamps a Speaker of the House, a U. N. Secretary, a holly wreath, etc. and ignored the centennial of Henry David Thoreau, one of the very few Americans whose philosophy has influenced world thought and action..."

It wasn't that August hadn't tried.

Way back in July, 1939, he had urged the postal department to print a Thoreau stamp, with no success. His ire against the department since then had been fueled again and again until it turned into something resembling a vendetta. His suggestion that Franklin D. Roosevelt also be honored with a commemorative stamp was rejected too, but with a valid reason. The laws didn't permit the postal authorities to use the likeness of a living person. It was the constant irritation of what Derleth considered tardy and inadequate postal service that burned him and erupted every now and then in a barrage of letters, seething comments in his columns, even more scathing remarks in flyers. One of these eruptions was over the cessation of the holiday mail service in Sauk City. When a petition to the postal department failed to restore the holiday services, Derleth issued another flyer. "...Just who is responsible for the end of this service in the first place?" he demanded. "Was it the simple, bullet-headed short-sightedness of some bureaucratic politician holding down a minority job somewhere between here and Washington? There is something here which has a bad smell – like the smell of a lazy public servant or a fat-bottomed bureaucrat...."

He sent a copy to the Postmaster General with a cover letter, this time with some success. He served as a self-appointed watchdog, pouncing on everyone concerned – including the senators and representatives – when the restored service was omitted or tardy. Copies of his March 28, 1960 "Wisconsin Diary" column about poor holiday service went to 33 senators, members of postal committees, and others. In 1963, he had 12 disapproving items from February to June in his column, ranging from the Gettysburg stamp to the contemplated zip code, in which, prophetically, he had little faith. "...I am dubious about its effectiveness," he wrote. "Heretofore, each time the experts in Washington have sought to 'improve' a service, the service has worsened. I will not be at all surprised to find delivery of the mail more disorganized than ever, once the zip code numbers are in operation...." (Fortunately, Derleth did not have to contend with the postal chaos of the '90s. He could get upset when the morning mail did not arrive until the afternoon.)[8]

The editors of the *MADISON CAPITAL TIMES* took much of the punch out of one of Derleth's 1963 columns criticizing the postal service, which prompted a threat from Derleth to drop the column. As with the book reviews, this was only another incident among many.

The battle waged over the book review seems to have been transferred to many other subjects in his Wisconsin Diary column after Derleth's brief vacation from the reviews. Evjue refused to run an item about the inequities present in the church where moneyed people were able to buy their way out of the sin of divorce, as opposed to the poor sinner, barred from the church's good graces for the same sin. Apparently Derleth was not able to get re-instated as a Catholic unless he could afford a substantial donation to make him welcome in church again.

Evjue cut out innocuous pieces of humor Derleth used to balance his column, thus spoiling the balance. The editor refused to run an item about an old Sauk City gentleman who picked up cigar and cigarette butts to salvage the tobacco for his pipe, although the fellow's name wasn't mentioned. He refused, also, to run one of August's defenses of long hair in school, which deplored "...the insistent drive of the inferior men for conformity,..." and pointed out that "...If Christ, Einstein, and Schweizter went to school to this kind of limited teacher, they would one and all have been commanded to have their locks shorn...." Since Derleth was careful to avoid any chance of libel in these items, he could not understand Evjue's censorship.

He made good his threat to resign in 1966. Evjue, spurred, no doubt, by a letter from a subscriber saying he'd renew his subscription when "Wisconsin Diary" was once again back in the paper, published an editorial including Derleth's item on the butt-scavenger as an example of material he would not publish! He also expressed doubt about another item he had deleted from August's column.

Derleth, without hesitation, asked if he was going to have to sue, or if Evjue would print a retraction.

So ended the column which one reader said she missed because it had helped make up for the lack of fine arts coverage and the scarcity of news about international affairs.[9]

Derleth's output of published books from 1960 through 1963 increased 50% over that of the last four years of his marriage.

Reviews of *THE HILLS STAND WATCH*, published in 1960 agreed that it was a pleasant, but not particularly distinguished book; the general consensus was that the plot was a bit melodramatic and thin, but the historic background accurate and full of drama. The local political maneuvering surrounding the Wisconsin Territory's bid for statehood, lead mining, and Indian raids on wagons transporting the lead, formed the background of the story. The illicit romance of Candance, an Easterner discontented with her marriage to David, a tradesman, and its tragic conclusion comprise the novel's romantic plot.

Derleth listed *THE HILLS STAND WATCH*, along with *SHADOW IN THE GLASS*, published in 1963, as part of his

Wisconsin Saga; *WALDEN WEST*, and *WISCONSIN IN THEIR BONES*, both published in 1961, were part of his Sac Prairie Saga.

Four juvenile books – one every year – were published during the four years following his divorce. *TENT SHOW SUMMER*, one of them, was written against the background of the Brooks' Traveling Stock Company. Derleth had been attending the company's shows over several years. He'd become a friend of the Brooks and had entertained the entire company at the Place of Hawks when they performed in the area. Again, a good example of how everything Derleth experienced or came in contact with sooner or later turned up in his writings.

Several poetry volumes, two collections of his short stories, a book about Solar Pons, a macabre tale, a compilation of short biographical sketches, a collection of his own Cthulhu fantasies written around ideas culled from Lovecraft's writings, and a portion of his journal were also published during those four years.

The stature of Lovecraft's work began to grow in the years since the founding of Arkham House, not only in the United States, but in England and other countries as well. In 1962 he was included in *SPINE CHILLERS*, a British anthology, indicating that Lovecraft was achieving the position of a classical horror author. His works, as well as other Arkham House books, were becoming collector's items. The printings had run from 100 – *THE SHUNNED HOUSE* – to 4,051 – *SLAN*. A run of the complete works of Arkham House would someday bring in $5,000 or more, according to the predictions of collectors at that time. The projection fell far short of the phenomenal rise of Lovecraft's fame, alone. In 1994, an original copy of one of Lovecraft's books was sold for $15,000.[10] Derleth's stature, too, has grown tremendously in the past 30 years, as has the success of Block, Bradbury, Asimov, and many others published by Arkham House. So the loyal fans had been making an investment as well as buying a book. Many of the fantasy fans had also purchased Derleth's *WALDEN WEST* and *SAC PRAIRIE PEOPLE*, indirectly helping to provide financing for Arkham House's expansion, and stretching their own literary awareness in the process. By 1964, there were 72 Arkham House books, six

Mycroft & Moran, and eight Stanton & Lee. The publishing houses, first operating out of the Place of Hawks, was being forced to add a warehouse for the growing stock.[11]

SOURCE NOTES
CHAPTER EIGHTEEN

1 Richard Bachhuber to A. D., June 10, 1958.
2 August Derleth, "Book of the Times", Capital Times, Oct. 4, 1962.
3 Ibid., August 24, 1961.
4 May 22, 1958; John Patrick Hunter, "Derleth slap at own book stirs dispute", Capital Times; Charles A. Pearce to editor, May 25, 1953.
5 A. D. to Ian Law, Nov. 25, 1958.
6 Note 2, Dec. 26, 1963; Aug. 2, 1962.
7 August Derleth, "The Thoreau Centennial Year", Dec. 20, 1962; Senator William Proxmire, Feb., 1961; A. D. to Sen. Robert LaFollette, July 26, 1946; A. D. to Postmaster General, Dec. 18, 1960; Bill Dutch, article in August Derleth Society Newsletter re: Derleth's postal conflicts.
8 William Evjue to A. D., Dec. 16, 1963; A. D. from Evjue, Oct. 22, 1952; Evjue to "Friends of Wisconsin Diary", Capital Times, Feb. 19, 1966.
9 A. D. Journal, n.d.
10 List of Derleth's books, SWHS Museum archives, Madison, Wisconsin, biographer's calculations; T. V. Olsen unpublished manuscript given to biographer; August Derleth Society Newsletter, 1944, p. 1.
11 A. D. to James Siegert, June 18, 1962.

Chapter Nineteen

...."I think Augie will be remembered for his poetry above everything else...."[1]

After his divorce from Sandra Winters, Cassandra wasted no time in worming her way back into Derleth's life. She made herself so indispensable, Derleth came near getting snared in the tender trap again. He might have repeated his mistake of marrying a woman far below his intellectual and cultural level, but for Rosella's ultimatum. If he married Cassandra, his mother vowed she'd leave. She had never liked Sandy but had not interfered with their marriage. She despised Cassandra even more than Sandy and was adamant about not living in the same house with a woman Derleth, himself, had described as a "trollop".

Rosella was not the only one who helped persuade August not to make the same mistake again. Close friends frowned on his lack of good sense in the matter. Cassandra, still married and with children of her own, presented the same problem Derleth had battled with years before with Maris. Much as he wanted to marry his "trollop" he finally came to his senses and rejected her.[2]

The children were growing up rapidly. April appeared to still be more malleable than Walden. Derleth, in his mother role, nagged at Walden, complained about him, experienced, perhaps, some of the frustration Rosella had gone through raising August. The man who could display amazing patience in his nurturing of writers and poets lost it with Walden when he dawdled at small tasks like picking up deadwood from the grounds. Walden had sneaked off on his bike to town when he was supposed to be doing chores, and Derleth grounded both him and his bicycle.[3]

Many of Derleth's ideas were unconventional. He refused to let the children "trick or treat" for UNICEF. He not only defended April, but attacked the school system when she was sent home for wearing slacks. He agreed with the ban on miniskirts in the dress code set by the principal, as they were far too revealing, but balked at the restriction against slacks.

When the First Lady came to Spring Green on her country beautification tour, Derleth was invited to the dinner given in her honor at the home of Helen and Dale O'Brian. His comment later was that he thought she was charming but that President Johnson ought to make her wear longer skirts, although hers was not a mini-skirt, but came to just above the knees.

"...I do maintain...the primary function of the school is to educate and that any undue concern with clothing, other than that it be clean and modest, is evidence of a mental attitude that could do with some psychiatric care...," he wrote to the District School Superintendent. He then threatened to turn the matter over to his legal counsel if April Rose were again sent home for wearing slacks.

When the issue of long hair hit the area schools, it also hit Derleth's "fan". He felt a teacher was hired to teach and advised teachers who concerned themselves with the length of a student's hair to change from teaching to barbering, and said so publicly in his "Wisconsin Diary" column in the *MADISON CAPITAL TIMES*.[4]

In late 1963, Derleth received a letter from the treasurer of the Wisconsin Regional Writer's Association asking if he would consider teaching a two-week writing class in July of 1964 at the Rhinelander School of Arts, currently in the process of being organized by Professor Robert E. Gard.

"...I'm starting a one-woman campaign to secure Wisconsin's ablest author for the novel and short story sessions," she wrote. "...Would you, if approached through the University, be interested and available?...."

She had been very impressed hearing Derleth speak at a conference, and having read his *EVENING IN SPRING* (his suggestion as a good introduction to his work) thought him the best possible choice for the job of writer-in-residence.

Derleth felt he could not commit himself for the two full weeks, although he was in agreement with the attempt of the Wisconsin Idea Theater to take university programs into the far reaches of the state. He was, as always, very busy. Rosella had had a slight stroke a week earlier and he didn't want to leave his parents or his children for so long a time under the circumstances. Besides, he doubted the University could afford to pay the amount necessary to make the position financially possible for him.[5]

Work on Lovecraft's letters was still going forward, although not as fast as Derleth would like. Don Wandrei, doing his own writing, taking care of his house and grounds, tending to the needs of his ailing mother and a handicapped sister, still found time to edit the letters. He found time to visit Derleth, too, especially during May, August's vacation and morel picking month. The two men shared a passion for the fungus growth. The letters they exchanged over the years contained surprisingly little Lovecraft and Arkham House discussions in comparison to their discourses on morels. It is difficult to ascertain which partner was more knowledgeable or more enthusiastic.

Derleth was more vocal about his morel expertise and considered himself enough of an expert to set the editors of *HARPERS* straight on some of the information contained in one of their articles on mushrooms, as well as adding almost as much extra information as was contained in the article.

The partners picked thousands of the delicious morels, which August loved fried in butter or smothering a steak. He often invited friends over, telling them he would supply mushrooms, if they would bring the steak.

He hung them carefully on strings and dried them in the attic, so he was well supplied year-around. Hugh, Rikki, Karl, John Stanton, Alice, George Marx, Peter Blankenheim and others were frequent morel-hunting companions over the years. Alice had her own favorite mushroom areas, August, his. They never invaded each other's "private" hunting grounds. Derleth picked morel, puffballs, shaggy morels and fairy rings – the four types with poisoned counterparts that had distinguishing differences easily recognized. He would not touch other varieties. He kept a careful count of each mushroom picked and where he'd found it, guarded the locations from villagers, considering them his own mushroom-picking areas and was not above protesting when the owner of the land got to the mushrooms first. His record years netted well over 10,000 morels.[6]

Derleth delighted in breaking records and establishing new

ones. After 20 years trying to surpass John Burroughs' record of 1,067 consecutive whippoorwill calls, he and Sandra finally did it in 1953 with 1,597 calls right on their own property. He noted in *Country Journal* finding a white lilac bush with two full-blown spikes of blossoms, a discovery he was unable to find a precedent for in the records; in 1964, he announced the purple martins arrived six days ahead of their schedule.[7]

Wandrei and Derleth shared another enthusiasm – good music. If Derleth had the opportunity, as he often made certain he did, to attend a symphony or an opera, his next letter to Wandrei would relate the program in detail, especially if it were the Minneapolis Symphony, from near Wandrei's home area. The music of Strauss, Schubert, Debussy, Mozart, and Delius delighted August. Derleth's favorite operas were "Der Rosenkavalier", "La Traviata", "Aida", "La Forza Del Destino", "Lucia di Lammermoor", "Salome", "Die Frau Ohne Schatten", "Othello", "Pelleas et Melisande", and "Carmen".

Derleth's lifelong dream of writing an opera himself materialized when James Drew, an Evanston, Illinois composer on the faculty of the School of Music at Northwestern University, sent Derleth a tape of his music so the author could familiarize himself with it. He later sent a tentative basic plot and character ideas based on a horror theme. Derleth wrote the libretto for "The Gable Window".

Dawson Taylor, a Detroit composer, wrote the ballad "Moonstruck" suggested by Derleth's poetry volume *OTHER SIDE OF THE MOON*, and when the Detroit library exhibited Dawson's album, August was asked to send *OTHER SIDE OF THE MOON* material to add to the exhibit.[8]

Derleth and Wandrei shared a love of gourmet food, too. A generous stream of delicacies passed between the Place of Hawks and Wandrei's home in St. Paul over the years, ranging all the way from hazelnuts off Derleth's trees to rare sausages, cheeses, Rosella's schaum tortes, chocolates, and Don's own black walnut chocolate cake. Both men would seek palate-pleasing, top-quality foods with the fervor and persistence of collectors. Augie loved Whitney's sweet crabapples and made a special trip to Ski Hi Fruit Farm to secure several bushels of them each year. There was a certain source of honey that he preferred and would go miles out of his way to get it for himself and friends. He would gift others like the Wisconsin poet, Edna Meudt, with bars of a superior chocolate, or chocolate covered marshmallows, his favorite. He also loved strawberries.

Rose and William did a lot of canning and August relished not only the food but the spicy bouquet permeating the house during canning season. German culinary skills were plentiful in Sauk City, and all through his life Derleth enjoyed such mouth-watering dishes as Grandma Volk's raisin pie, Aunt Annie Ring's "Dausch" (cut-up pancakes with hot or cold blackberry sauce), Mrs. Schwenker's macaroon kisses, Rosella's raised doughnuts, prune whip or banana cream pie, coffee kuchen, and elderberry syrup. Many of these delectable desserts cropped up in Derleth's juvenile fiction, especially those most biographical, such as the Steve and Sim stories. Derleth often made special trips to the Baraboo or Mineral Points area for chop suey or pasta.[9]

Busy as the growing Arkham House affairs kept him, Derleth still found time to become involved with three Wisconsin writing organizations during the sixties: the Wisconsin Fellowship of Poets, the Wisconsin Regional Writers' Association, and the Council for Wisconsin Writers.

At the beginning of the decade, he had launched a new publication, a poetry magazine which included many Wisconsin poets as well as those out of state. The first issue was favorably reviewed in the December 1950 issue of "Indian P. E. N." "Hawk & Whippoorwill" for Derleth was a labor of love. Funds for three years work on this project were made possible by the Wisconsin Arts' Council and the National Endowment for the Arts. The poets ranged from total unknowns to such acclaimed names as Susanne Gross, Edna Meudt, and Jesse Stuart, winner of an Academy of Poets $5,000 award. Subsequent issues were published whenever time and money permitted.

Although Derleth had the magazine printed in England, where costs were lower, he still lost $1,700 on the venture and had to discontinue publication in 1963. Yet, he never regretted the loss, feeling "Hawk & Whippoorwill" was both illuminating and entertaining and well worth the price. Through it, he gave encouragement and opportunity to many poets.

175

Derleth tended to follow his own discipline in writing poetry. He credited Professor Oscar Hodkins, one of his college instructors, with impressing upon him the conviction that, "If it doesn't communicate, it isn't art"; one of the reasons, perhaps, he could never appreciate some of the modern approaches to painting, music, or poetry. He scoffed at the idea of awards being given to someone like Aram Saroyan for a one word poem. To Derleth, this was pretentious, nonsensical, and demonstrated his belief that when creative artists adapt unrecognizable signals to their communication, they actually have nothing to say.

Derleth wrote poems fast, scribbling in his little notebooks as he hiked or rode, ideas of poems in an almost undecipherable script. These he expanded, worked and reworked at least a score of times before he would release them for publication. His notebooks numbered in the hundreds by the time he died.

His poetry appeared first in little non-paying reviews and soon attracted the notice of critics and other poets. Edgar Lee Masters thought his poetry better than his prose, as did August's life-long friend, Karl Ganzlin, who, along with many other people, believed that Derleth will be remembered for his poetry about everything else. The praise of his love poetry spurred August to put out a record of his reading some of the *PSYCHE* poems.

Stephen Vicent Benet wrote that he liked the Wisconsin poems in *HAWK ON THE WIND*, and it was among the top manuscripts submitted for the Yale series, but there was no room for more than one manuscript a year, and that one had already been chosen. William Rose Benet described August's poetry as something akin to "...improvisation on the piano...with flowing theme, molded rhythm, close observation and the pulse of life...." Another critic said he had "...clear eyes for the American scene and a quiet, limpid style that is neatly wedded to his observation. The complete absence of fuss, the sense of control, the deft, yet unspectacular handling of imagery – these qualities not common in modern poetry...." A Mexican fan liked Derleth's poems so well he attempted to translate them into Spanish for publication.

Jesse Stuart said of his *SELECTED POEMS*, 1944,

"...These poems have the music of the wind over Wisconsin and the beauty of an April plum petal...."

Many of August's poems appeared in such prestigious textbooks and anthologies as *PROSE AND POETRY OF TODAY, THE BEST POEMS OF 1943, AMERICA THROUGH LITERATURE, AN AMERICAN TREASURY, LITERATURE IN AMERICA* and others.

Derleth's association with the Wisconsin Fellowship of Poets resulted in the compilation of poems for two anthologies sponsored by the organization.

Also in 1963, Derleth had been asked to serve on the organizational committee for the proposed awards of the newly conceived Council for Wisconsin Writers, spearheaded by Colonel Herbert P. Schowalter and Al P. Nelson, a well known author and teacher of creative writing from Delafield, Wisconsin. These awards would be backed financially by the Johnson Wax Company of Racine, Wisconsin. Derleth agreed to serve, but made several immediate suggestions, aware, even then, "...that such a project could run into trouble without clear defined rules, ethical conduct, etc...." He suggested a top award be given for the "best work" – according to the judges' choice, based on literary excellence and published in that calendar year; that the work could be a short story, essay, article, book, poem, etc.; that all categories of writing be considered; and that the judges' panels should not be loaded with academic personnel. The reason for the suggestion to cut down academians was that Derleth felt most of the big grants like Guggenheim, Rockefeller, etc., go to people from the universities because they are judged by academic personnel. He believed his own Guggenheim grant had been awarded on the basis of the prestige of the people who recommended him. Those recommendations were the extra weight that swung the award in his favor, he felt. Derleth, himself, recommended several writers after his own prestige was established. Among them were Ray Bradbury, science fiction author, and Donald Emerson, a Milwaukee juvenile writer.[10]

SOURCE NOTES
CHAPTER NINETEEN

1 Biographer's interview with Karl Ganzlin, Riverside tavern, Sauk City, Wis.
2 A. D. to Inez Weaver, June 2, 1957; A. D. Journal, 15, 24, 25 April, 1957.
3 Biographer's observations and conversation with Derleth on her first visit to Place of Hawks; interview with Waldon Derleth, August's son, same day, August, 1968.
4 A. D. to Gerald A. Eyler, Feb. 28, 1969; Capital Times, Nov. 14, 1969.
5 Wisconsin Regional Writers' Association Treasurer to A. D., Nov. 8, 1963; A. D. to WRWA Treasurer, 11 November, 1963.
6 A. D. to editors of Harper's, March 30, 1962; "Morels and Ideas", Milwaukee Journal, May 8, 1960, pp. 3, 4; Pete Blankenheim tape, Derleth Room, Sauk City Library.
7 A. D. to J. J. Lankes, Nov. 27, 1954.
8 A. D. to Donald Wandrei, Jan. 16, 1960, April 21, 1965; James Drew to A. D., April 10, 1960; Dawson Taylor to A. D., March 4, 1960.
9 Derleth's favorite food information is culled from many of his books; his journal contains page after page of mention about the delicacies he most enjoyed, where to get them, etc.
10 James Boyer to A. D., May, Jan. 6, 1961; August Derleth, "On being an all-around bookman", (lecture notes); A. D. address to National Poetry delegates, 1971; Hawk and Whippoorwill Recalled, Vol. 1, #1, summer, 1973; biographer interview with Karl Ganzlin, Riverview Tavern, Sauk City, Wisconsin; Jessie Stuart to A. D., Sept. 24, 1935; Robert E. Esteran to A. D., Sept. 13, 1946; A. D. to Col. Herbert Schowalter, Feb. 16, 1966 and July 7, 1967; Ray Bradbury to A. D., Nov. 22, 1949.

Chapter Twenty

"...It is sad, but neither of us can go back to begin again...."[1]

In late 1962, Derleth had lunch with Marcia Masters. She had kept in touch over the years, often sending gifts for Rosella and the children, chocolates for August. It wasn't until their meeting in Chicago that the magic of their romance 20 years earlier, sparked back to life briefly. Marcia, less frightened than she had been then, took the initiative and wrote an impulsive love letter after their meeting. *"...I would like to go back to the beginning of time, to the beginning of all things, where you are. I would like to blend into those hills again. Just seeing you did that. I am filled with razzle-dazzle wonderful puddles-in-the-spring feelings, and through finding you, I have found myself...."*

And another: *"...It is so strange to be my age and to be assailed by giant emotions. I was wrapped in the arms of a giant once. Perhaps that makes me different forever. Many lesser things, the ridiculous vanity, superficiality, even fear, are burned away...."*[2]

This time it was August who took a second look, from the mountain of years and heartbreak and disillusionment since their romantic interlude: the financial burden of his parents and children, not to mention his publishing company and his saga. The second look colored his response to the "spontaneity and elan" of Marcia's letters.

"...I am serious about not marrying again," he wrote. *"I don't think anyone could induce me to go through it once more. What we have in common looks enchanting from a distance but on a day-to-day basis, the prosaic would wash it out. Perhaps in a very real sense, I am not suited for marriage; the very pressure and verities of my work make it mandatory for me to make swift decisions not subject to anyone's demur, and that you will agree, is not a satisfactory thing in a marriage...."*[3]

What he did not tell her but no doubt weighed heavily in his decision was that he had turned his back on all the lovely ladies

179

who pursued him, and chose, instead, to fall head over heels in love again with a young boy – someone he could train and mold into a suitable companion, who would not interfere with his freedom, or his work. When he saw the boy he called Mara, he knew instantly that this was an excellent prospect for his affections. What he didn't realize was that his relationship with Mara was the beginning of what would become the most satisfying alliance of his personal life; one that surpassed all past and even future amours; a mutual love that survived beyond their sexual relationship to the day he died, and even afterwards.[4]

So strong was August's feeling toward this young man, a correspondent living over a hundred miles away from Sauk City became aware of them simply by reading a letter from August. The name Mara was mentioned only casually. He's in love with her, the correspondent realized suddenly. Her fingers, holding the letter, felt a strange vibration. She met Mara a few years later, and had another shock. Mara was not a young lady, as she'd assumed. It wasn't until after August's death, a decade later, that she discovered her psychic flash had been 100% correct. August was a bisexual and was indeed in love with Mara.[5]

Mara, like most of Derleth's lovers, was the inspiration for several poems, among them "Morel Morning", which ends with the following revealing lines:

> *"...and remembering last year you were along*
> *on such a morning, picking morels too*
> *and the hour is suddenly charged with love*
> *as were I speaking to you of all that binds us*
> *   each to each*
> *through the morels thickly phallic in my hands...."*

Protective as he'd always been of his lovers, he seemed unable to resist confiding to some of his pen-pals. To one he wrote, in 1960, "...I have found myself embarked on a most absolutely incredible amour, which only demonstrates anew that even a man of 51 isn't safe from the insanity of love...."

Again, as with his other affairs, Derleth poured out his feelings in poetry. The book resulting was *THIS WOUND*, "Poems for Mara". The poems combine love and nature, but the titles – "Nightmare", "Drunk", "Anguish", depict anything but an emotion of gentle breezes and fragile flowers. They speak, rather, of love and loyalty, of envy and frustration, of adventure and lust, and always, of the mating hawk.[6]

His relationship with Mara caused him less stress, less guilt, and gave him more joy and contentment than any of his entanglements so far. His production increased considerably during the Mara years, as did his outside activities. He had no need or desire for anyone else; not until years later when Mara, like Marty, fell in love and married a girl more his age, was August alone again.

Marcia and August kept in touch, meeting for lunch when Derleth was in Chicago, corresponding and when Derleth initiated the establishment of a vanity publishing house to provide a New York outlet for his reprints, Marcia's poetry volume, *INTENT ON EARTH*, containing poems she had written about her father, Edgar Lee Masters, and a reprint of her work, *GRANDPARP FLEW IN*, were published under his vanity label.[7]

Derleth was not the only one who poured out his love and agony in poetry. Years earlier, when Marcia left Sauk City for California, she spent most of her time there thinking about August, agonizing between her love for him and her fear that marriage would not work for them.

After Derleth's death, the author – seen through Marcia's love and fascination, her fear and her pathos, her graphic poetry – emerges as both a phenomenon and a simple country boy. Her sonnet "Wind around the moon, IV", captures his magnetism, irresistible charm, humbleness, incredible ego, and his complexity.

August was:

"...a man of wind and sky and harvest gods...
Scribbling his wild flower verse..."

while they hiked and then

"...Lay down with love among the flowers and roots."

They swam in the dangerous currents of the Wisconsin. Marcia loved his home, the view, the birds. Yet she,

"...scorned his boorish manners,..." and confessed she
"...never could submit
To ultimatums or tyrannies

As if the manuscript had all been writ
For his tremendous stride and heart and wit."
"...I would not succumb
To his gigantic, frantic, fairy tales...
Picking up the crumbs
Flung...by his famous and wild-wooded thumbs..."
"...He was quite marvelous, a man of song,
And intellect as wide-branched as the woods.
He strode the hills, his massive feet in thongs,
His spirit rich with grassy solitude
And unencumbered by man's attitude;
A spirit free as prairie winds or birds.
I fled his golden wrath of hair, his moods
Our hilltop feast too soon effaced by words
That stung like bees upon a flower disturbed..."

Marcia compares their story to Arcady which conceals reality behind hills of "...lyric green...." Though she

"...found [her] love in that illusive sheen.
The music of the winds filled his breast;
He lived above the wordly, sly, and mean.
Yet wasps were in his tongue. Bewitched, oppressed,
I fled to seek the mountains of the West...."

Marcia found a place out of Tuscany. She called it a magical place and with some supernatural help, and a lot of soul-searching, decided against marrying Derleth. It wasn't an easy decision, her poem reveals, as:

"...Day after day I thought of him I left...
My tyrant genius, furious, bereft,
recounting all my faults and his own woes...
in silver prose and poetry too lovely to describe
In letters of five-thousand words arrived..."

Here, Marcia used "poetic license" to reveal that he did write the letters begging her to come back to him. Duplicates of the rough drafts were sent to her long after Derleth's death, and could have sparked her to add the last portion of the sonnet, "Shadow on the moon".

"...If you had been a simple singing man...."
"...But hawks as well as buttercups bred you
If I a poet's child, had not known grief,

182

Not had a cradle tipped by storms that knew
No end – I should have loved your country eaves,
And spent my life beneath your golden leaves."
She then admits:
"In autumn...
I would forget the battle of our wills
If you were here, my sun-crowned, storm-tongued friend.
But you are dead. It is too late to mend
My foolish ways or yours..."[8]

SOURCE NOTES
CHAPTER TWENTY

[1] A. D. to Marcia Masters Schmidt, Oct. 28, 1963.

[2] Marcia Masters Schmidt to A. D., no date.

[3] Note 1, Op cit.

[4] A. D. Journal, 2, 6, & 8 Jan., 1954.

[5] A. D. to biographer, November, 1963; interview with Edna Meudt, July, 1971.

[6] August Derleth, This Wound, Poems for Mara, (Iowa City, 1969).

[7] A. D. to Inez Weaver, Sept. 20 and 27, Oct. 1, 2, 6, Dec. 14, 1968, Jan. 3., 1969; to Sonia Green, Sept. 24, Oct. 3, 7, 14, 24, 30, 1968.

[8] Marcia Lee Masters, Wind around the moon, Part IV, Flight to a Haunted Palace, and Shadow on the moon.

Chapter Twenty-One

"...I'd sooner see a man killed than a deer, providing he is one of that so-called 'sporting kind' who kill for pleasure, not for meat..."[1]

Another writing venture was initiated when Derleth took a trip to attend a State Historical Society banquet held at the Northernaire, a plush resort located in Three Lakes, Wisconsin, June, 1963. His introduction to Carl Marty's fabulous home for wild animals at the wilderness resort struck an immediate response, for August had been a lover of nature all his life.

During the banquet, August and Carl left the other diners to have a quiet conversation at the bar. From their exchange, a book about Marty's three dogs was born. Rusty and Ginger, cocker spaniels, and Bernese, a St. Bernard, had helped Carl gather and nurse injured and stray animals and restore them to their natural habitat. The resort owner's love for wild animals and the work he was doing through the Villas-Oneida Wilderness Society had reached far beyond the borders of his own county and state. Carl Marty had even been approached by Walt Disney Productions about the possibility of using some of his wild creatures in a movie. Carl refused Disney's offer because his main concern was for the well-being of the animals and not for their exploitation.[2]

Carl Marty believed Derleth's knowledge of nature and wildlife was second to none. Sauk City, itself, appears more nature-minded than most towns. A sign on the cemetery gate on Lueder's Road across from the Place of Hawks forbids the use of artificial flowers on graves during the flower-bearing months from spring to fall. There was no spraying of poisonous chemicals allowed in Sauk City. A sign at the foot of Winnie Street near the river, requests visitors to stay in their cars because this is an eagle-feeding area.[3]

August mourned the passing of a familiar tree almost as much as the passing of an ancestor. At one point, Standard Oil

Company announced their intention of destroying an eighty-year-old sturdy elm and a giant maple tree, both standing on the corner of Main Street across the bridge from Sauk City. To this, August issued a flyer "On Trees", advising the oil company that it would be easier for the city to get along without the Standard Oil Company than to sacrifice the trees. In response, the trees were spared.

He plagued Governor Gaylord Nelson about the indiscriminate cutting down of trees on the highways around Sac Prairie, hinting that the highway personnel who hated the trees might become impotent. (Freud wrote that trees are phallic symbols, signs of sexual prowess.)[4]

August displayed a DDT sticker on his car and was quick to advise Senator William Proxmire of the plan of Swift & Company to produce a deadly insecticide named Parathion and to protest against it.

Derleth's reputation for being an authority on nature had spread all over the country. It was routine for him to get a call or letter from some well-known naturalist asking for ways to identify a leaf, bird, fungus growth, or the location of species such as the cardinal flower. Allen DeVoe, a prominent naturalist and author of several nature books appealed to August for information about crows to confirm facts gathered elsewhere as he completed an article for *Reader's Digest*. DeVoe, in a review of *VILLAGE DAYBOOK*, said of Derleth, "...He is so vividly alive and sensitive – so sharply aware of the wonderfulness of things, so alertly mindful of...the glory of God...that he injects his every page with this sense of wonder and delighted relish...."

August was not at all reticent about correcting other naturalists. He pointed out errors in *Nature Magazine* and once refuted one man's writing in *ENCYCLOPEDIA BRITANNICA* concerning 125 varieties of the genus Penstemons. He created an uncomfortable relationship between himself and the Madison Ornithological Society when he stood firm about his sighting of a Goshawk on two consecutive days early in February which was unusual, and the members of the society refused to believe him. He corrected Howard Mead, publisher of *WISCONSIN TALES AND TRAILS* on mistakes about morels, which Howard had resourced from the Wisconsin Conservation

Department and the Milwaukee Public Museum.

Derleth's inclination to correct people permeated to all areas of his life. He disagreed with the *Saturday Review* editors who published John Ciardi's article using the word "presently" to mean "now" or "at present". Derleth even said *WEBSTER'S DICTIONARY* was wrong on that usage, one that he maintained had been obsolete for centuries. He also criticized the editors of *TIME MAGAZINE* for calling Coulton Waugh's book, *THE COMICS*, a "...'notable, fact-finding job'....", pointing out the many omissions, incomplete history and partial facts.[5]

It was understandable why Derleth would appreciate Carl Marty who, over the years, had rescued hundreds of wild animals. Fox, deer, possum, beaver, raccoon, wolf, porcupine, otter, skunk, coyote and even bear were saved from hunters' bullets.

The book, *FOREST ORPHANS*, came from this relationship in 1964, and *MR. CONSERVATION*, seven years later. Marty purchased thousands of copies of the books to sell at Northernaire and throughout the area. The proceeds were used for the welfare of the "misunderstood wildlife" of the northwoods.

Derleth's association with Carl Marty led to his acceptance of a teaching position at the Rhinelander School of Arts in 1965. Mr. Marty had generously offered Derleth and his family use of a villa, free of charge. August would need to work with Carl on the second book. The children would enjoy the wildlife, the swimming, the horseback riding, tramping through the woods, and it would give their grandparents back home a rest. In addition, August could investigate possibilities for several juveniles of the "home-place" variety, set in Rhinelander, Three Lakes and Eagle River.

One of the first tasks Derleth undertook after arriving with Rikki and the children at the villa, was to autograph 400 copies of *FOREST ORPHANS*. Walden went fishing. Later, they all watched a little fawn come from the woods to be fed from a baby bottle by Carl Marty.

With all his lecturing, teaching experience and his own book on *WRITING FICTION* (published 18 years before) for reference, Derleth's class was no problem. Commuting seventy miles round trip daily was. Unsettling also was the need to dash home on the weekend to open as many as 200 letters, pack and send the books ordered (which he did with the help of Rikki and both children) and then motor back to Rhinelander. Reading stacks of students' manuscripts, many book-length, was also a problem. Derleth's critiques were thorough, often ruthless, always emphatic. Yet, his work with the writers paid off. Many found publishers after taking his class. Among them were Frances May, Ruth Pockman, Topsy Gregory, Kenneth Kingery, and Sara Lindsay Rath. Though often cruelly sharp, Derleth also displayed a patience and kindness over the years. He would rather experience pain, than cause it. This sensitivity under his bluster and braggadocio was not always appreciated.[6]

Though it had been Rosella's ill health that prompted him to turn down the teaching position three years before, it was William Derleth who died first. He'd been having spells of dizziness and mental disorientation, off and on for over a year. In September, 1965, he suffered a pulmonary occlusion attack and died shortly after.[7]

When his brother-in-law, Colonel Oliver Andersen, left the military service in January, 1966, and visited the Place of Hawks with Hildred and their son, Lari, Derleth started to think about taking another trip to California. Arkham House sales were averaging 1,000 books a month since 1964; it was a good time to take a vacation.

In June, he left for the West Coast with Rikki and the children. They went sight-seeing, enjoyed Disneyland, visited Mark Schorer briefly, and were entertained at the home of Frederick Shroyer, the man responsible for inviting Derleth to the Pacific Coast Writer's Conference in 1953. While there, one of the most gratifying honors was bestowed on August. Through the efforts of Luther Norris (a Hollywood hotel operator and author of several books on Alaska) an organization was formed called the Praed St. Irregulars. It was for pastiche creators, as Derleth's Solar Pons was a pastiche creation of Sir Arthur Conan Doyle's Sherlock Holmes mysteries. The Praed St. Irregulars were "...dedicated to the proposition that (some) detectives are unequal(ed) and that the immortal and living Solar Pons shall assume pedestaled stature beside his great master, Sherlock Holmes...." Each member was given a name. Derleth was titled

"The Agent" because he was the source of the adventures. "The Pontine Dossier" was the official publication. By 1969, there were 600 members. Fritz Leiber, Professor Shroyer, Forrest J. Ackerman, Ellery Queen, Vincent Starret, A.E. Van Vogt, Ray Bradbury, Robert Block, Boris Karloff, Basil Rathbone, and many other mystery buffs became members at one time or another. There were scions of the Praed St. Irregulars in England, Singapore, and on the continent.[8]

Another honor August received was a framed cross – The Mrs. Ann Radcliffe Literature Award "...to Wisconsin's most distinguished author for his own work, for his efforts in publishing the work of H.P. Lovecraft, the 10th Century Poe...." presented at the annual Count Dracula Society Awards Dinner in California after he had returned to Wisconsin. It was accepted for Derleth by Robert Block.[9]

Besides his *BEAST IN HOLGER'S WOODS*, the Rhinelander set juvenile, Derleth was working on a Wisconsin Regional Writer's anthology, *WISCONSIN HARVEST*, a rewrite of a junior profile of Wisconsin, and the last third of *RETURN TO WALDEN WEST*.[10]

Derleth utilized the Hodag, a legendary hoax created for the citizens of the Rhinelander area years earlier by Eugene Shepherd. Shepherd had manufactured a reptilian creature with horns down its back to fool and frighten the natives. August asked Dorothy Guilday, a junior high teacher and president of the Wisconsin Regional Writers Association, to check the juvenile book for correct names of streets, locations of buildings, etc. It was Dorothy who was a liaison for the Rhinelander School of Arts, helping Robert Gard coordinate it, gaining support of the Rhinelander University Women and Cedric Vig, Superintendent of Schools, arranging the use of the junior high for the classes, and greasing the operational wheels of the workshop.

August's relationship with her is significant in that, it was her resemblance to Sandra that drew Derleth's attention; it was her intelligence, her educational background, and her interest in and knowledge of literature that helped cement their friendship. Paradoxically, Dorothy was the type of woman Derleth had always shied away from, yet the kind who best matched his social, educational and interest levels.

189

When Derleth needed a young Indian girl to step into the scene and steal the credit for catching the villains and solving the puzzle of the beast, he used a young Dorothy Guilday. He even dressed "Dody", the character, in a plaid shirt and blue jeans, one of the outfits Dorothy wore at the workshop that season.[11]

One of the more pleasant aspects of teaching at Rhinelander was the opportunity to meet other established authors: Studs Terkel, a Chicago radio personality and author of WORKING, a best seller; TV Olsen, a prolific Rhinelander native with many westerns, two movies, historical fiction and nonfiction to his credit; Mark Connelly, legendary playwright; Tere Rios Versace, fiction writer, whose FIFTEENTH PELICAN was the basis for the "Flying Nun" TV series; Archibald McLeish, poet, world-famous unofficial U. S. Diplomat, friend of Eleanor and Franklin D. Roosevelt, author of many travel articles and foreign food critiques; Alvira Vicsey, talented ballerina; and many other successful literary and artistic personages.[12]

SOURCE NOTES
CHAPTER TWENTY-ONE

[1] A. D. to Inez Weaver, Nov. 12, 1959.

[2] Carl Marty to A. D.; Summer, 1961.

[3] A. D. to Carl Marty, no date.

[4] A. D. to Ian Law, Feb. 19, 1960; Derleth "On Trees", flyer, SWHS archives, Madison, Wis.; A. D. to Governor Gaylord Nelson, Feb. 19, Feb. 17 & 19, Mar. 11, 1960; from the governor, Mar. 9, 1960.

[5] A. D. to Harpers' editors, Mar. 30, 1962; from Alan Devoe, Jan. 18, 1943; DeVoe review of *Village Daybook* SWHS archives; A. D. to "Saturday Review" editors, Sept. 1962; to "Madison Capital Times" editors, Nov. 26, 1947.

[6] Biographer's experience in classes at Rhinelander and in writing daily articles about the School of Arts for the Rhinelander daily newspaper.

[7] A. D. to Inez Weaver, July 23, 1967.

[8] Kay Price, "Praed St. Irregulars Owe Their Identity To Derleth's mystery tales". Madison Times greensheet, Thursday, Apr. 24, 1969.

[9] Scroll in the SWHS archives.

[10] Note 7, Nov. 18, 1968, July 23, 1967.

[11] August Derleth conversation with biographer re: his juvenile *THE BEAST IN HOLGER'S WOODS.*

[12] Biographer's opinion.

Chapter Twenty-Two

"...Your material comes from the stuff that will always be around...love, life on the village paths, under the trees, in the season...and people, people, people...."[1]

In late November, 1967, after returning to the Place of Hawks from Rhinelander, Derleth had tired spells and then suffered a slight coronary attack. He went into the hospital a few days later, and by December 17th, had lost 20 pounds, had contracted a virus infection with a fever, and felt very weak. It wasn't till after Christmas that he left the hospital.

August's vast energies were being depleted and six months after his hospitalization, he was still going to bed tired, sleeping badly, and waking up tired. Nevertheless, his output was tremendous. Arkham House sold 15,000 books in 1967.[2]

In 1967, the guest writer-in-residence at the Rhinelander School of Arts was Jesse Stuart. Derleth invited a small group to a dinner party at the Claridge Inn to welcome Jesse, whom he had not seen for 23 years, though they corresponded regularly. The two sat at the opposite ends of the table and shouted compliments, boasts, bits of information about their current projects, and no one else could break into the conversation.

During the course of the next two weeks, the authors had an opportunity to really enjoy their solid friendship which had grown through letters, shared readings, and appreciation of each other's work. Of the two, Jesse seemed more impressed by Derleth, although the Wisconsin writer had a profound respect for the Kentucky one, both as poet and regionalist. August had been working on one of the poems on Thoreau during a writing session and approached Jesse with the finished piece, waiting with obvious trepidation as he read it.

"What do you think?" Derleth asked, the moment Jesse put the pages down.

"Perfect," Jesse answered.

"Are you sure? You really think so?" Derleth persisted.

"Absolutely perfect," Jesse repeated.

Derleth pointed out a line here, there, trying to break Jesse down, but Jesse remained firm.

Derleth relaxed, finally, his whole face glowing with pleasure and satisfaction.

He could hardly have expected harsh disapproval from the man whose letters over the years abounded with glowing tributes:

"...When writers are counted in the future, I'm sure you will be in there, standing up...you're an American DeFoe...."

"...Your material comes from the stuff that will always be around...love, life on the village paths, under the trees, in the season...and people, people, people taken as they are in your day and time...The sheer weight and variety of what you have done...will grow with the years. It will build up. My friend, Wisconsin and the Midwest has only one August. The U. S. has only one August, unique and alone...."

Derleth had been nominated, two years earlier, for an honorary degree from the University of Wisconsin. He had little hope of getting it with a majority of 28 votes needed. As anticipated, the nomination did not pass. This news got Jesse all worked up. He had received nine such degrees from Kentucky Universities and colleges.

The two authors had much in common, love of their home area, love of poetry, love of nature, love of simple pleasures. They also shared a love of eating. Both, due to recent illnesses, were on diets under doctor's orders.

Virginia Karow, one of Rhinelander's superb cooks, famed for her chicken with Indian wild rice, prepared a feast for her two creative writing instructors. Derleth had to down pills all afternoon to settle his stomach after that meal. Virginia didn't get away with just taking pills to cure her stomach ache. She landed in the hospital for a gall bladder operation. The first thing she saw when she awoke from the anesthetic, was a huge bouquet of yellow roses sent by August and Jesse.

August was in the habit of sending flowers for almost any reason. To one of his amours he sent a single rose every day. To several friends, like Effie Bachhuber and Erna Johnson, he sent three bouquets for their birthdays and signed the cards with affectionate messages from three different men.

Eating too much had always been a problem with Derleth. Even as he worked, he was in the habit of nibbling on candy, nuts, popcorn, etc. His eating habits were not the daintiest, either. Eunice McClosky Laconske wrote a biographical sketch of him, accusing him of picking up bacon with his bare hands along with a long line of anecdotes about Derleth's lack of table manners. A business colleague of August's often relates the story of having dinner with Derleth when after he finished he took out his teeth, washed them in a water glass, wiped them and wrapped them in a handkerchief and put them in his pocket.

Derleth's own teeth had given him trouble for years and his false teeth never did get comfortable enough for him to wear them all the time. That may have been why he "wolfed" down his food. Even Rosella Derleth admitted she could never break August of some of his bad eating habits, like dipping his little finger into hot tea, coffee, or soup, to test the temperature.

As far as Derleth's manners in other respects, they were as paradoxical and controversial as the man himself. He cared nothing for what people thought of his actions. He simply did pretty much as he pleased. Yet he was inordinately sensitive to the opinions of some like Lovecraft, Stuart, and even strangers he admired.

He admitted to being vindictive, vituperative, downright vicious, at times. He could, on the other hand, be kind, thoughtful, charming and courteous in situations where a lot of people would not have bothered – as with the very old, and the very odd people in Sac Prairie. He scorned the country club crowd, needled people in his life like Sandra's doctor's wife, Esther Trautman, by calling her Mrs. Vanderbilt; and to anyone who stepped on his toes or got in his way, he could be publicly contemptuous and even cruel, making many enemies in the process. He was a man with fine, cosmopolitan, excellent tastes in art, literature, and music, yet at the same time, a rough product of his blacksmith and saloon operating ancestors.[3]

In 1964, Derleth was asked to be one of the judges for the first Council for Wisconsin Writers' awards. The next year he entered two books himself, *WISCONSIN COUNTRY* and *COUNTRY PLACES*. A junior historical novel, *FEATHER IN THE WIND*, by Beverly Butler, was chosen for the top award.

Derleth felt that if one of his books had not won, then Susanne Gross's *TERN'S BONES* (poetry) should have. He was very bitter. He admired Beverly Butler as a person and for her successes in juvenile writing, but he felt this book simply wasn't of the same quality as his entries.

Leslie Cross, book editor for the *MILWAUKEE JOURNAL*, had been so positive that Derleth would win the Council's 1965 award for best book, he had asked August to send him a copy of the acceptance speech in advance.

"...The judges guiltily tried to throw me a sop in the shape of a plaque for my work as a whole. I can't eat plaques and this...(one) still has never materialized...," said Derleth two years later.

His contempt for the plaque he didn't get made him less than receptive to a letter from a member of the Board of Directors of the Wisconsin Regional Writers' Association, asking him to send a book list to the president of the organization. The WRWA board wanted to sponsor Derleth for a newly established Governor's Award. When Derleth received this new award, another plaque, it was like rubbing salt in a wound. He thought the thing was hideous. At the age of thirty, he might have valued it. At 57, it meant very little. Nevertheless, he found a spot for it atop the fireplace, along with his collection of grotesques – little carved monsters created out of the fertile imagination of one of Arkham House's weird tale authors, Clark Ashton Smith. The award had come too late to mean anything, or to do him any good. Significantly, it was a mere token carrying with it no monetary stipend. August felt that most people judged the honor of awards by the accompanying monetary prize.

Of the numerous awards presented to August while he lived, it would be the Governor's Award and The Guggenheim that were chosen by the Sauk City Chamber of Commerce for mention on a huge memorial plaque erected in Derleth's honor after he died.[4]

Derleth had sixteen of his own books published from 1964 through 1967. Seabury Publications had requested he join their book list, upsetting Duell. The $1,000 advance Seabury offered on each completed manuscript weighted the scales in their favor.

Despite all the pluses, Derleth's blood pressure shot up to 190/120, his highest in a decade. The time he needed to answer his staggering volume of business and personal mail and a bit of softening of his crusading fervor due to age, caused his vitriolic letters-to-the-editors and his flyers to decrease in number. Still he managed on occasion to get very upset and say so in no uncertain terms. In 1966, for example, he wrote to the editors of *NEW REPUBLIC*, published in Washington D.C., to set them straight on the reason Joe McCarthy had beaten Bob LaFollette, Jr., in the election for Congress. *NEW REPUBLIC* claimed McCarthy's win was accomplished through the help of a bloc of Milwaukee Communists' votes. A lie, Derleth refuted, and set about to correct the misconception. According to him, all of Wisconsin didn't have enough Communists to influence any election. McCarthy had won because of the Democrats who crossed over with their votes in the primary, thinking their candidate could defeat McCarthy whereas LaFollete might not be able to do so. The crossover boomeranged, helping to elect McCarthy rather than defeat him.

Derleth's political opinions were still as strong as ever, and he still minced no words, voicing them. Long before Watergate, Derleth warned against Richard Nixon. He felt Nixon was untrustworthy and an opportunist. He accused Nixon of using slander, dirty innuendo, and outright smears in the 1952 and 1956 campaigns. He felt Helen Gahagen Douglas was one of the best representatives, and Nixon had accused her of Communist leanings, thus defeating her bid in the Senatorial race. The author, on the other hand, greatly admired Franklin D. Roosevelt.

August protested the draft. He would never vote for a military man like Truman, Stassen, Taft, or Mac Arthur, he said. One year, he voted for Norman Thomas, socialist, in protest.

As unimpressed as he was with Truman at first, he later changed his mind about Truman's leadership and praised it in a review of Melvin laird's *A HOUSE DIVIDED*, in 1963.[5]

Derleth disagreed again with the Council for Wisconsin Writers' decision for their best book award, 1966, which went to what he considered a very competent historical biography. He felt, however, that two excellent and more creative meritorious works were passed over. They were Bently's novel, *THE COMPETITORS*, and Mme Fredges *THERE WE WERE AGAIN*, a memoir. The chairman of that judging committee was definitely a historian.

In 1968, Derleth knew, even before the annual award dinner, that his entry – *COLLECTED POEMS: 1937-1967* had minimal chance of being named best book. In the summer of 1967, a council board member had told August that there was a definite move on to give the award to an author of a very "good dog story".

In response to a letter from the WRWA treasurer expressing dissatisfaction with the quality of judges being selected to judge works for the award, Derleth wrote:

"...Your letter arrived here with singular appropriateness,....I have just finished composing my letter of withdrawal from the Council for Wisconsin Writers, insisting my name be removed from all letterheads, although I do not intend to mail this letter until the 24th and then only if my *COLLECTED POEMS: 1937-1967* is not awarded top place...."

Derleth's poetry had elicited praise from many poets all over the country. Robert Clauber, editor of the Beloit Poetry Journal in his *MILWAUKEE JOURNAL* review, had praised his book. Only two years earlier, Derleth had received the Midland Authors' Kenneth Montgomery Award for "...continuing distinction in poetry..."

Ten years earlier, The Milwaukee Press Club had made Derleth a "Knight of the Golden Quill", an honor bestowed upon Wisconsin men who had distinguished themselves as writers, so he wasn't entirely without recognition in his own state. That his reputation was even firmer overseas is evident for he was selected, a few years earlier, as a life fellow of the International Institute of Arts and Letters in Switzerland. Early in 1965, Derleth made Cleveland Amory's "First of the Month" column in the *SATURDAY REVIEW*. Amory called Derleth "...the country's number one writer...." These are a small sample of the many recognitions given him.

Derleth, however, desperately wanted acclaim from his home territory. The money was important to him, but more important the principle involved. Derleth felt the odds were stacked against him, and that a definite conflict of interest was present. Both the author of the dog story and chairman of the judges worked on the same newspaper. They were also good friends. Derleth distrusted a chairman who had blatantly demonstrated his ignorance by telling the other judges he didn't care for poetry and had not seen any that appealed to him since reading the verses in *ALICE IN WONDERLAND*. Derleth said there had been no indication that any of the award judges but one, Edna Meudt, had even read his collection. Edna told August she had been advised outright that the committee shouldn't consider his poetry collection for top place because it was a collection, because Derleth was so altruistic that he would rather give the award to someone else, that he really didn't need it. August accused the Council of being "...Milwaukee oriented..." since, in the prior years, the awards had been given primarily to Milwaukee writers. He wrote to Colonel Schowalter, co-founder of the Council, that most of the judges for this year's award, except Edna Meudt, were "...utterly without the authority or the wisdom to pass judgment on books...."

When the prizes were announced at the Council dinner later that month, August's entry received the $250.00 poetry award, but the $1,000 "best book" award went to the author of the dog story. Derleth was noticeably upset. A full table of about 12 people, among them Edna Meudt who headed the committee of judges for the poetry award, kept their seats as others rose in a standing ovation for the best book winner.

True to his intent, Derleth resigned from the Council charging that it had failed to achieve its stated goals and obligations fifty percent of the time. As he predicted, his reaction was labeled "sour grapes".[6]

Three years later, in an address before the delegates to the annual convention of the National Federation of State Poetry Societies, where he was named "Honorary Chancellor" of the organization, he revealed the wistful hope he entertained that,

"...Perhaps, someday, someone, will assess my life in poetry and conclude that it had left a visible, infinitesimal mark on the history of poetry in America and in the mid-century...."[7]

Many prominent literary critics and successful authors

already were predicting Derleth's poetry would withstand the test of time. Universal and public acknowledgment will come later, after he is officially declared the only classic writer to emerge out of the 20th century.[8]

SOURCE NOTES
CHAPTER TWENTY-TWO

1 Jesse Stuart to A. D., Feb. 6, 1969.
2 A. D. to Jessie Stuart, 1969.
3 Dorothy Guilday, interviewed by biographer; re: event; Biographer's eye witness of event; Note 1, op. cit.; interview with Virginia Karow; Derleth's vanity press publisher to biographer; Eunice McClonsky's unpublished article on Derleth; Rose Derleth interview by biographer (see Chapter 1 source notes).
4 Leslie Cross letter to A. D., June 13, 1966; A. D. letter to Herbert Schowalter, July 9, 1969; to Inez Weaver, Jan. 25, 1966; WRWA board member to A. D.; A. D. to WRWA board member; biographer's visual research.
5 SWHS Museum archives, list of published Derleth books; A. D. Journal; A. D. to Inez Weaver; A. D. to Editors of New Republic, Washington, D. C., 1966; August Derleth, "Book of the Times", Madison Capital Times, 1963.
6 A. D. to Colonel Schowalter, biographer's visual research; A. D. to Professor Robert E. Gard, March 26, 1968; to Schowalter, March 27, 1968; "Derleth quits writing group, criticizes judging", Milwaukee Journal, Mar. 25, 1968; Col. Schowalter to A. D., March 21, 1968; Leslie Cross to A. D., March 27, 1968.
7 Derleth address to National Federation of State Poetry Societies, SWHS Museum archives, (miscellaneous papers), Madison, Wisconsin, 1949.
8 Biographer's prediction.

Missing Journal dates and dates of letters to and from August Derleth resulted from biographer's incomplete notes, and a loss of actual copies of those items, journal entries and letters, beyond her control. When her lawyers accidentally discovered that the failure of Derleth's lawyer to renew copyrights on all of Augie's works, as requested by the U. S. Copyright offices, and informed April and Walden Derleth of the fact, the children not only moved quickly to remedy the mistake, they froze the Derleth papers in the Wisconsin State Historical Society's

Museum archives to prevent anyone access to them until the year 2020. Only then will it be possible to verify some of the material in Chapter 22, and elsewhere throughout the book.

Chapter Twenty-Three

"...I thought I had done...with all the fantasies and dreams of love....[1]

By 1968, Derleth was firmly entrenched as writer-in-residence at Rhinelander School of Arts. People were coming from all over the states to study under him and many other fine artists at the workshop.

One new student that summer, was an incredibly lovely, beautifully dressed, young, married woman of about 25, who was in no time attracting the attention of many male students as well as staff members. She managed deftly to turn her admirers away. She devoted most of her time catering to the older members, both teachers and staff. She'd carry refreshments to them and fetch things they needed, also treating them when there was a cash bar. She did not, however, seem especially enthusiastic about getting much knowledge about the art and craft of writing. Neither did she talk about her own writing, as most of the other students did.

By the end of the first week, she was still a mystery. Why was she there? It wasn't until a few nights before the end of the two-week session that her purpose was made very clear, and it had nothing to do with writing.

A local lumber baron and his wife, Iris Ford, were having a party at their luxurious home for the School of Arts staff. When August arrived, he headed straight for the long table piled with an incredible array of gourmet food. With his usual ravenous appetite for rich and fattening food, he lopped off a large slice of a giant-sized Roquefort cheese. By the time he reached the end of the table, he had enough food for three or four people piled on his plate in spite of the fact that he had been eating generous samples of the delicacies as he went along.

No one interrupted Derleth as he wolfed down every crumb and headed for a fountain of champagne across the room. It wasn't the champagne that had caught his eye. It was the luscious looking desserts arranged on the table around the base of the fountain. Again, he filled a plate, and was half-way through a piece of dark chocolate layer cake, when who should appear out of the shadows of a far corner but the mystery lady. She sailed past the long table and headed straight for August. Whatever she said must have been a mouthful. Food forgotten, August stood mesmerized for a moment, then quickly abandoned the plate of goodies to follow her into a secluded alcove off the room. There they stayed for the remainder of the evening, oblivious of everyone but each other. So engrossed was Derleth, under such a strong spell, he even allowed the young lady to feed him champagne out of her glass.[2]

That August now knew why she was attending the school was written all over his face as he padded in her wake like a love-sick puppy, almost drooling with anticipation when they left Rhinelander together a few days later.

Rosella Derleth had gone out to California to visit Hildred and would not be back until September 27th. April and Walden were in school all day. Thus there was ample opportunity for Caitlin, as Augie called her, to spend hours in Derleth's arms, locked in his studio several times a week. August let nothing and no one interfere with their loving. When they were apart, they talked for hours on the phone.

August spent sleepless nights, paced the floor for hours during the day, thinking about Caitlin, wondering how long this fire that burned so fiercely could last. Obsessed with her, haunted by her, driven by his desire for her, he wrote poems to her, and letters he never meant to send.

She brought a record with her one afternoon, asking that he listen to the lyric in "My Lord and Master". Shaken by an "...incredible tide of passion and protectiveness after two hours of loving," he played the record. "My Lord and Master" was a frank and warming love letter from her. He could not help reflecting that when she was there with him, he was scarcely his own master.

The flames of passion and obsession consuming both of them burned more brightly every day. August chafed at not being able to have her all the time, yet his daily journal entries contained numerous references to some things in their relationship that disturbed him. He was complete putty in her hands.

He lost his head buying things for her. His "powers of concentration" were "made ragged" by "the constant intrusion of her" into his thought. He was "...clearly out of control for the first time in his life...." When she criticized one of his poems saying she had "...curious objections..." to his writing about "...her naked loveliness..." he realized her manner indicated "...a subtle drift toward emasculation...."

He thought perhaps Caitlin, herself, might not be conscious of it. The slow process of emasculation continued, as was noticeable both in her phone conversations, and in their passionate coupling. Nevertheless, Derleth "...after a week's agonizing appraisal...," surprised Caitlin by telling her he would finance the establishment of a six weeks residence in Las Vegas for her to seek a divorce. If at the end of that period, she decided to marry him, he would fly out and marry her there, and they would honeymoon in England.

Caitlin was speechless. Three days later, they celebrated a month's anniversary of the first time August kissed her. The following day, Caitlin announced they would be married in a year. August was "...shaken...." He felt like "...a little boy who has been reaching for the moon for years and has suddenly been told he would get it, beginning to wonder whether he could adequately take care of it...."

One day later, she veered away from the decision that they would be married in a year. And the day following, she broke a promise to visit him. He was convinced that "...it was a ploy in her emasculating game...." If she continued in this vein, he decided, he would end their affair promptly, feeling it was "...far better a clear severing right away instead of a protracted agony later...."

Caitlin drove August to the airport in Chicago on the 27th of September to pick up Rosella. At home, August told his mother that he was considering marriage if Caitlin went to Las Vegas for a divorce. He tempered the shocking news by telling Rosella he strongly doubted that Caitlin would seek a divorce. Rosella had been complaining about the age gap between them (35 years), a fact of which August was only too painfully aware.

Loss of sleep, hours on the telephone, hours in his bed with Caitlin, hours more of mental and emotional turmoil over his situation, interfered with his many commitments.

His daily journal entries were more about Caitlin, and what he was going through, than about the stars, flora, fauna of previous days. August viewed their situation as an observer while still involved in the physical, mental and emotional action, probing the causes, the effects, the meaning of this, "...mad possession...."

On one occasion, after long thought about their "...admirable mutual appeal..." on a major plane between his masculinity and her femininity, on a secondary plane between her lesser steak of masculinity and his pronounced femininity, they agreed they were astonishingly complementary. Few men and women, for lack of some components in their nature different than what he and Caitlin shared, were able to have such a rich relationship.

On one of his hikes, he was so immersed in his thoughts about Caitlin, he walked right up the railroad bridge tracks without being aware of a train coming. Had the engineer not blown his whistle, Derleth might have walked right into it.

As their affair intensified, other situations arose between them that he recognized as obstacles against their achieving a happy-ever-after future together. August was shocked and disturbed on several occasions by Caitlin's fierce assertiveness and jealous rages. One occurred after she overheard him calling his ex-wife Sandy "honey" over the phone; another over the visit of a neophyte poet and student, Sara Rath. Sara was a young, devoted, attractive, rather naive fan of his. Caitlin was "at him" for days about the visit.[3] Years later after Derleth's death Sara told her story to a class of young students and reporters of her walk in the woods with August. She was relaxing on a blanket when he proceeded to discard all his clothes except his socks and to dance under the trees. She said she was shocked and embarrassed and pretended to be asleep. Perhaps August was trying to demonstrate in his own individual fashion, that a poet, especially, must discard facades, coverups, non-essentials, and deal with the core, the naked realities of life.

Sara's poetry revealed her talent, but although she was married, and the mother of two children, she seemed but a child, herself. Possibly the incident, occurring at a time when he was pouring all his emotional and physical energy into his affair with Caitlin, may have had nothing to do with sex as far as Sara was concerned. Or would it? Given the contrasts and contradictions already apparent in Derleth, there could be many more yet undiscovered.

If trying to create a romantic mood, it seems the sight of a 59-year-old, aging, overweight, leprechaun prancing about in nothing but his socks, would be more apt to have tickled Sara's funnybone than plucked at her heartstrings.[4]

August shared the progress of his affair with Mara. Although now Mara was living in a different city, they were in touch, still sharing their triumphs, their problems, still very close. In one journal entry, August wrote that as with Caitlin, he knew he would never find anyone equal to Mara. "...These two together just precisely satisfy my needs on every plane...." There is no indication that Caitlin knew about Augie's relationship with Mara, or that her lover was bisexual. It is doubtful August continued his physical relationship with Mara during his involvement with Caitlin, or after Mara married. There are, however, many indications that Mara and August were very close emotionally, right up to the day of Derleth's death. Given Caitlin's unreasonable jealousy, it seems doubtful she would have allowed such a liaison, were she aware of it. Mara, on the other hand, fully approved of their affair, even cheered them on.

By November, another disturbing "portent" popped up; Caitlin's obsession with her plans to remodel his house, once they married. He had, during their first weeks in Rhinelander, been very aware of Caitlin's wardrobe, and realized what an expensive proposition just keeping her supplied in dresses would be. The past months since her seduction of him, he had gone overboard for her with an extravagance entirely alien to a man who had for years been forced to squeeze every penny to finance his publishing houses and pay off his house loan. Even given the fact that his income was up and he'd been able to save $6,000 of it, his sudden extravagance seemed way out of character. Now here she was talking about thousands of dollars worth of changes. She was planning an addition to a room for herself with a bathroom containing a sunken bathtub. A complete renovation of the parlor furnishings downstairs was next on her list.

207

Her expectations and plans set off alarms in Derleth alerting him to the impossibility of a happy marriage.

These portents, although disturbing, were not the basic reason for his quandary. Here he was, about to break up a family again, something he'd vowed he would never do. He was torn apart and utterly incapable of anything other than battling this tortuous conflict that "...left him suspended in a void somewhere between his principles and his desires...after but three months of intimacy he already felt that he could not contemplate life without her...."

August's misery in the coming months intensified as Caitlin added additional conditions for the marriage, such as expecting him to shave and shower everyday. One day they had no sex at all as she warmed up to the things she needed and the things she wanted. August realized Caitlin would eventually confuse her "wants" with her "needs", and was acutely distressed, exhausted, and unable to accomplish anything else the rest of the day. Also, on the days August and Caitlin's sexual encounters were at their peak, they left him with such high blood pressure and rapid pulse, it took several hours and a second blood pressure pill to calm himself down.

Gradually the occasions, if not the intensity of their couplings diminished somewhat. They still grasped every opportunity to steal away from Sauk City to Madison for shopping, necking in out-of-the-way booths at restaurants, or in the back seats of movie houses. They went to great lengths to accomplish these trips without anyone's knowledge, like two teenagers skipping school and keeping an eye out for any truant officer who might spot them. When one drove the other crouched down out of sight going in and out of Sauk City. Shopping was done with eyes of one on the merchandise, the other's scanning the store for familiar faces as more jewels and more gowns were purchased.

Caitlin soon began to change other areas of August's activities. When a reprint of *EVENING IN SPRING* was imminent, Caitlin insisted he get a new jacket for the book and raise the price of it. Another time she suggested he pick the best of the 68 poems he'd written to her for publication. After discussing her suggestion with his attorney and finding him in favor, August lost no time putting the book, *CAITLIN*, together. Then she suggested he do the same thing with the long, passionate, love letters he'd written to her when they were apart. Again, his attorney agreed with her idea. A limited edition was published, but almost immediately recalled. What prompted the recall is not clear. Most of the letters contained very specific, graphic material and might have triggered even closer speculations about Caitlin's identity than they had anticipated.

Both lovers welcomed the opportunity to attend the 1969 session of the Rhinelander School of Arts. There they could be together for two whole weeks. By that time, Caitlin had already discussed her desire for a divorce with her husband.

Caitlin and Derleth planned to go directly to bed for several hours of "...sexual dalliance..." after arriving at the Claridge Inn, where they'd reserved two adjoining rooms to ward off any suspicions and speculations. They would seek out a secluded romantic setting afterwards to dine, and then turn in to sleep in each others' arms all night. August tried to push aside all his apprehensions about marriage to her, and her revelation on the trip up to Rhinelander, that she meant to have a child with him. He was still shying away from marriage, telling Caitlin she should think very seriously about giving up a man she could manipulate for one she could not easily manipulate.

Their carefully laid plans were foiled when they arrived at the inn. Dr. Robert E. Gard, Studs Terkel, Dorothy Guilday, and several other staff members were in the lobby to welcome them.

Derleth, seeing the staff member who had just spent ten days of fasting in a Washington jail (with four other Wisconsin mothers for attempting to meet with President Nixon to ask him to pull America's troops out of Vietnam), quipped to the group, "I was ill at ease about my biography being written by a jailbird!"

Although the lovers' plans had been thwarted, they managed to make up for it in the days that followed. They made love that first night while watching the T.V. broadcast of the astronauts landing on the moon. The weeks ahead were filled with classes, jewelry shopping, socializing, and other group activities, but they enjoyed many interludes of being along together, and for the first time since the beginning of their affair, slept wrapped in each other's arms at night.

After the first weekend, a staff member scolded him for not entering school by the front door and stopping at her desk to pick up mail, notices, important papers. She was tired of having to hunt him down to deliver his messages. She pointed out that they were advertising, not concealing their involvement by sneaking into the school through a back entrance like two naughty children fearful of being caught with their hands in the cookie jar.

August laughed, and sitting beside her on the bench, confided that he and Caitlin had spent the weekend further north, exploring the beauty of the forests and enjoying the warm hospitality of the inns and people. He told of how, when he and Caitlin entered one cozy country restaurant for dinner, the customers beamed their approval at the old gentleman's solicitous care as he guided Caitlin to the one empty table. Since no one knew them, they abandoned all pretense, and behaved the way lovers do, holding hands and kissing. The expressions of disapproval and disgust they faced, leaving the inn, had them chuckling the rest of the evening.

The Rhinelander School of Arts, teeming with poets, authors, artists and entertainers, presented a far more cosmopolitan atmosphere than small town Sauk City residents were able to provide. As the days flew by, August and Caitlin became much less secretive about their affair than they had dared to be at home. By the time the annual staff dinner was held, most of those present were well aware of it.

Professor Gard, as was his custom, rose to welcome the diners and to introduce each with a few words about them. He asked the staff members to respond to introductions with an addition to his little speech, a one-word description of their primary life's goal. When Derleth's turn came, he shouted, without a moment's hesitation, "LOVE!" The next person was August's "secretary".

"...And this beautiful young lady is...ah, uh, mmmmm," he coughed, grew very crimson in the face, but just couldn't spit out what her role on the staff really was. He didn't need to, fortunately, a ripple of giggles, very faint at first, rolled around the table, increasing to a roar of laughter as Derleth, and even his "secretary" joined in to rescue Bob from his sticky situation.

The incident triggered a state of frank, relaxed discussion among the diners. Derleth's conversation with one of them, as related in his journal, was probably one of the most honest ones he'd ever been comfortable enough to make at a social gathering. He went so far as to discuss his need to control, and what relation it might have to the ego and the id. When the subject turned to sex, August stated, "...I have no inhibitions, had few all my life sexually, that if I wanted to masturbate, I did so without guilt; if I wished to make love to a member of my own sex, likewise; if I wished to make love to a woman, again, likewise, the only condition being that sexual pleasure must rise from love, or at least a deep and genuine affection...."

August and Caitlin left the affair early to take a walk, and make love in their rooms at the Claridge Motor Inn. Later, they joined a group of the other staff members gathered in the Claridge lounge for after-dinner drinks and more conversation. When the subject of Derleth's biography arose, Derleth shivered perceptibly and said, "Please don't, Dorothy. It's too morbid."

None of the group except, perhaps, Caitlin, was aware that August had to go into the hospital for extensive tests and possible surgery after he returned home.[5]

SOURCE NOTES
CHAPTER TWENTY-THREE

[1] August Derleth, "Overture", <u>Caitlin</u>, p. 11.
[2] Biographer's conclusions as she witnessed what was happening.
[3] A. D. Journal, August 30, 1968, pp. 21-ff.
[4] Sara Rath, "There She Is! That's Her, You Dummy", Insight Section, <u>Milwaukee Journal</u>, November 1, 1968, p. 44; Biographer's opinion.
[5] Note 3, p. 278.
[6] When the biographer's lawyer discovered that Derleth's attorney had neglected to renew all the copyrights on Derleth's books, letters, papers, etc., and informed the Derleth children of that fact, they immediately froze all the material until the year 2020. Only then will it be possible to verify some of the material in Chapter 22 and elsewhere throughout the book.

Festive group in Claridge Lounge following a Wisconsin Regional Writers Association Banquet. From left, a portion of camera-shy Caitlin's chair; August Derleth; Dorothy House Guilday, president of WRWA; Elvira Vecsey, Ballerina; Dorothy M. G. Litersky, Derleth Biographer; and Studs Terkel, best-selling author and prominant Chicago radio commentator. Photo was taken by Jeri Schwartz, professional photographer.

Chapter Twenty-Four

"...Jesus, he's a tough old bastard..."[1]

An otherwise delightful two weeks at Rhinelander had been haunted for Derleth by the knowledge that he must go into the hospital for a gall bladder operation. He dreaded facing the ordeal. He'd had hypertension since 1940, knew his chances of living to a ripe old age were not good, in spite of the longevity of his ancestors. His presentiment of a premature death often crept into his writings. He'd expressed the hope to last long enough to be of maximum help to the children.

One of the first things Derleth did after returning home was to call his lawyer to add a codicil to his latest will, drawn up in 1969. Lyle Von Behren had been designated as guardian of the person and estate of his children in the event Derleth's sister and brother-in-law were not able to serve in that capacity. Since Lyle no longer resided in Wisconsin, Derleth had to name someone else. He chose Gregory and Kathleen Mulcahay, whom the children knew and liked. Kathleen had volunteered to help after Rikki took a job in Milwaukee. She typed manuscripts, chauffeured August about. Her husband, whom August had known since Gregory was a young boy, was a local entrepreneur – not yet 30 – making his way up the ladder of financial success.

Derleth entered St. Mary's Hospital in Madison in late August. The surgery went well. August seemed at first to be recovering and out of danger. His doctors then brought him new x-rays of his gall bladder, pointing out what they thought were two additional stones in the bile duct which would also have to be removed. August, still a bit hazy from the first operation, trusted their decision, and consented to the second surgery. It was one of the worst mistakes of his life, Derleth said. They operated again on the 18th of August. Caitlin and Mara were both there, waiting to see that he was all right before leaving, so he could sleep and begin to recuperate. August tried to get out of bed the second day and collapsed. He was muddled, then lapsed into unconsciousness. When he awakened to a darkened room a few days later, he heard chanting, smelled incense. Tufts of light floated toward, then receded from him. A voice, speaking Latin, announced the absolution of all the sins of Derleth's life. He realized he was receiving Extreme Unction, the last rites of the Catholic Church.

One of the doctors had told Hildred that August would not live, causing her, Rosella, Walden, April, and many others much sorrow. Derleth's hallucinations lasted for over a month. He saw large bats, spiders, and owls floating across the walls. He imagined he arose every day, went to his desk, and sat all day writing letters. When Rikki Meng came to visit, Derleth would ask if Rikki saw the piles of letters alongside of his typewriter. Rikki soon learned to say yes.

Caitlin was at his side for 50 of the 87 days in the hospital, "...shining like a star...bathing his fevered face, etc...." So, also, to a lesser degree, came Mara and Edna Meudt. A red rose arrived every day without fail, peaking the curiosity of the hospital staff.

When the hospital issued a bulletin that August was in "...dangerous condition, but not critical..." cards and letters poured in. Cassandra wrote as did Mark Schorer. Derleth had come to terms with his anger against Mark, and felt pity rather than rage.

The doctors put a hole in his chest, using a very thin auger in a glass tube. Although sedated, and in pain, he heard one of the doctors remark, as they left the room, "...Jesus, he's a tough old bastard...." It perked Augie up for the rest of the day.

Edna Meudt spent many hours at his side, bathing his fevered brow, waiting on him. She spent at least an hour advising him not to marry Caitlin, and giving her views on their relationship.

August's secretary, Mrs. Mulcahy, also dropped in regularly to discuss the things going on in the publishing houses and the Place of Hawks.

Marty came too, and the two rejected suitors talked, as always, of Cassandra.

Only when he was out of danger did he learn he had a collapsed and punctured lung, pleuritis, hepatitis, peritonitis, moniliasis, and protens. He'd had a total of four operations. He also had $28,000 worth of private nursing care.[2]

Cards and good wishes poured in from all over, expressing essentially the same sentiment as that sent by Mel Ellis and his wife, albeit not all were as Derleth – oriented.

"...So that is Gwen's and my wish for you – that you may stroll along, kicking at the fallen leaves and seeing a goosepack high and going south..." Ellis wrote.[3]

August received a heartbreaking letter from his daughter begging him to obey the doctors so he could come home. April, always so dutiful as a young child, chafed considerably under August's strict hand when she reached her middle teens and became increasingly rebellious during his long illness. He had let her go out in a mixed crowd at fourteen, but forbade her to date any one boy. He forbade her to "...hang around..." with her friends after school, though she was older, now (older than Sandra, her mother, had been when he first made love to her). Perhaps this was the reason he kept such a tight rein on April. He knew only too well what could happen to a beautiful young teenager without proper restraints. He was aware, too, of the crush April had on Rikki, when she was not yet fifteen. August had thought then that if they fell in love and wanted to marry, after she was 18 and had finished high school, he would not object. He could ask for no better son-in-law than reliable, intelligent, industrious, hardworking, gentlemanly Ricardo Meng.

April had had her ears pierced while he was gone, without his permission. He ordered her to remove the earrings and grounded her until the holes were healed. Though April protested against his rules, she loved August dearly, as shown by the heartbreaking letter she wrote to her father, begging him to obey the doctors so he could come home.[4]

August was released the 19th day of October. His sister Hildred and his secretary, Kathleen, had to help him up the stairs. Both secretaries and Alice had done their best to keep the publishing house operating smoothly. Hildred, too, lent her services when necessary. They were not, however, about to handle the 500 books stacked in his studio, waiting to be reviewed, nor the 500 letters waiting to be answered.[5]

On November 12th, he was back in his studio bed, making love to Caitlin.[6] By December, August was on his feet, putting in a full day's work at his desk, even hiking and driving. His knees were too shaky for stairs, and he was forced to use a cane. A blood clot on his left knee had not yet dissolved.

He began to catch up with everything except his journal and the 500+ letters. He regained fifteen pounds, but still watched his diet, determined to keep his weight at 190.[7]

Incredibly, in spite of the illness and his new romantic interest, nine of his books came out in 1968. Two serious works, *EMERSON OUR CONTEMPORARY* and *RETURN TO WALDEN WEST* were still in progress.

The Emerson biography, like Thoreau's, was a book Derleth had wanted to do for a long time. He believed reading Emerson was profitable for everyone, but especially for the young, and agreed with J. Donald Adams that "...The early reading of Emerson made easier...some of the most difficult decision...because Emerson fortifies the will to make the best and most out of life...."

Two smaller volumes, *THREE STRAW MEN*, a juvenile, and *THE LANDSCAPE OF THE HEART*, poetry, were being prepared for 1970 publication.

The expense of his illness was enormous. His lack of output during that period and his reduced work schedule after coming home prevented Arkham House from bringing out some of the books planned for 1971. It was this that really hurt financially.

Nineteen hundred sixty-nine ended with the prospect of still another serious operation ahead. The doctors feared he might have an abdominal hernia of major proportions.[8]

Even before his near-death and long hospitalization, August wrote *A HOUSE ABOVE CUZCO*. It was a tale built around the visit of Benton, a biographer, to the house of Avrel Miller, a famous midwestern author who had deserted his native area to live in the Andes Mountains above Cuzco. Benton is puzzled by a book of poetry titled *CAITLIN* and wants Avrel to solve the mystery for him. Avrel refuses, but his wife helps reveal the secret. The complexities of the story point to many layers of intent in the writing.

"...I'm hardly a subject worthy of a biography. A literary curiosity, perhaps; no more....", the words of Avrel, are definitely the sentiment of Derleth about himself.

"An author's relation to his work is always interesting to his public," Benton replies. "The precise degree of reality in his fiction is something many readers like to know...."

Exactly. And Derleth, after years of confessing that this book or that poem, was autobiographical, with most of the characters drawn from real life, set out in this book to deny that his fiction reflected reality.

In another sense, *A HOUSE ABOVE CUZCO* was a very real attempt to protect those people closest to him. The success of his effort will have to be judged by posterity, though even he seemed to doubt it.

"...If one suppresses the truth, guessing could be so much worse," Mara, Avrel's wife, comments.

"Could it? I wonder." Avrel replies.[9]

When the proofs came for correction, Derleth, to further confuse prospective biographers, changed the original names in it. He managed to include the names of some of his lovers – male and female. "Mara" was one of his male lovers![10]

SOURCE NOTES
CHAPTER TWENTY-FOUR

[1] A. D. Journal, 1 August to 19 October, 1969, pp. 60-ff.

[2] Note 1, op. cit.

[3] Mel Ellis to A. D., n.d.

[4] April Rose Derleth to A. D., no date.

[5] Note 1, October 19.

[6] Ibid., 12 November, 1969.

[7] Ibid., Dec. 1969.

[8] August Derleth, <u>A House Above Cuzco</u>, (New York, 1969), a summary.

[9] Note 1, n.d.

[10] Ibid.

Chapter Twenty-Five

"He often maintained a hawk shouldn't lie down with the sparrows because the sparrows only seek to destroy the hawk...."[1]

Arkham House sales kept climbing in 1970: 2,661 books in April alone, and if the trend continued they should reach 22,000 for the year. Derleth's own writing, however, was only 200,000 words an unheard of low. He'd recuperated enough by May to pick over 7,000 morels. His recovery was interrupted by still another bout of surgery in August – a 15-inch gash across his upper abdomen to repair a ventral hernia with wire. This time he kept right on working as he recuperated in the hospital.

RETURN TO WALDEN WEST was out and *PUBLISHERS' WEEKLY REVIEW* called it a "...lovely, compassionate, deeply felt book...." In September, Derleth made a package deal with Ballantine for Lovecraft's work from *LURKER AT THE THRESHOLD* to the recent *TALES OF THE CTHULHU MYTHOS*, along with some of his poems. The $4,000 advance would be used toward publishing the third volume of Lovecraft's *SELECTED LETTERS*, at a price of $7,500 for 2,500 copies.[2]

One of the things Derleth's bouts of illness seemed to have accomplished was to make Sac Prairie sit up, finally, and take notice of their most illustrious native. The board of education named the library of the middle school "August Derleth Library and Research Center". In October, the twin cities honored him with an August Derleth Day.

Over 300 people – neighbors, friends, editors, writers, students, dignitaries, people from all over the state and from as far away as California and Florida came to the testimonial dinner. The Place of Hawks was thrown open for a pre-dinner gathering. Rosella and April presided at the coffee and sherry table. Derleth kept busy autographing books. The guests prowled all about the comfortable, friendly home and the autumn colorama of the grounds.

Frank Lloyd Wright had once called it a barn.

"...Well, there's a bull inside of it...," August admitted.[4] When empty, the house seemed huge, and like Grandfather Derleth's smithy hayloft, full of mysterious nooks and shadows and during a high wind, low moans and screeching wails. Mounting the staircase, one could easily see where the house itself, complete with a cemetery across the street, might have inspired some of Derleth's spinechillers.[3]

August's sticking to his home place did in no way isolate him from the world. The world came to him. Through the Place of Hawks over the years, passed a steady stream of visitors from all over. The author's work drew them like a magnet to see for themselves the Sac Prairie he had preserved between the pages of his books, or to meet the man who had done more than anyone to nurture fantasy writing. At least one of his fans – William Dutch, an educational administrator from Chicago – was so enchanted with the area as seen through the author's eyes, he decided to settle in a nearby community when he retired. Dutch spent his retirement years working to attract other people to Derleth's work.[4] Sac Prairie natives also visited the home at one time or another to partake of Derleth's special brand of hospitality, as big and warm and friendly as the home, itself. Groups of students, women's clubs, girl scouts, writers, many others picked the spot for a tour. Often the out-of-town visitors were also escorted around the twin cities, shown the old harness shop converted into a woodworking shop after the horses gave way to tractors. Hugo Schwenker still worked there with skillful hands that fashioned beautiful roomy cabinets, some of which Derleth used to store his ever-increasing stacks of manuscripts. Those tours also included the railroad trestle, Bare Ass Creek, Lang's corner, the Riverview Ballroom, the bluffs and the marshes, all the spots already so familiar to the readers.[5]

Guests at the dinner, held in the Riverview Ballroom, were entertained with excerpts of Derleth's books by local readers who took the parts of several of Derleth's better known characters – Aunt May, Grandfather Adams, Gus Elker, and Margery, to name a few.

Greetings and testimonials were presented by Governor Warren Knowles, Senator William Proxmire, Lt. Governor Jack

Olson, Representative Vern Thompson, and many other local dignitaries.

Dr. Robert E. Gard gave the main address. Derleth, in his brief response, said an author is made, not born. He acknowledged the help of many of the people in the room. The proximity to Madison had also been a factor in his success. In Madison were available all the cultural and educational facilities he needed. The State of Wisconsin Historical Society Museum archives had been a constant source of material and had aided in the sale of many of his books.

To all appearances, that night of the dinner, August was fully recovered from his horrendous hospital experience. One concerned fan, inquiring whether August was feeling okay, sparked a "show and tell" demonstration by the author. He lifted one leg high and balanced on the other, right there in the middle of the ballroom for several minutes. It was August's fascination with the matching bracelet, choker, and earrings the woman wore, that convinced her he was right back in stride. She knew what he was thinking as he gazed at her sparkling antique jewels, and commented on their beauty. He was thinking how wonderful they'd look adorning the neck of his gorgeous Caitlin.[6]

Derleth had not, however, gained back his old strength and drive. Even as he planned his schedule for the year ahead, a note of foreboding crept into his correspondence. The horror novel he planned for January would most likely be his last in that genre. In January, 1971, working on *THE WATCHERS OUT OF TIME* he said the Lovecraft pastiche would also be his last. Time was running out for him, he stated in another letter.

In February he learned he would need still more corrective surgery. Though it would be a minor repair, Derleth decided to put it off as long as possible, eighteen months or more.

His own production was down, although Arkham House continued to flourish. His working capital had soared to $13,000, and his personal savings to $6,000, the largest amount of money he had ever had on hand.

In May, he picked 7,330 morels in an all-out attempt to break his 1968 record of 10,000. He felt he may have done so if a drought had not drastically reduced the number available.

Rikki was back on the job as general manager, not yet as proficient as Derleth in handling all the Arkham House business, but Derleth felt he soon would be. Rikki was a tremendous help, and his presence would free Derleth for another session at the Rhinelander School of Arts in July, and later in the year or in early 1971, for a trip to England he'd been wanting to make for several years.

The trip would probably be his honeymoon. Caitlin no longer made any attempt to hide their relationship. She had confessed her love for Derleth and announced she wanted to get a divorce. Her husband begged her not to leave him. Caitlin turned a deaf ear to his pleas. She meant to marry Derleth, and nothing would stop her.

Scott Meredith, famous literary agent, was handling a lot of Derleth's material now, with satisfactory results, and that, too, eased his workload somewhat. For perhaps the first time in his adult life, the financial treadmill had slowed to almost a stop.[7]

Although Derleth had sworn he would have nothing more to do with the Council for Wisconsin Writers, his *RETURN TO WALDEN WEST* was entered and took the award for "best non-fiction book by a Wisconsin author in 1970". He received $500. Instead of heeding his advice against having a best award, the council was now giving two best awards.[8]

One thing Derleth's consternation with the committee had accomplished, was to pinpoint the desirability of securing impartial judges. The 1970 annual banquet brochure indicated that North Dakota judges had picked the winners![9]

Lin Carter, a prominent author in the science fiction and fantasy genre, visited Derleth in late June. He noted that Derleth seemed to have approaching death on his mind, although he was not ill. On the contrary, Derleth enjoyed a hearty meal, so hearty he felt a bit uncomfortable after it. Derleth told Carter he had enough manuscripts planned ahead to keep Arkham House going for several years in the event of his death.[10]

Derleth had been preparing for eventual death in several ways. He'd been worrying for months about his old friend, Hugh, being alone in his shop without a telephone in case he should become ill or have an accident with his carpenter tools.

Derleth ordinarily checked on his old friend once or twice a day, but while he was in the hospital, he could not. If something happened to August, who would keep tabs on Hugh? No amount of argument or pressure would make Hugh consider putting in a phone, so Derleth decided to jolt his old buddy with the realization that he was getting on in years. He managed to secure a key to the woodworking shop, and on several occasions when Hugh was away from it, entered and moved a tool here, turned the pages of an open book there, not too obviously but just enough to upset Schwenker's neat, structured environment. Fortunately, Derleth had confided his plot to a mutual friend and instructed her to set Schwenker's mind at rest concerning his apparent lapses of memory, if Derleth died.[11] He need not have been so concerned. In 1992, Hugo Schwenker was still going strong, fishing, working in his tidy shop, chatting with his occasional visitors about Derleth, and viewing through his window, Water Street, the heart of Sauk City.[12]

SOURCE NOTES
CHAPTER TWENTY-FIVE

[1] A favorite comment of Derleth's, in speeches, and letters, as well as in private conversations.

[2] A. D. letter to Duane Rimel, May 21, August, 17, September 14, 1970.

[3] Biographer attended banquet honoring Derleth, October, 1970, Sauk City, Wisconsin, Riverside Ballroom.

[4] Interview with William Dutch at the Firehouse Restaurant, Sauk City, July, 1974.

[5] Lin Carter, "A Day in Derleth Country", August Derleth Society Newsletter.

[6] Note 3, op. cit.

[7] A. D. Journal and letters, specific information out of reach, at present.

[8] Biographer interviewed members of the Council for Wisconsin Writers in 1970; A. D. letter to Col. H. Schowalter, June 25, 1968.

[9] Brochure for the 1970 annual Awards Banquet of the Council for Wisconsin Writers at Milwaukee, Wisconsin.

[10] Note 5, op. cit.

[11] A. D. Journal, n.d.

[12] Biographer visited Hugo Schwenker's woodworking shop on Water Street, Sauk City, 1992.

Chapter Twenty-Six

"...Today I am – tomorrow I was...."[1]

Before his illness, Derleth had been dreaming about the possibility of his enjoying at least ten years of married bliss. Hovering so close to death in the hospital, never regaining his old vitality, emphasized the tenuous hold he had on life. The ugly wounds on his body were a constant reminder of that frail thread, and a repugnance to him. Although he seldom complained about the trusses and corset he had to wear, they were not the kind of adornment a lover would welcome. But more than that his real problem was not cosmetic but a dilemma. His deep conviction that he had a right to anything he pleased as long as it did not harm anyone else was on trial again.

Derleth endured many tormented hours trying to come to some decision about marrying Caitlin. They spent long rapturous hours in his studio. August was well aware of the strong anima (feminine side) within him. His closet sexual activities were not generally known, in spite of the many people who suspected there was something very interesting going on in the Place of Hawks. Until Caitlin, he had always been in complete control of almost every situation. He had to, in order to walk the very thin line between his secret life and his visible one. Few dared to give voice to their suspicions. At the slightest hint of slander, Derleth was sure to sue. He knew too much about the private lives of Sac Prairie people. Their fear of his wrath served as a shield protecting him against discovery.

August had not realized how strong his inner feminine anima was until the day Caitlin assumed the aggressive role in their coupling. He was amazed at his extreme pleasure and his utter helplessness as she took control of him. He was also horrified. Caitlin's subtle aggression, which had seemed so delightful that night she crashed the staff dinner to reveal her desire to have an affair with him, was far from subtle now. His greatest fear arose: he would never be in control of his life again.

To have this woman for a few years – ailing, debilitating

years – perhaps still facing more surgery, would be the most unkind thing he could do to her. To continue the clandestine relationship could also destroy her life and her reputation. He could dream about leaving Sauk City to start life over somewhere else with her, but his heart, his life was buried in his home town. To give her up was out of the question. As long as she was willing and satisfied with the status quo, he would never have the strength to resist her. She would wipe out Derleth, the prolific author; Derleth, the giant; Derleth, the genius – turn him into something less than a man.

He could no longer deceive himself about someday writing the rest of the books planned for his saga, either. The drastic loss of energy had cut deeply into even his less serious writing. There wasn't enough time left, even if he recuperated.[2]

Shortly after he had left the hospital, he visited a Sauk City woman who had just lost her mother to offer his condolences. She told him that she had no reason to stay alive. She'd nursed her mother for years, had no other relatives or friends, and was fearing old age and being placed in an institution. That for her would be her worst nightmare come true. "I'm going to die, Augie," she said simply and a few weeks later she did.

Her death did not surprise August. It emphasized what he had learned so much about in Indian lore. It was common practice for older, ailing members of tribes, to simply lay down and die, usually on an elevated platform in their sacred burial grounds.

How easily she had solved her problems, Derleth thought, when he heard the news about her death. Would that his dilemma were that simple.[3]

*****

Derleth awoke from his nap. The sun was already sinking.

Tic-toc, tic-toc. It was almost 9 p.m. Rosella must have told the children not to waken him for dinner if he was asleep. Six hours. That was the longest nap he'd ever taken. His regular night's sleep was less than that.

He got up and stretched. He felt wonderful. The tension had left his neck and shoulders, his head was clear.

He padded over to his desk, sat down. There was something he needed to do. He picked up the phone.

226

"Hello, Karl?" They talked for half an hour. Derleth told Karl he was going to die, "Take care".

He talked at length with Rikki Meng, on the evening of July third. He called Edna Meudt, too. He told her he was not feeling well, and seemed to have some difficulty breathing. His voice was husky. A dry cough interrupted his words, and here, too, he indicated he did not expect to live very much longer by his parting remark: "...If we do not talk again, Edna, take care...."

Sometime during the following 4th of July morning, August went outdoors to sit under a special tree on his property that he had chosen to substitute for a platform in a sacred burying ground. His death certificate stated the cause of his demise was "an apparent heart attack".

August had finally found the way out of his catch-22 situation. Ironically, though he had defended homosexuality and bi-sexuality throughout his lifetime, at the end he proved profoundly afraid (as most homophobics are) of his gentler side – the anima within.[4]

SOURCE NOTES
CHAPTER TWENTY-SIX

[1] <u>Man Track Here.</u>
[2] A. D. Journal.
[3] Ibid.
[4] Conclusion of the Biographer. Loren E. Pederson, <u>Dark Hearts: Forces that Shape Men's Lives</u>, 1991. From Chapter 7 p. 197ff, "Men's Sense of Love": "...Friendship between men is further burdened by the fear of phallic or genital relatedness, which is also known as homophobia – the fear of being homosexual...."; "...(this causes men to avoid expressing tenderness toward other men.); "...Although acting out against homosexuals is seen as a form of homophobia, it might just as well be called 'feminophobia' since it seems far more to characterize men's fear of their anima (the feminine in men.)"

One of the last two pictures of Derleth, taken at Edna Meudt's farm during a Wisconsin Poets Society meeting. Many see the tiny optical illusion behind his left shoulder as a "death head". Can you pick it out?

Photo by Dale O'Brian

Epilogue

"...Less than this my lone path is:
a deermouse track in winter's snow -
less than any mark of hare or crow.
Than the last falling leaf from the
most crabbed, most aged tree
in the least wind, than the last pebble
dropped into the stillest pool,
than the most secret ways of
the foolish, obscure bee,
no path of mine is now as much,
nothing of mine is more...."[1]

Sunday, July 4, 1971, in the marshes the whippoorwills were surely crying, but August Derleth was not there to hear them. No more would his firm footfalls resound against the trestle of the old railroad bridge. Time, for Derleth, had finally run out.

Five priests were present at the Requiem, and he was buried in the cemetery across the street from his Place of Hawks: the very cemetery where once he'd danced with Marcia Masters. The inscription on his gravestone was Thoreau's:

"...I wish to live deliberately, to front only the essential facts of life, and see if I could not learn what it had to teach, and not, when I came to die, discover that I had not lived...."[2]

The waves of grief spread clear across the country in varying degrees of intensity, from the first tortured "...Aug is dead..." of his beloved Caitlin to the regretful notices on the literary pages of the New York newspapers.[3]

The Rhinelander School of Arts' session later that month was overshadowed with the grief of having lost Derleth. When a hawk swooped low above the string of canoes carrying students down the Wisconsin River, two of the canoers – Sara Rath and Derleth's biographer – were convinced it was Augie, giving a final, farewell salute.

231

In December, thousands of miles away from Sauk City, two of Derleth's workshop friends sat side-by-side and shivered as they watched "Lagoda's Heads", one of August's macabre short stories being presented on television in a series of three short tales edited by Robert Bloch. Both felt as though Derleth had reached out from the grave to touch them.[4]

The obituaries, the memorial tributes, the attempts of people in all walks of life to eulogize Derleth and show his death was loss to each of them, re-echoed the grief. In a memorial issue of IS IV, the man emerged, as Tom Collins, editor and publisher noted, "...in a kind of mosaic...."

August was called: "A simple, honorable man, a most complex personality"; "a walking paradox...an arrogant man...a roaring exhibitionist"; "a dynamo of whirlwind energy"; "kind and sensitive"; "a bright dash of color...on the Wisconsin literary scape"; "humorous, incredibly generous"; "hack...artist...genius"; "scrupulously fair in his dealings"; "oak...massive and somewhat rough"; "great naturalist"; "virtually a Renaissance man"; "completely natural, completely outspoken"; "great, good-natured bear"; and his work "kind and non-violent".

"...Derleth loved life...There is not a writer today who doesn't owe a debt of gratitude to August Derleth for enabling so many of his fellow professionals to find a certain amount of enduring fame between hardcovers...."

"...The man was more important than anything he wrote...."

"...He was a master of superb characterization, with a keenly honed insight into the frailties of human nature...He was an original, an individualist...He was the most damning paradox...."

"...Clearly a man of great constitution and energy...a firm conviction that he stood first – 'first among equals', like a Roman Emperor."

"...Straddling Wisconsin like some rough, latter day Titan, August Derleth was indeed huge, in every way...."

"...A complex and talented, talented man, a genius whose love for life and appetite for work were as outsized as his frame, a serious writer who gave up everything in behalf of his friends and thereby gained immortality...."[5]

"...Contrast was the key to August Derleth...He could be

rude, tactless, and have damn little regard for other people's feelings...His acts of kindness and generosity – and they were many – were usually private and anonymous...Whether you read his books, then met the man – or met the man, then read his books – you were stunned by the contrast...The paradoxes extended to his work...He flaunted convention...You can't measure an extraordinary man by ordinary standards. There were no limits to August's range...He was unique...The Wisconsin scene was richer for his presence; it is poorer for his absence. And we'll never see his like again...."[6]

The Wisconsin Fellowship of Poets, with a grant from the Wisconsin Arts Council and The National Endowment for the Arts, published a new poetry magazine entitled *HAWK & WHIPPOORWILL RECALLED*, with the first issue devoted to the memory of August Derleth.

One of the poems – "Before Leaving" – by Catherine Case Lubbe tells of a June gathering of poets at a farm where the last pictures were taken of August. Her film was bad. Nothing could be seen but a bit of blue. She begged the film processors to try again, "...and there he stood, all the color, the life and strength of him, the radiant spirit and joy of him...."

An aura of ominous portent clung to still another picture taken that day by Dale O'Brien, (whose photos appear in several books about Wisconsin), of Derleth with a sugar maple, a cemetery urn, and over his right shoulder an optical illusion seen by some viewers as a death mask, by others as nothing but a few squiggly lines on the fallow field in the background.

Frances May writes of the same day when "...Poems sparkled/ like the best red wine/ all in his Merlin spell..."

Chad Walsh wrote, "...How the pages of his memory cover/ His state like a sectional map..." and likened him to "...Paul Bunyan singing...."

Gerti Sennett "...heard his harps and chords/ The ringing bells of him...."

Jo Bartels Alderson wrote of his "...momentous virtues and gigantic faults..." and hoped her words were as real as Derleth's.

Anne Stubbe mused, "...Upon the quality of late September love/ This man, whose passion/ Like a flambeau, lightened portals/ Unto corridors of death."

Marian Paust wrote, "...Your songs seeded in forests; where your feet led you,/ and the marsh reeds repeated them/ wherever wild flowers glistened,/ mushrooms exploded through loam, and hawks surfed on blue sky...."

To Inga Caldwell, he was "...star material...."

Russell Ferrell believed "...there flowed in his veins; a sweet sap/ dripped from a thousand spigots/ by aspiring poets/ and young writers...."[7]

Other poets published odes and eulogies in other publications. James Wade, in *WHISPERS*, a fanzine, wrote "Sauk City: Two Gentlemen Meet at Midnight", fashioned after the poem "Providence: Two Gentlemen Meet at Midnight", written by Derleth about the ghosts of Lovecraft and Poe meeting in the city where both had lived. In Wade's poem, the long conversation takes place between Derleth's and Lovecraft's spirits, with Derleth wondering "...Did I create you Howard, or did you make me...?"[8]

Jeanette Schlatter, freelance writer, visited Sauk City some time after Derleth's demise and was appalled to learn that no memorial had as yet been planned for their most illustrious son. She suggested they get busy.

Embarrassed at the oversight, the Sauk City Chamber of Commerce, of which Derleth had been member and president, hastened to correct it; but what would be a fitting tribute?

It so happened that about the same time they were clearing away a large stand of trees alongside the Wisconsin River, directly adjacent to Kleinert's Park and the old Bare Ass Creek area. They had planned a baseball park in honor of another illustrious former citizen – Jack Voll – who had contributed much of his time as well as financial help for the little leagues and other city ball teams.

A hasty change of plans was made, and the Father of Sauk City Baseball lost out. A huge plaque was erected at the site in 1976, and an appropriate ceremony held, announcing the dedication of the August Derleth Park.

Mercifully, Derleth did not have to suffer the massacre of dozens of the trees he loved so dearly, or know that his name was to be forever linked with the atrocity of their removal.[9]

An August Derleth Society was founded during 1977 by

Richard H. Fawcett, and a quarterly newsletter established. The society sponsored taped interviews with close friends and associates of August for deposit in the Sauk City Library. Members conducted tours through Sauk City and held a two-day seminar for the tenth anniversary of Derleth's death. They also worked toward establishing an honorary degree for Derleth from the University of Wisconsin.[10] Another memorial that August hoped for was the establishment of the Place of Hawks as a Wisconsin writers' shrine. To this end, Derleth designated that the first option to buy after his children no longer wanted the house, should go to the State of Wisconsin Historical Society, where he also left his personal papers, his priceless collection of comics and memorabilia, and his unpublished manuscripts.

August's dream of having the Place of Hawks preserved as a writers' shrine has not yet materialized. A few years ago, the State of Wisconsin designated it as a Wisconsin Historical landmark, and in 1996, the National Historical Society also dedicated August's home as a national landmark. Derleth's biographer has long had the dream of seeing his home and grounds become an author's haven where those writing about this classic author and his many talented accomplishments can research and study in the same place Derleth did, surrounded by his gigantic collection of books. It would be a perfect place to experience the ambiance of Derleth's warmth and hospitality, and enjoy the grounds he so loved. To that end, she sent a small sum in lieu of flowers to the family of August designating it as "seed money."[11]

At Northernaire in Eagle River, Wisconsin, Carl Marty issued a memorial flyer saluting "...a great friend of the voiceless..." and inserted one in each of the copies of *FOREST ORPHANS* and *MR. CONSERVATION* he had for sale.[12]

In a joint meeting of the Wisconsin Regional Writers' Association, the Wisconsin Fellowship of Poets, and the Wisconsin Academy of Sciences, Arts and Letters, Derleth was the first author to be named in their dedication of the Wisconsin Authors' Hall of Honor at Fort Atkinson, 1973.[13]

Along with the glowing tributes, the eulogies, were rumbles of discontent in the Lovecraft fanzines.

Through the distribution by Ballantine Books, the H. P. L. Cult began to resemble that of Tolkien. Mint first edition of

THE OUTSIDERS AND OTHERS were going for as high as $300, and letters and other memorabilia of Howard P. Lovecraft were possessively sought after by many.

Derleth's tight reign on Lovecraft material from the beginning and the mounting cost of the Lovecraft first editions irritated the fans. Many had been accusing Derleth of getting rich on Lovecraft. Many questioned Arkham House's legal right to Lovecraft's material. Even after death, the people on the plains were throwing stones at the mountain, the sparrows trying to diminish the hawk.

There was a more serious charge against August, which one fan called "...literary piggybacking...." In stories such as "The Dark Brotherhood" and others published in *THE WATCHERS OUT OF TIME*, Derleth had used story themes set forth by Lovecraft, and wrote the manuscripts himself. They were, in a sense, like pastiche, but fans resented Derleth's highlighting Lovecraft's name on the covers of some of these books, giving the impression that they were primarily by Lovecraft, or at least collaborations with Lovecraft.

Other fans felt Derleth changed and distorted Lovecraft's concept of the Cthulhu Mythos, the background of many of Lovecraft's stories.

Lovecraft's biographer, L. Sprague de Camp, wrote: "...Derleth made considerable changes in the mythos...developed a whole pantheon of benign deities, the Elder Gods. These oppose the Ancient Ones and sometimes help men in their struggle with the Great Old Ones. In Lovecraft's Cthulhuvian Universe, mankind has no powerful friends to speak of...I have found his contributions to the Cthulhu Mythos in some way superior to Lovecraft's and in others, inferior. His style is smoother, less crotchety and affected; on the other hand, his powers of imagination, while substantial, come nowhere near the feverish intensity of Lovecraft's. Derleth liked to tidy up the loose ends of the mythos...His bringing in of the Elder Gods on mankind's side, which probably reflects his basic Christian orientation...further diluted the effect of Lovecraft's original and powerful concept of the 'mechanistic supernatural'...."

Other criticisms of Derleth surfaced here and there. The most virulent of these, perhaps, was written by Vernon Shea, one of Lovecraft's "family" and a long-time correspondent of Derleth's. In spite of the sharp critical tone of Shea's article, he tempered it with "...I suddenly realized how indebted I had been to Derleth, for his correspondence, for his encouragement, for the stories of mine he had used in his anthologies...." (Derleth had also guided Shea, step by step, through Shea's first attempt at an anthology.) "...It's what one leaves behind that matters and Augie definitely went out on the plus side...the fantasy field will never be quite the same without him...."[14]

When the giant fell, and all hope of their ever going back to the beginning was snuffed out, Marcia Masters wrote:

"An Elegy
to A.D.[15]
"It was a kind of cowslip, meadow love
That took in earth and sky
It was the flight of birds,
The sound of rain.
It was our wild, exuberant shadows
Across the country road—
The way we danced around those small town tombs,
As if no world of stone and dust,
Could make us die.
But you are dead who said
I was a bird, a star, an April rain,
Though something lingers in my blood:
Some celebration in the sun
As if my dance with you were not quite done...."

SOURCE NOTES EPILOGUE

[1] August Derleth, "Man Track Here", Collected Poems, 1937-1967.

[2] Mike Miller, "Kindness Praised at Funeral Rites"; quotes from Eulogy by Fr. Joseph Cox, Madison Capital Times, July 8, 19, 71, p. 1.

[3] Edna Meudt, Wisconsin Academy of Poet's Review, Vol. 1a, #2.

[4] Personal experience of biographer while canoeing down the Wisconsin River in one of eight canoes. Sara Rath and biographer pointed simultaneously at the hawk, low over their heads; personal experience of biographer and Dorothy House Guilday, at the home of the biographer in Palm Beach Co., Florida.

[5] Tom Collins, "IS IV Memorial issue", October, 1971, in back of title page; tribute throughout issue.

[6] Ted V. Olsen, untitled piece written for The Racounteur's Newsletter, a male writers' club in Wisconsin.

[7] "Hawk and Whippoorwill Recalled", Vol. 1, Summer, 1973.

[8] James Wade, "Sauk City: Two Gentlemen Meet at Midnight", Whispers, Vol. 3 #2 Aug. 1977.

[9] Interview with Jeannette Schlatter, Rhinelander School of Arts, 1976.

[10] Biographer is a charter member of the August Derleth Society. Her name is inscribed on the dedication plaque in the Sauk City August Derleth Room in the basement of the city library.

[11] Biographer to Derleth's family.

[12] Mr. Marty sent a copy of his memorial to August Derleth insert to biographer, 1971.

[13] Leslie Cross, "No finis for August Derleth", Milwaukee Journal, Sept. 26, 1973; "Derleth chosen as top state writer", Sac Prairie Star, Sept. 27, 1963, p.1.

[14] Sprague DeCamp, Lovecraft, a Biography, pp. 428 ff; Harry Warner, "A unique writer", IS, IV; Richard L. Tierney, "The Derleth Mythos", Meade and Penny Frierson, (fauzine) 1972; Prof. Dick Mosig, "Myth Maker", Whispers, Vol. 3, #2, Dec. 1976, pp 49ff; J. Vernon Shea, fanzine, p. 9.

[15] Marcia Masters, "An Elegy To A.D."